"Brilliant. Invaluable for writers and filmmakers. Eric Edson's book will change the way screenwriting is conceived of and taught."

— Michael Hauge, Hollywood script consultant, author:
*Writing Screenplays That Sell* and *Selling Your Story in 60 Seconds*

"Laser-sharp insight. A great tool for any screenwriter, novice or journeyman. I could not imagine a more thoughtful and thorough analysis of screenwriting."

— Michael Peretzian, Senior Vice President, The William Morris Agency

"Like discovering a new continent. This book may well be the best cure for writer's block ever written."

— Jessica Davis Stein, novelist: *Coyote Dream*

"The Rosetta Stone for translating story ideas into powerful screenplays. I've made over 40 movies and I wish I'd had *The Story Solution* as a guide for every writer I've worked with."

— Steve White, President of Feature Films, New World Entertainment

"Bravo! Eric Edson compellingly makes the case for his unique approach. An engaging, enjoyable read that will make any student of screenwriting a better writer."

— Jon Stahl, Professor and Chair, Department of Cinema and Television Arts, California State University, Northridge

"A brilliant presentation... a tremendously valuable contribution to writers everywhere."

— Michael Wiese, director, producer, publisher

"Strikes off into new territory. A remarkable teaching tool."

— Tom Rickman, screenwriter, Academy Award nominee: *Coal Miner's Daughter*, WGA Award winner: *Tuesdays with Morrie*, Emmy Award nominee: *Truman*, *The Reagans*

"A clear path to a Hollywood sale."

— Erica Byrne, screenwriter: *Hunter, Silk Stalkings, La Femme Nikita*

"*The Story Solution* lifts the veil from screenwriting — it's more than a tool, this new process takes writers into the breach of successful commercial storytelling."

— Stephen V. Duncan, co-creator of *Tour of Duty, A Man Called Hawk, The Court-Martial of Jackie Robinson*; Professor of Screenwriting, Loyola Marymount University; author of *Genre Screenwriting and A Guide to Screenwriting Success: Writing for Film and Television*

"As I write this, I'm knee-deep in a pilot I've been developing for 20th Century-Fox that has been, I'll be honest, kicking my ass. Then I read an advance copy of *The Story Solution*, and it's like the smoke dissipated, the angels emerged, and everything became clear. Thank you, Eric Edson."

— Chad Gervich, writer/producer: *After Lately, C*
author: *Small Screen, Big Picture: A Writer's Guide to*

"Many books on screenwriting will gloss over or just lightly touch on the hero's journey. Eric Edson dives in with a depth rarely seen. *The Story Solution* takes apart the journey with thoughtful insight and relevance — you'll be amazed at what you find."

— Matthew Terry, filmmaker/screenwriter/teacher,
columnist for HollywoodLitSales.com

"A passion for storytelling is what drives Eric Edson's *The Story Solution*. Outlining 23 steps toward heroism, Edson reveals the universal elements that all great characters make to achieve their arcs. Filled with dozens of cinematic examples, as well as invaluable chapter summaries, exercises, and suggestions to consider, the book becomes an invaluable interactive resource for any storyteller, regardless of the medium."

— Stefan Blitz, editor-in-chief, ForcesOfGeek.com

"*The Story Solution* takes the reader on a very in-depth journey. Eric Edson does a phenomenal job of giving very valuable tools. Well thought out and precise, with excellent examples from top films. It quenches your thirst to understand story and how to make yours work better on every level. A must-read for screenwriters."

— Jen Grisanti, story/career consultant at Jen Grisanti Consultancy Inc.,
author: *Story Line: Finding Gold In Your Life Story*, writing instructor for Writers
on the Verge at NBC

"Writers are like explorers who occasionally find themselves lost in a pitch-black story forest. It's always a comfort when someone hangs a lantern along the way to help us through. Eric Edson's book, *The Story Solution*, has given us 23 lanterns that burn very, very bright."

— Todd Klick, Director of Story Development,
author: *Something Startling Happens: The 120 Story Beats Every Writer Needs To Know*

"Eric Edson's dual gifts as a professional screenwriter and brilliant teacher of screenwriting are fully engaged in this book. He makes the complex accessible through lucid prose, a wealth of contemporary examples, and exercises that work. One of Mr. Edson's students described him as 'amazing, concise, and able to convey concepts in a very understandable way.' As is the man, so is the book."

— Linda Venis, Ph.D., Director, Department of the Arts, UCLA Extension
Program Director, Writers' Program, UCLA Extension

"Mandatory reading for every serious-minded filmmaker. Eric Edson's preternatural understanding of cinematic structure, channeled into *The Story Solution*, will help newcomers create a solid foundation, but it's guaranteed as well to enlighten even the most experienced screenwriter."

— Michelle Morgan, screenwriter/producer: *Imogene, Middle of Nowhere, Girls Just
Want To Have Fun*, on *Daily Variety's* list of "10 Screenwriters To Watch"

"*The Story Solution* just might be your secret weapon to constructing a script that will set you apart from the scores of submissions that land in Hollywood's daily in-box. With a solid approach to structure as well as a validated career as a writer and a teacher, Eric Edson deftly leads writers through his unique scripting process one progressive, dramatic, example-filled step at a time."

— Kathie Fong Yoneda, consultant, workshop leader, author: *The Script-Selling
Game: A Hollywood Insider's Look at Getting Your Script Sold and Produced*

ERIC EDSON

# *the* STORY SOLUTION

23 Actions All Great Heroes Must Take

Published by Michael Wiese Productions
12400 Ventura Blvd. #1111
Studio City, CA 91604
tel. 818.379.8799 | fax 818.986.3408
mw@mwp.com | www.mwp.com

Cover Design: Johnny Ink  *www.johnnyink.com*
Interior Book Design: Gina Mansfield Design
Illustrations: Niki Kaftan
Author Photograph: Victor Balog
Indexer: Bruce Tracy

Library of Congress Cataloging-in-Publication Data


Edson, Eric, 1950-
The story solution : 23 steps all great heroes must take / Eric
Edson.
    p. cm.
Includes filmography.
ISBN 978-1-61593-084-5
1. Motion picture authorship. 2. Motion picture authorship--
Handbooks, manuals, etc. 3. Motion picture plays--Technique.
4. Characters and characteristics in motion pictures. 5. Heroes
in motion pictures. I. Title.
PN1996.E37 2012
808.2'3--dc23

                                        2011038439

FOR DIANNE
THE GIVER OF GIFTS

# ACKNOWLEDGEMENTS

———— ❧ ————

I thank all the gifted students who taught me to see.

I thank Michael Hauge — man of wisdom, accomplishment, and generosity — who also, on the side, is one hell of an editor.

I thank my brilliant colleagues in the California State University, Northridge, Department of Cinema and Television Arts, who each day reveal to me the power of mission.

I thank Dr. Linda Venis and my compatriots at the UCLA Extension Writers' Program for the chance to share this extraordinary journey that is a writer's life.

I thank Michael Wiese, Ken Lee, Matt Barber, Gina Mansfield, and all of the stunningly talented people at Michael Wiese Productions for their full faith and support.

I thank Michele Samit, esteemed comrade in arms, who taught me how to preserve a poet's soul beneath that required alligator's hide.

I thank the producers, directors, writers, executives, agents, and actors with whom I have worked — people who prove daily that courage is indeed grace under pressure — many of them generous of heart and a few not so much, but master teachers all.

I thank my friends for those deep bonds of affection that revive and restore.

I thank my family — Dianne, Elise, and Owen — for their unconditional support through hours both dark and light, who discovered the hard way what "obsessive" really means.

And most especially I thank Isla and Kenneth Edson, who first showed me what love looks like, and without whom this book truly would not exist.

# TABLE OF CONTENTS

———— ⊘⨉⊘ ————

# INTRODUCTION

———— ⊗ ————

## NEW TOOLS FOR WRITING GREAT STORIES

Whether you're new to storytelling or you've already got some screenplay or novel writing experience, this book demonstrates a fresh way to create dynamic stories that will glue readers, agents, and producers to their chairs. *The Story Solution: 23 Actions All Great Heroes Must Take* offers a unique plot building template that can advance your writing skills into the "sold" category.

Claims I make for this book I consider promises, so don't think for a second that I take this stuff lightly.

For more than twenty years I've been getting paid to write movies and television, including seventeen feature film scripts on assignment. Currently I'm Professor of Screenwriting and Director of the Graduate Screenwriting Program at California State University, Northridge. For over a decade I have also lectured through the UCLA Extension Writers' Program, the largest writer training center in the world.

And most sincerely I say — if you choose to work in this magical medium of storytelling, for the screen or for the printed page, you can save years of trial and error in the pursuit of strong plotting craft by applying the concepts explained in this book.

I will use the language of screenwriting here, but do remember that these principles work equally well for novels.

Hard truth: 95% of all screenplays by newcomers don't work. And most of these scripts fail for the same reason. They simply do not contain enough active, audience-gripping dramatic action to sustain a whole feature film. Even with riveting characters and dazzling dialogue, many writers remain clueless about how much sheer plot is required to hold an audience enthralled for two whole hours.

After reading thousands of scripts and discussing screen story with writers, film executives, producers, and directors at all of the major Hollywood studios — and after closely analyzing many hundreds of films — I've gleaned an important insight. *Every* commercially successful movie contains the same detailed pattern in screen storytelling, consisting of 23 specific, linking story actions I call Hero Goal Sequences® that must be included in a script if the movie is to become a hit.

(NOTE: There's actually a small range in the number of Hero Goal Sequences® necessary, never fewer than 20 or more than 23. But for simplicity's sake, I'll use the high end number of 23 when referring to the Hero Goal Sequencing paradigm.)

Anyone who ever sat down to write a feature-length film knows that Act Two, the seventy-page middle section, is a killer. Scripts rise to glory or fall into obscurity based on what happens in these middle pages. The second act remains an incredible challenge and a vast desert wasteland strewn with the bleached bones of many hopeful writers who did not make it through to the other side.

Wouldn't a more unified, consistent, and user-friendly story paradigm be enormously helpful?

Of course the imponderable power of talent helps a lot in writing, as in all things. But truth be told, talent is not the deciding factor in who will bag a script sale and who won't. Hollywood hardly ever buys a completed screenplay to be shot without rewrites anyway.

Hollywood buys, then develops, stories.

Writer-director Lawrence Kasdan observed, "The American movie tradition is about narrative." In other words, about well-built plots.

It comes down to this. Movies that work always work for the same story structure reasons. It doesn't matter if it's *Inception* or *Avatar* or *The Dark Knight* or *Juno* or *Men In Black* or *The Departed* or *The Proposal* or *Iron Man* or *Pretty Woman* or *Ray* or *The Hangover* or *Erin Brockovich* or

*Fight Club* or *Walk the Line* or *The Devil Wears Prada* or *Up*. No matter the genre, if a movie is a hit, if it gives people the kick they come to the cineplex to get, then I maintain that that film contains the same 23 progressive story actions as every other successful movie.

An outlandish idea, perhaps. At the very least, spooky. But absolutely true.

Offered here is a clear, linking chain of highly specific, understandable Hero Goal Sequences® that drive your story forward with no holes or gaps. Steps that tie every part of your story together, creating for your reader a unified and emotionally exhilarating ride.

If your screenplay captivates a producer and sweeps her along eager to find out what happens next, then the chances of getting that script sold shoot way, way up, yes?

Please don't assume I'm proposing some kind of cut-and-paste formula for cranking out technically perfect but soulless stories. No. When using these tools you still get to work hard, sweat buckets, strain your brain and mine your creativity, just like before. But this book makes it possible to take any idea you may have for a movie, virtually *any* conflict-based story idea at all, apply this approach to plotting, create answers for all issues raised by the Goal Sequencing paradigm, and know with confidence that you've written an audience-engaging, potentially successful movie.

And if your script lacks these required 23 steps it will most likely never make it out of the agent's or studio reader's slush pile.

Pretty tall talk?

The following chapters will prove it.

This book has been organized into four parts. Part One lays out the key conceptual reasons why the ritual of storytelling means so much to all of us, the essential role that conflict plays, and how savvy screenwriters and novelists can best use these ageless human truths in building stories with Hero Goal Sequences® that will wow agents and producers.

Part Two explores ways to build your characters, and investigates the universal character categories that serve writers in the creation of story. It also includes tools to develop characters progressively throughout these 23 story actions, and how the dialogue you write for them should sound.

Part Three reveals the ways in which character is plot and plot is character, explains the basic elements of screen story structure that then become foundation for the more detailed 23 sequences template, and how a strong Hero Growth Arc fits perfectly into the 23 Hero Goal actions to give your script thematic depth and get it noticed.

Part Four then reveals in detail, one by one, the 23 linking story sequences all hit movies share, offering up the most powerful plot outlining method you will ever encounter.

The beating heart of this book remains throughout a demonstration of how understanding and using Hero Goal Sequences® can greatly improve the work of any writer.

> *"There's no more enjoyable existence than having a passion to write a story."*
>
> ~ Quentin Tarantino

*part one* Laying
The Foundation

*chapter one*

# THE SCREENWRITER'S GOAL

———— ❧ ————

You wake up one bright, chipper morning, lift the shade to see squirrels frolicking on the fence outside, and *Bam!* It hits you.

The perfect new idea for a movie.

This is it. Breakthrough time.

Without even stopping to nuke yesterday's stale coffee, you scurry to your desk, pounce on the keyboard, and let those fingers fly. And yes! Script pages start pouring out.

Bless sudden inspiration. It's a thrilling source of creative energy, a jolt like no other.

Until about page forty-eight.

Pause.

Chin scratch. *Now* what does the hero do? Press iron? Text his girlfriend? Take a nap?

Uhh... don't have a clue.

And once again that eternal truth gets revealed: *no plan, no Oscar.*

It's a fact of the writing life. To really give any new story a fighting chance, mapping out in advance exactly how your plot will develop — from first page to last — remains essential for success. Launching into a project without a well-considered roadmap most often leads to another half-finished screenplay or novel dropping into the bottom drawer, never to be seen again.

Well, there's a concept I call Hero Goal Sequences® that can conquer the bottom drawer.

This paradigm offers the best story-building tool anywhere. And it works for novels as well as feature film scripts.

A fine story is an elegant tapestry woven from many interlocking, brightly colored threads. Each strand by itself means nothing. Only when interlaced to realize a carefully planned pattern do all the threads join and become art.

## STORY RITUAL

According to Noah Webster, ritual means "Any formal customary observance, prescribed form or... ceremonial procedure."

A *prescribed form*. That's screenwriting in a nutshell, and Hero Goal Sequences® on the nose.

Understanding the ceremonial way we enjoy storytelling allows us to demystify the basic concept of all narrative writing, which is that *every good tale ever told is made up of a series of prescribed steps through a ritual structure of story that speaks to the very way we experience life itself.*

This is why story architecture, or the ordering of plot events, remains so critically important for screenplays.

## WHY WE WATCH

Watching a really good movie is a kick like no other. Imagine how diminished life would feel if suddenly we didn't have motion pictures any more.

But in order for us to write effectively we must understand the primary, personal reason why each member of the audience sits there enduring those pre-show countdown commercials waiting for the feature to begin.

So why *do* we go to the movies?

To be entertained. Sure.

And to experience those adventures we probably never will know in real life. Yes.

We go to laugh. Absolutely. We go to cry. The stunning international success of *Titanic* is based on nailing that reason down cold.

But the answer to this question contains our basic purpose as storytellers, so we need it distilled down to its simplest form.

*We go to the movies to feel deeply.*

We go because we want all manner of emotion to wash over us. That's what successful motion pictures do. Dramas or comedies, they lead us to touch our inner humanity and experience a catharsis of feeling.

Everything a screenwriter sets out to accomplish begins with the focused, simple, paramount goal of leading an audience into a meaningful experience of feeling deeply.

## EVERY TALE A MYTH

Good movies command our attention with intriguing heroes and the seemingly insurmountable problems they must overcome. But every well-conceived story also has a larger personal impact on us because underneath the plot, every movie offers some object lesson in the way we should live our lives.

Whether it's a good film or an awful one, we search out the message inside the story. We can't help ourselves. The human brain arrives at birth hardwired to seek meaning in everything. And the way people respond to storytelling originates right here, in our common need to find the significance of all experience.

So, consciously or unconsciously, an audience will dig into each film story seeking the point, whether any theme has been intentionally put there by the screenwriter or not.

We owe audiences nothing less than our best and most true observations of life.

Every movie made is a *myth* about a hero who confronts staid social customs in an attempt to change them — or who sets out to protect valued ideals in order to preserve them.

Myths hold meaning. And screenwriters must know how meaning gets conveyed in a movie.

## THEME AND WHERE TO FIND IT

The message inside a myth is called the "theme," and in any screen story theme can most often be found within the human frailties of the hero.

When a writer constructs some fictional hero to face a daunting journey, she builds into this character a personal flaw or failing. Then along the way, while the character struggles to overcome this shortcoming in order to achieve her story goal, the theme of the film emerges.

Whether it's a big action extravaganza or the small exploration of a relationship, what your hero learns about how to improve his own inner emotional life will be the gift of significance presented to the audience.

Think of a screen story as the hero's emotional journey of growth from immaturity to maturity. Each hero's tale is a voyage that parallels our natural passage through this world.

Many great film artists build cinematic narratives around a character who overcomes wrong-headedness in his relationships with others to discover the truth about who he really is. Author and top Hollywood script consultant Michael Hauge calls this progressive discovery of personal truth the hero's inner journey: a transformation from *identity*, the state of hiding behind a self-protective mask, to *essence*, where the hero at last reaches an unmasked, emotionally honest and fulfilled existence.

In the sweet romantic adventure *Shrek* we're introduced to a gentle ogre who lives alone deep in the swamp. He wants only to be left in isolated peace. If anyone intrudes into Shrek's domain, he scares them away. By so doing, Shrek gives people exactly what they expect from an ogre, and it allows him to hide his true wounded feelings of rejection.

Shrek thinks he prefers to live in solitude. But when his swamp gets invaded by scores of fairytale creatures driven from their own homes by Lord Farquaad, the only way Shrek can evict them is to sally forth on a grand adventure and fetch a princess. Along the way, this loveable ogre learns that in order to achieve genuine happiness he must risk revealing his true heart to others.

We all fear the pain of rejection when we commit to emotional openness. But accepting some suffering in life is necessary to live fully. So at last Shrek musters the courage to honestly declare his feelings to Princess Fiona, and his candor allows true love to enter his world.

We find the theme of *Shrek* revealed through the hero's personal character growth: in order to find love, we must be willing to accept some pain and remain emotionally open.

Many films build their themes around explorations of love. One of the most studied movies ever made, *Citizen Kane*, presents an unspoken thematic question in the very first scene when Charles Foster Kane dies alone in his palace, Xanadu. We wonder how a man who possesses absolutely everything money can buy could end up dying alone.

And we discover that throughout his life Kane longed to be loved. But he was never able to give love in return.

"He never gave himself away," friend Jedediah Leland says of Kane, "He never gave anything away. He just left you a tip." Wanting love without giving it is mere vanity. So when Charlie Kane's unresolved character flaw of self-centeredness results in a lonely death, the meaning of the movie emerges: in order to receive love, we must first give love freely to others.

But what about films that stay on the surface of life? What's the theme of, say, an early Bond movie? This charming one-dimensional hero lived only to triumph over the bad guys. And he never lost. So the message in any early Bond film has to be: good always triumphs over evil.

From shallow genres come shallow themes, but we must note that there *is* a theme, even in a James Bond movie.

Today Bond has been overhauled to make this iconic character more interesting and he has finally been given human flaws and inner conflicts that allow new 007 stories to contain deeper themes about love and the hollowness of revenge.

So the screenwriter's goal is to design from beginning to end a captivating, meaningful journey for a troubled hero — a journey that leads the audience to discover some universal human truth and experience strong emotion.

## SUMMING UP

- Before you dive into writing screenplay pages, it's important to think through your story idea completely and create an effective outline with Hero Goal Sequences®.

- A story communicates to an audience through a prescribed ritual of presentation. This makes screenplay structure, or the ordering of plot events, critically important in movies.

- Everyone longs to feel deeply, and screenwriters must allow people to participate emotionally in each story.

- In every tale told the audience will unconsciously seek out a meaning whether the writer actually has one in mind or not. So good movies must deliver a carefully crafted, true message about life. Movies communicate what's good and evil, right and wrong, and every screenwriter bares the responsibility to offer a meaning under her story that reflects human truth.

- The specific message of each film is called its "theme," and it resides within the character flaw of the hero. How the central character must grow as a person in order to resolve the plot conflict reveals the theme.

**EXERCISE:**

Off the top of your head, write down three first names.
For example:
  1. Elenora
  2. Clifford
  3. Henrietta

Now to each name assign a job or primary life pursuit that seems to fit the name. The job can be ANY human endeavor.
  1. Elenora — Correspondent for the British Broadcasting Corporation.
  2. Clifford — Fine dining restauranteur.
  3. Henrietta — Junior high school gym teacher.

Next, assign to each character a THEME WITH AN EMOTIONAL CONTENT using the following theme statement form which implies a dramatic action:
In order to _____ you must _____

_____.

For example:
  1. Elenora — BBC Correspondent: In order to <u>find meaning in life</u> you must <u>search with your heart as well as your head</u>.
  2. Clifford — Fine dining restauranteur: In order to <u>recover from tragic loss</u> you must <u>honor the past by living in the present</u>.
  3. Henrietta — Junior high school gym teacher: In order to <u>find true love</u> you must <u>first truly love yourself</u>.

Result: you now have planted the seeds for three captivating, meaningful journeys about troubled heroes who can lead an audience to discover a universal human truth and experience strong emotion.

Pick one, and start developing your story.

*chapter two*

# How We Feel
# a Film

———— ⊘ ————

The early pages in any successful script are all about winning the trust of your reader.

A producer hunkering down in his leather chair to read your screenplay must *allow* you, the storyteller, to sweep him away on whatever ride you've got in store. It's necessary to begin the journey by convincing that producer it really will be worth his while to jump on in through Alice's looking glass with you. So you must make things personal. You need to lure, tempt, trick or cajole every reader into an emotional relationship with your hero as soon as possible.

Your reader needs to care deeply before she can be brought to feel deeply.

How is that done?

By appealing to the universal goodness in human nature. Successful writers build stories that engage our better instincts and tap into a natural human predisposition to feel concern when we see another person in trouble.

But in order to bond with any hero in hot water, the reader must first, on one level or another, *like* them. So the most critically important step when beginning every screen story is to introduce the hero in a way that fosters immediate *character sympathy*.

This remains true no matter the story's genre, or whether the lead is a classic good-guy type or some moody, morally questionable Anti-Hero.

## MAKING YOUR HERO SYMPATHETIC

Hollywood spends a lot of money trying to convince you to like the hero. Movie stars get paid vast sums, in part, because the producers rely on a star's track record of infusing into every role they portray a warm and sympathetic personality to which people are instinctively drawn.

Think back to the beginnings of films that have stuck with you. When did you first know you cared about the hero?

Immediately upon meeting the decorated young war hero Michael Corleone (Al Pacino) in *The Godfather*, we're given reasons to like him. The same is true for the astronaut Jim Lovell (Tom Hanks) in *Apollo 13*, the almost-princess Giselle (Amy Adams) in *Enchanted*, and even poor Sweeney (Johnny Depp) at the start of *Sweeney Todd*.

But of course, every time I emphasize to students the vital need for creating sympathetic heroes, there's always someone who wants to play the exceptions game.

"Well, hey, what about *Groundhog Day*, or *As Good As It Gets*, or *Heathers*? None of those heroes are in the least bit likable!"

And I reply: *Take a closer look.*

When we first meet Melvin Udall, the hero of *As Good As It Gets*, he drops a little doggie down an apartment garbage chute because it's peeing in the hall. And Melvin (Jack Nicholson) says awful, insulting things to everybody who crosses his path. So isn't this character the grotesque opposite of sympathetic?

Personally, I find Melvin Udall to be one of the most brilliantly conceived, completely sympathetic screen heroes ever written.

From the start of *As Good As It Gets* we're shown that Melvin is a man locked inside a prison called Obsessive-Compulsive Disorder. His personality isn't his fault, he was born that way, so he suffers at the hands of unjust injury.

And at least he has the guts to confront people. He insults them to their faces — a quality that sometimes the rest of us wish we had.

Then Melvin becomes the first man to recognize waitress Carol's (Helen Hunt) true inner beauty. We like Melvin because he has the good sense to be drawn to a woman we already care about.

The fact that Melvin is a highly successful romance novelist reveals the truth of his inner being. He longs desperately for love, but trapped within a psychological condition that — as manifest in Melvin — drives everyone away, he can only suffer.

While we laugh at Melvin's off-handed nasty barbs, our hearts break for him, too. We're rooting for Melvin to bust free from his self-imposed isolation and find his way to happiness. He quickly earns our sympathy.

Inventing a hero we care about does not mean creating a flawless person. We see more of ourselves in people who mess up, who say dumb things at exactly the wrong moment. Those are the qualities we feel comfortable with. Bridget Jones (Renée Zellweger) we like. Erin Brockovich (Julia Roberts) we like. Andy Stitzer (Steve Carell) in *The 40 Year Old Virgin* we like.

## KEEPING CHARACTER SYMPATHY IN BALANCE

As important as flaws and weaknesses are, you must be careful to balance those flaws with strengths.

Remember the 2002 romantic comedy *Life or Something Like It?* Probably not, because few people saw it. This film tells the tale of a local TV newswoman who, while on assignment one day, hears from a homeless street prophet that she has only a few days left to live.

The hero, Lanie Kerrigan (Angelina Jolie), is an annoyingly shallow person, impressed with her own small-time local fame and bleach blonde hair. She's engaged to one of the dumbest, most narcissistic baseball players in movie history and she thinks her life is perfect just the way it is. But after hearing the prophet's prognostication about her imminent demise, Lanie begins to rethink her relationships and accomplishments and eventually comes to see the meaninglessness of it all.

*Life or Something Like It* tanked at the box office. In my judgment it failed commercially because the script as written gave us a hero so selfish and vain the filmmakers landed too far inside flawed character territory. Lanie Kerrigan possesses no redeeming qualities whatsoever, and the audience can't help feeling maybe her quick and painless death would be best for all concerned.

For an audience to ride the emotional white water rapids of your movie you first must get them into the canoe. When a person finds your hero sympathetic, they *identify* with that character. They project themselves into your hero as their surrogate for the adventure ahead. Then the audience climbs aboard eagerly and commits to your emotional movie ride.

Now they trust you.

## A RECIPE FOR CHARACTER SYMPATHY

Identification with a sympathetic hero should take place as early in the script as possible. Page two is good. Page one is better.

But exactly how does a writer create character sympathy?

Fortunately there's a recipe, a list of nine ingredients for use in creating a sympathetic response when bonding an audience to your hero.

The more sympathetic attributes included, the more richness, power and depth you give to the most important character in the movie. As a general rule, never write *any* screenplay without using at least five. And you're probably better off including six or seven.

Here are the personality traits and story circumstances that create character sympathy for an audience:

## I. COURAGE

Not optional. Your hero has got to have guts.

Every lead character who connects with an audience, who gains and holds our emotional involvement for two whole hours, must reveal from the outset their courageous nature. Moviegoers only stay interested in brave heroes. We admire people who face the world with courage and we come quickly to care what happens to them.

We identify more readily with flawed people, yes, but those flaws cannot include a lack of courage because only brave people take action, and only action can drive a plot forward.

Scripts about just plain folks without guts, people who remain frightened and unsure of themselves and who never get around to pursuing a plan, simply don't grab our imagination. If a hero can't get up the spunk to take charge of her own fate, the writer has created a *passive central character*. This remains one of the major reasons so many new original screenplays don't sell.

Using Hero Goal Sequences® will automatically turn passive heroes into active ones.

Every movie lead worth her salt wants something. Something highly specific. And she must have enough guts to take the risks necessary for chasing after it. *The hero makes the story happen.*

The same goes for smaller stories and family dramas, too. A gentle bravery must be seen in the hero there as well.

In *Unforgiven*, we first meet hero William Munny (Clint Eastwood) struggling to eke out a living for his two kids on a small pig farm somewhere on the desolate Great Plains. Since his wife died, Munny struggles on alone to support his young children (courage). Even in the face of impending financial ruin he attempts to be fatherly and gentle with his kids (more courage). We soon learn that Munny is a recovering alcoholic. Now in loving honor of his wife's memory, Munny continues to hold onto his sobriety so he can do his best raising their children alone (yes, more courage). It quickly comes out that in bygone days Munny was a notorious gunman who possessed an almost death-wish fearlessness when facing down other killers (twisted courage).

All this we learn about the hero of *Unforgiven* within minutes of meeting him.

We're first introduced to Erin Brockovich as she's interviewing for a job in a doctor's office. We learn Erin is unemployed, a single mom, and she's diligently trying to support her three children (courage). She fights an uphill battle to gain the doctor's interest in her as a potential employee (hopeful courage).

We find out Erin lost her last job because she missed work when her child was extremely ill, demonstrating Erin's complete commitment to her children's well-being (courage). Her ex-husband was "useless," so she got rid of him (courage).

She's always very honest and forthright (courage) but she ends up trying too hard and doesn't get the job. Then her car is smashed by a speeding Jaguar and Erin hires a lawyer to seek damages (courage). After losing the case because she's too honest on the witness stand (courage), Erin isn't shy about telling off her attorney (courage). Then Erin pushes onward hunting for a job, any job, so she can feed her kids (courage).

And the title credits haven't even ended yet.

The heroes in a great many scripts by newcomers do not exhibit courage up front and it's clear from the start that these screenplays are in trouble.

## 2. UNFAIR INJURY

Life is seldom fair.

How does it feel when you get passed over for that promotion and watch the job go to some incompetent suck-up? Injustice stirs our passions like few other things.

And for a screenwriter, that's just great.

After courage, the second quickest way to bond an audience to your hero is to place that character in a situation where blatant injustice is inflicted upon her. A good 75% of successful movies start with the hero experiencing some form of Unfair Injury.

In *Working Girl*, hero Tess McGill (Melanie Griffith) labors long and hard as a savvy secretary who keeps her incompetent stockbroker boss out of trouble with his clients. She asks only for an opportunity, the chance at a promotion which she richly deserves. But her male stockbroker co-workers steal Tess's good ideas, abuse her talents, mock her, and try to con her into bed. No one takes Tess seriously. Still she struggles courageously on, a victim of Unfair Injury.

See how it works?

At the start of *Wall Street* up and coming stockbroker Bud Fox (Charlie Sheen) gets stiffed for payment owed Bud's company on a stock trade by an unscrupulous client. A cowardly supervisor forces Bud to pay for the loss personally, even though it wasn't Bud's fault.

I could fill this book with examples.

Unfair Injury also puts the hero in a position where he's compelled to DO something, take action in order to right a wrong — an excellent place to start any movie story.

### 3. SKILL

Very, very few films are ever made about incompetent losers.

We admire people who possess the grace, expertise, and mental acumen required to become masters of their chosen work. It doesn't matter what your hero's field of endeavor might be, as long as he's expert at it.

We can forgive a great deal if, when it's time for him to get down to business, a hero delivers the goods.

William Munny in *Unforgiven* isn't merely a former gunslinger. Back in his drunken killing days he'd been one of the very deadliest gunmen anywhere, one of the most feared and fearless. Munny used to be the best.

And similarly, in any cop movie or professional warrior/fighter story, the hero can be introduced to the audience as a drunken burnout, even a lousy husband and unreliable father, as long as he is brave and respected and when the mission/case/fight starts, the hero's professional skills remain top drawer.

This is even the situation in *The Wrestler*, when Randy "The Ram" Robinson (Mickey Rourke) proves to us that for all his faults, he was and remains one of the best showmen in professional wrestling.

This character sympathy tool works just as well for heroes from more humble walks of life, too. In *Collateral*, hero Max (Jamie Foxx) isn't just a cab driver. He's the cleanest, most street-savvy and time-accurate cab driver anyone has ever met.

Novice scripts all too frequently begin with the lead character getting fired from some lousy job because he screwed up. Then the hero bee-lines straight to his favorite sleazy bar and fires down a row of shots while his bartender buddy tells him what a hopeless jerk he is. After that, he hangdogs it on home where his girlfriend blasts him with a withering harangue about how he's a fool, lousy in bed, constantly stoned, and an all-around lazy ass. Usually the hero receives this verbal thrashing while watching television and sucking up a brew, occasionally interjecting, "But gee, honey..." Then after his girlfriend storms out with her suitcase in hand, this hero lights up a joint, sinks back into the sofa and says something like, "Bummer, man."

He has displayed no courage, everything bad happening is his own fault, and he isn't good at a single thing. But the audience is now expected to care what happens to this guy next. Sorry, we don't.

(*TIP: When any story requires your hero to get fired, make sure the reason for her being canned is not her own fault. Make it an Unfair Injury.*)

At first glance you may think Ned Racine in *Body Heat* is an exception to this "good-at-what-they-do" rule because in his chosen profession, lawyering, Ned (William Hurt) appears less than competent. But take a closer look. His real reputation has been built as a Casanova, a smooth and charming ladies' man who beds women as naturally as most of his friends ride bikes. This is Ned's true skill, and in the Casanova business, in his hometown at least, Ned has no equal.

### 4. FUNNY

We warm to people who make us laugh. We're naturally drawn to folks with a humorous view of the passing parade. True wit is smart and filled with human insight. So if you can possibly bestow upon your hero a robust and playful sense of humor, do it.

In *Die Hard*, Officer John McClane (Bruce Willis) has his hands full as he battles an office tower full of terrorists. But John frequently breaks the tension by cracking wise.

*Erin Brockovich* takes on a multibillion-dollar utility company in a life or death class action law suit, but she frequently tosses off cute quips of sardonic wit.

It won't be right for all movies. Sister Helen Prejean (Susan Sarandon) in *Dead Man Walking* can't josh too often while visiting prisoners on death row.

But generally, wit works well as a character component for lots of dramatic movie leading roles. Even among patients at a madhouse, roguish convict Randle Patrick McMurphy (Jack Nicholson) exercises a cutting wit in the riveting drama *One Flew Over the Cuckoo's Nest*.

Take care, however. Creating a hero with a sense of humor is one thing. *Making fun of the hero* is something else altogether and should be avoided.

### 5. JUST PLAIN NICE

Where you can, simply show the audience that your hero has a good heart.

We can easily care about kind, decent, helpful, honest folks, and we admire people who treat others well, relate with respect to people in humble walks of life, and who defend the weak or stand up for the helpless.

Remember Rocky Balboa's (Sylvester Stallone) carefully tended pet turtles, the street waif he mentors, and the painfully shy girlfriend he courts? Even though he's just a palooka, Rocky offers the world his caring and generous heart.

I'm not suggesting that you write characters who always put themselves dead last, or belittle themselves, or apologize endlessly. This sort of behavior only reveals low self-esteem.

Being a good person doesn't mean volunteering for servitude. Just plain nice will do.

In the first scene of *Men In Black*, Agent K (Tommy Lee Jones) stops a van full of illegal Mexican immigrants as he searches for an incognito space alien criminal. Going down the row of frightened people, Agent K remains kindly, and in Spanish tells each illegal not to be afraid. When K figures out which one is the space thug he sends everyone else back on their way unharmed as he quips sincerely, "Welcome to the United States."

Agent K's only beef remains with criminals from outer space. To everyone else he's respectful and kind. A nice guy. A brave guy. A skilled guy.

What's not to like?

There are heroes who are not nice, of course, like Melvin Udall in *As Good As It Gets*. But when creating heroes where nice is not an option, writers must provide other strong reasons to root for them.

### 6. IN DANGER

If when we first meet the hero he's already in a situation of real danger, it grabs our attention right away.

Danger means the imminent threat of personal harm or loss. What represents danger in a particular story depends on the scope of your tale.

Most Action-Adventure movies start with an energetic sequence called the Action Hook. These hooks often involve immediate life or death risk for the lead.

But in smaller stories where physical life or death isn't an issue, upfront jeopardy might be the danger of crushing failure, as in *A Beautiful Mind*, or permanent spinsterhood, as in *27 Dresses*, or the loss of a life-fulfilling mate, like in *Legally Blonde*.

The beginning of *Ray* finds young Ray Charles (Jamie Foxx) standing alone by the side of a Deep South country road waiting to board a bus. Ray, of course, suffers the Unfair Injury of blindness. The bus driver treats him badly because he's black. Then as soon as Ray gets to Seattle, he's quickly robbed by a slick guitar player and sexually abused by the honky-tonk manager. Then another bar maven right away turns Ray on to drugs.

Danger abounds.

### 7. LOVED BY FRIENDS AND FAMILY

If we're shown right off that the hero is already loved by other people, it gives us immediate permission to care about them, too.

How many movies have you seen that begin with a surprise party or other bash being thrown for the hero by a room full of adoring friends, as in *Tootsie*, *Working Girl*, or *The Punisher*? Or affection gushing for the hero from a doting mom, dad, sibling, mate, child, or best friend, like in *Apollo 13*, *The Brave One*, *Edge of Darkness*, and *Contact*?

### 8. HARD WORKING

Heroes we care about have an enormous capacity for work. People who work hard create the rising energy needed to drive a story forward, like Peter Sanderson (Steve Martin) in *Bringing Down The House*, Maggie Fitzgerald (Hilary Swank) in *Million Dollar Baby*, and Jake Sully (Sam Worthington) in *Avatar*.

How many movies can you name where the hero is lazy or unengaged? Even Roger Greenberg (Ben Stiller) in *Greenberg* works hard at building a doghouse, pursuing a woman, and figuring out his own life as he commits himself to a path less traveled.

### 9. OBSESSED

Obsession keeps brave, skilled, hard-working heroes focused on a single goal, which is enormously important to any story. A driving obsession creates the plot — and that keeps your screen-play on track, rising relentlessly to a powerful climax.

Just be sure that your hero's obsession remains a worthy one.

There are other qualities of character that can help create a hero audiences will root for, but these are the never-to-be-ignored basic nine. Use them liberally, no matter what genre you write.

Remember, we must bond emotionally even with heartless Anti-Heroes.

At the beginning of *Scarface*, small-time criminal Tony Montana (Al Pacino) is certainly not a nice person. But look at the character sympathy tools used to make us care anyway: he's incredibly brave, very good as a professional criminal, of-ten funny, suffers from the double Unfair Injuries of poverty and place of birth, is loved by his sister Gina (Mary Elizabeth Mastrantonio) and best friend Manny (Steven Bauer), lives sur-rounded by danger, works day and night, and is obsessed with success.

Eight out of nine isn't bad.

Once you've hooked a reader into caring about your hero, your story can really begin.

## SUMMING UP

- Early in every script, writers must win the trust of their audience and invite readers to become emotionally engaged with the hero by creating character sympathy.

- When an audience accepts a hero as sympathetic, they can then identify with that hero, project themselves into the character as their surrogate for the story adventure to come. Through identification, audiences can experience the emotional journey of a hero across boundaries of sex or species as long as that hero remains recognizably human at his core.

- Character sympathy should be kept in balance by not making the hero overly flawed or overly perfect — just human enough for viewers to care about her.

- It's important that audience identification take place as quickly as possible to get viewers emotionally inside the movie world. So in the opening moments of any film, screenwriters must include these character attributes and circumstances to build hero sympathy that will foster identification:

  1. Courage
  2. Unfair Injury
  3. Skill
  4. Funny
  5. Just Plain Nice
  6. In Danger
  7. Loved By Friends and Family
  8. Hard Working
  9. Obsessed

**EXERCISE:**

Get the DVD of any commercially successful American movie with one hero in it. You can check for the level of box office success at BoxOfficeMojo.com.

From the point where the hero first enters the story, study the next ten minutes of the film. Write down both character STRENGTHS and WEAKNESSES demonstrated by the hero. Then answer the following questions:

1. How many of the nine hero sympathy tools are used at the beginning of the movie?

2. How are the hero's weaknesses presented so as not to harm hero sympathy?

3. Are any sympathy tools used besides the nine listed in The Story Solution?

4. After spending ten minutes with each hero, are you drawn to keep watching the film or not? Why?

5. If the hero is portrayed by a movie star, what personality characteristics of the star himself help bond you to the hero?

# chapter three

# HOW CHANGE GRIPS AN AUDIENCE

———— ⊘⊘⊙ ————

Most people work pretty hard avoiding change. Some of us even fear changing the really lousy parts of life. But then we get to go to the movies.

At the cinema we cut loose and enjoy change. With zero personal risk, we insist on it. One major reason why everybody loves the movies so much is that *the language of film is a language of constant change.*

Skilled screenwriters hook an audience through identification with the hero, then hold them in thrall by manipulating the story to provide a relentless flow of transformative events.

Whether a movie comes on big and loud or small and whispery, an audience expects each hero to end up someplace very different from the home ground where the story began.

At the start of *Forrest Gump*, Forrest (Tom Hanks) is a slow-witted handicapped kid who gets bullied all the time. He hasn't got a snowball's chance of ever amounting to anything. By the end of the movie he's a famous self-made millionaire tycoon war hero, as well as a wise, loving husband and father. Change.

At the start of *Bridget Jones' Diary*, Bridget is a low-level office drone lacking in self-worth, romantically attracted to cads, and unable to find any man willing to marry her. By the end she's a self-possessed, nationally renowned TV newswoman in love with, and loved by, a wonderful and wealthy barrister. Bridget and her world have changed completely.

The only powerful piece of dramatic writing I can remember that's about a lack of change is Samuel Beckett's classic stage play *Waiting for Godot*. And it's revealing to note that even though *Godot* was made into a film, I don't know two people who have ever actually seen the movie version. No change.

Cumulative story transformation is built from a series of smaller changes that take place step by step throughout the whole story. An audience will only remain emotionally involved in a movie if they experience units of change at regular intervals.

And here's the kicker: *the number of smaller changes needed for any film story to succeed dramatically is both quantifiable and constant.*

The function of change as the central driving dramatic force in all movie plots is not random. The size and purpose of story events required for each unit of change to work well is not random either. You can, in fact, predict exactly the number and degree of story change bumps needed, and you can time almost to the minute when those bumps should appear.

Soon I will show you the exact number of "change units" needed for every feature film. This yardstick is so precise you will always know in advance whether or not your script will work emotionally for an audience.

These units of change are Hero Goal Sequences®.

Every successful motion picture story you've ever enjoyed can be broken down this way. Once you learn to identify these units you then have a tool to build your own gripping, effective screenplays. No more guess work. You can instead know exactly how to shape a script for the maximum dramatic punch.

I realize there are lots of people who want to conceive of the creative writing process as an eternally unfathomable thing. These good souls will naturally resist any practical analysis of story "pieces" for fear their creative spark will somehow be extinguished.

But compare the idea of 23 Hero Goal Sequences® to the progressive chapters in a book. Each passing chapter lays the groundwork for the next. They link and build on each other.

The mere concept of an organizing tool called "chapters" does not in any way inhibit or limit what the book can be about, nor does it diminish its power, its originality, or its artistic achievement.

A symphony usually requires a series of prescribed movements. The movements come in an expected order, and these parts, too, build on each other. This organizational concept has served composers very well for centuries.

So before jumping to any conclusions about where this book is leading, ponder Mozart. Or Dickens.

We will consider in later chapters the exact use of Goal Sequences for designing strong stories. But for now, simply keep in mind that planning dramatic change effectively is an essential component of great screenwriting.

## THE NEED FOR HIGH STAKES

High stakes motivate any hero to pursue big change.

Consider, if you will, a friendly Friday night card game you've got going around your kitchen table.

Poker night with your buddies. Horsing around, laughter, beer. Everybody buzzing and no one's really paying much attention to the current hand being dealt.

Then suddenly Lorraine drops a clattering fistful of chips in the middle of the table.

Silence falls. Everyone realizes… that's the fattest pot they've ever seen. Lorraine grins.

All eyes turn toward sweet, soft-spoken Jerry, next in line for the bet. He wipes a sweaty palm on his pant leg. Deciding if Lorraine's bluffing or not now means serious money.

Not to mention that until a couple months ago Jerry and Lorraine were married. Before she taped a "Dear Jerry" note on the aquarium tank and ran off with the pool man.

The jocular mood of the evening evaporates. Everyone waits to see what poor Jerry will do.

Lorraine radiates an irksome confidence behind her golden tan, gives off that needling smell of chlorine she always has about her these days. Jerry looks pale.

He clears his throat. Then slides out every last chip he's got. His rent for next month. "It's not like you haven't lied before," Jerry mutters.

Lorraine runs her tongue across collagen lips.

Then oh so slowly, one by one, she lays down her cards.

Are we curious to find out who wins?

Sure. Because this poker game isn't just about the money anymore. Although there are plenty of bucks on the table, additionally this showdown is about a broken heart, a dream shattered, a love betrayed, and the possible loss of a home. All of which raise the stakes.

Audiences are far more interested in what happens next when the hero stands to lose something important. And the more urgently a hero wants something, the more willing they are to take any big risk necessary to get it.

A guy who is a total slob might suddenly set out to clean up his act after he falls desperately in love with a compulsively neat woman. And a young lady addicted to drugs may finally find the courage to quit after she learns she's pregnant.

The greater the need, the higher the stakes, the more riveting your script.

Let's say you're thinking of having your hero dye her hair bright red in Act Two. A new coiffure will be a nice visual change.

So is that a good story idea or not?

It depends. If your Hero is simply changing her hair color on a whim, there's no burning necessity. It will just slow things down.

But in *The Pelican Brief*, Darby (Julia Roberts) stops to dye her hair while she's hiding out alone in a New Orleans hotel room. Killers are closing in. She's desperately trying to conceal her identity in order to escape. And being by herself in the hotel room is all the more bitterly painful because just an hour ago Darby witnessed the man she loves being blown to pieces by a car bomb.

In this case the hero changing her hair color is an urgent action fueled by incredibly high stakes. She must change her appearance and vanish into the crowd or die.

Big stakes raise the temperature of everything and we can't pull our eyes away from people who are experiencing ever higher levels of emotional heat.

## TYPES OF HIGH STAKES

Since having something important at stake draws an audience ever more deeply into your story, we need to know the various kinds of stakes that make the hero's desire for change as gripping as possible. Here's the list:

### I. LIFE OR DEATH.
List finished.

What's at stake for the hero must be on the level of nothing less than life or death. Only the highest motivation will drive the lead forward through all the insurmountable obstacles to come and keep viewers riveted to the very end.

But aren't there lots of films where the possibility that the hero might get killed isn't even a consideration? Like in most comedies?

Of course. And in dramatic writing there are two subcategories of life or death stakes.

### I. LIFE OR DEATH STAKES, TYPE A
The literal kind.

Here, if the hero fails, he's burnt toast. *Finito.*

This represents perhaps 80% of all commercial motion pictures produced by Hollywood.

Look at any of the big studios' summer release schedules. You'll see very few films where the possible outcome for the hero is anything less than to stay alive or get dead.

## 2. LIFE OR DEATH STAKES, TYPE B
The metaphorical kind.

When someone experiences a soul-wrenching defeat or loss from which they never fully recover, we often speak of that person as having "died inside." Or that they're among "the walking dead." Even though they continue to breathe and work and eat, we recognize such a person as a mere shell of their former self.

Besides physical death there can be a death of the spirit.

Anyone who has ever fought for the ultimate prize of true love knows that quest, too, is a matter of life or death.

*Serendipity* is a romantic comedy about Jonathan (John Cusack) and Sara (Kate Beckinsale), who meet, spend a few gloriously romantic hours together, and feel the lightening bolt strike. But Sara sets up a test for Jonathan in order to see if fate really intends them for each other. Unfair Injury strikes and causes Jonathan to blow Sara's test. They are parted.

Years later, both are within hours of marrying someone less worthy. Separately, Jonathan and Sara sense they might be marrying the wrong person because maybe, just maybe, destiny's True Intended for them was lost years before.

In the desperate few hours before matrimony, each takes off on a mad hunt for the other.

What charm *Serendipity* possesses grows out of the way the filmmakers play off of the metaphorical life or death stakes built into a there's-only-one-true-love-for-me philosophy: either lovers recognize their preordained perfect match at the instant they meet, or the chance for ultimate happiness vanishes forever.

And the fact that Sara and Jonathan are both only hours away from marriage to the wrong people raises these emotional life or death stakes to the maximum wattage.

There are hundreds of movies with impending weddings in them because that's where some of the highest emotional stakes in life can be found. Theoretically, at least, weddings create a permanent union. So the looming stakes of personal fulfillment or eternal loss rise to a level of spiritual life or death.

In the middle of the romantic comedy *Working Girl*, hero Tess McGill goes to a blue collar bar in the low-rent New Jersey neighborhood where she has always lived, to attend a wedding shower for her best friend, Cyn (Joan Cusack). Tess was born into this working-class world, but she's now scheming to become a successful business executive.

Tess arrives at Cyn's wedding shower in a tailored suit with her hair and makeup strictly high class — looking very different from her home-front friends. As the whole party watches, Tess's boyfriend Mick (Alec Baldwin), a commercial fisherman, gets down on one knee and asks Tess to marry him — even though just two days earlier Tess caught him in bed with another woman. Put on the spot, Tess answers with a tepid "maybe."

Storming away from the bar, Mick rails that Tess made a fool out of him. Tess retorts, "I'm not steak. You can't order me." Mick declares that until she gets her priorities straight, they're through. He huffs off.

Now Tess walks down to the Hudson River and gazes out across night waters to the glowing lights of Manhattan on the far side. It's crystal clear she no longer belongs in this working-class world. She can't go home again.

Those twinkling lights of New York City are now Tess's only hope to become the free and self-possessed person she longs to be.

The stakes of Tess's upcoming business deal have just become — metaphorical life or death. The highest stakes possible.

I've read scores of screenplays by newcomers with plots involving heroes who are working toward a job promotion, just like Tess McGill. But often what's missing is that if the hero doesn't get the desired promotion, nothing will change. Life will go on as before and there's no price to be paid if the hero doesn't succeed.

Recently I read an otherwise well-written script — except it was built around this plot: a handsome, brilliant, rich young man works as a mid-level executive in his mother's huge corporation. He maneuvers for a promotion but does not get it. With pique the hero quits his mom's company and sets up a business in direct competition against his mother. Helped by his very rich friends, right away the hero bags a big deal and his company grows larger than mom's. The end.

What was at stake for this hero?

Absolutely nothing.

When he doesn't get his promotion from mama he's still rich, still handsome, and still heir to a vast fortune. Even when he leaves his mom's company he remains the apple of mama's eye, still in a privileged position and helped by everyone.

*Events* take place in this story, but there's no *change*, nothing to lose, no issue of deep importance at stake for the hero aside from his own ego.

Compare that to the setup in *Legally Blonde*. Here the hero Elle Woods (Reese Witherspoon) also hails from a rather privileged background. But Elle is deeply in love with Warner — who dumps her when he heads off to attend Harvard Law School. Shattered, Elle decides that the only way to land her man again is to get into Harvard Law herself and prove to Warner just how classy she can be.

Everyone sees Elle as an air-headed blonde without a chance in Hades of making it into Harvard Law. But through smarts and hard work, she does get in. Then when Elle follows Warner to law school she finds everyone at Harvard also assumes she's a dumb blonde. Warner quickly becomes engaged to an "old money" snob... and Elle's goal of marrying Warner slips further away than ever.

She's rejected and humiliated even though Elle shows a warm and caring heart and goes out of her way to help people. Elle now stands in for all of us who have ever seen ourselves as misunderstood and undervalued... which is just about everybody.

Elle's quest after Warner becomes a battle to resolve for a lifetime her own worth as a person, her spiritual life or death.

See the difference that high stakes make between these two stories?

Also note the character sympathy tools used in *Legally Blonde* to connect us emotionally to the hero. All nine sympathy enhancers are employed: Courage, Unfair Injury, Skill, In Danger, a Nice Person, Funny, Loved by Others, Hard Working, and Obsessed.

## ONLY THE HERO CAN MAKE CHANGE HAPPEN

Change is certainly critical in each screen story, but the source of energy pressing to make that change happen is key as well. It must come from the hero and no one else.

To be special, to be brave, to be a cut above ordinary folks, your hero must seize his own fate and actively work for a solution to the conflict he faces. If anyone else solves your hero's problem for him, your movie will fizzle.

Elle Woods in *Legally Blonde* begins her journey as a young woman who plans to make a career out of living for surfaces; getting her nails and hair done, and designing the perfect pink wardrobe. This is all that's ever been expected of Elle.

But when Warner dumps her and goes off to law school, our hero is suddenly losing forever the one man who defines her life.

So the hero musters all her courage and fights back.

That's how every good movie begins. Into the life of a sympathetic hero plops a Big Problem, igniting in the hero a strong desire to create a change that will solve the problem. The lead sucks up her courage and sets out to beat the Big Problem or die trying, physically or metaphorically.

By the end of *Legally Blonde*, Elle Woods has altered her whole world. No one thinks Elle a dumb blonde anymore. She single-handedly wins an important criminal case, graduates at the top of her law school class, and she bags Warner, who by now is groveling to get her back.

But Elle's inner world has matured as well. She at last sees clearly that what she wanted at the beginning of the movie, Warner, isn't really worth wanting at all. By the end she no longer desires to be just an ornament on some man's arm. She's become ambitious and respected. Elle tells Warner that if she's going to make law firm partner by 30, she needs a boyfriend who isn't such a complete bonehead.

Oh, how Elle has *changed*.

But here's the key reason we're so entertained as we watch this hero achieve her transformation. *She does it through her own willpower and actions.*

When we observe bad things happen to a hero who just stands there and doesn't fight back, it's only interesting for a short while. When we see a character create his own destiny through personal choices and strong efforts, we remain enthralled to the end.

Part of the great value of Hero Goal Sequences® is that they will ensure your hero never becomes passive. Every screenwriter must learn how to spot passive central characters because they sink scripts faster than concrete shoes sink gangsters.

*House of Sand and Fog* tells the story of Kathy (Jennifer Connelly), a young woman evicted from her recently inherited home because the city has made a mistake about unpaid taxes. Her house gets auctioned off to a refugee Iranian, Colonel Behrani (Ben Kingsley), who sees the bargain-priced dwelling as a last hope for his struggling family. Kathy tries to tell everyone that a mistake has been made. Colonel Behrani fights back.

In its initial theatrical release this film did very little business at the box office. I believe there are two primary reasons.

First, the lead character of Kathy, as written, is not sympathetic. She's churlish, ungrateful, stupid, uncourageous, self-pitying, and bad at the most basic tasks in life. On the other hand, Kathy's adversary Colonel Behrani possesses the qualities of courage, love, strength, kindness, and charm. Our emotional sympathies are completely out of whack. We like the adversary and don't like the hero. Trouble ahead.

Secondly, *the hero is passive*. When the going gets tough, Kathy's solution is to attempt suicide. But she proves as incompetent at suicide as she is at everything else. When that doesn't work out for her, she just slumps into a state of complete passivity and stops taking any action at all. Throughout the entire third act the hero of *House of Sand and Fog* is either unconscious or wandering in an aimless daze. Literally.

Since Kathy does nothing to resolve her own conflict, it becomes the action of the hero's married boyfriend, a demented cop we also dislike, that drives the movie forward to a climax.

The coffin nails for *House of Sand and Fog* are an unsympathetic hero, and a passive hero. The heroes we want to watch are active, not reactive.

## SUMMING UP

- Audiences enjoy movies that give them what they often avoid in life: change. The emotionally loaded experience screenwriters seek to create in a film story is always built around a concept of constant dramatic plot evolution.

- The big change in a screen story, from the hero's situation at the start of the movie to his very different situation at the end, is constructed from a series of smaller changes that take place step by step through the movie. The exact number and content of these actions are predictable and have been named Hero Goal Sequences®.

- High stakes are essential for dramatic change to be effective. The only story stakes powerful enough to grip an audience throughout a film are literal life or death, or metaphorical life or death — when the hero risks losing something life-defining like true love, self-worth, or personal fulfillment.

- Only the actions of the hero can successfully push story change forward. Responsibility for making things happen in the plot of a movie cannot be turned over to any other character.

- Passive Heroes who do not take action to solve their own problems must be avoided.

## EXERCISE:

Choose any two commercially successful American movies that have one hero in the story. First, read the questions below so you know what to look for, then watch the first twenty minutes and last twenty minutes of both films carefully. Answer the following questions:

I.  What is the hero's ordinary life situation at the start of each story? Be specific and include geography, friends, conflicts, work world, housing, attitude, dreams, happiness/unhappiness with a mate (or the lack of one), what's wrong in her society, disappointments and joys, emotionally guarded or not, etc.

2.  What is the hero's life situation at the end of each movie? As compared to his ordinary life at the beginning, how has the HERO'S EXTERIOR WORLD CHANGED? How has HIS INNER PERSONAL LIFE CHANGED?

3.  How is the hero personally instrumental in making this CHANGE come about?

4.  What's AT STAKE for the hero in accomplishing the goal that drives each story? Are those stakes life or death — either literally or metaphorically?

5.  How many clear, individual moments of CHANGE in the hero's circumstances do you see unfolding as the story progresses in those parts of the films?

*chapter four*

# CONFLICT IS KING

———— ❧ ————

$A$ll screen story structure exists to drive some worthy hero onward through ever more daunting conflict toward an important goal. There's just no tale to tell without this battle.

So take a tip from the World Wrestling Federation: the bigger, meaner, nastier the brawl, the better.

The opposing force character required to create conflict I'll call the adversary. This term covers characters ranging from a decent person who needs to stop the hero for perfectly understandable reasons (Dr. Bruner in *Rain Man*), to a psychotic killer who just enjoys murder (crazed hitman Anton Chigurh in *No Country for Old Men*).

Movie conflict is two people pursuing mutually exclusive goals who smash into each other, physically and emotionally.

A hero and adversary collide either while chasing after a single goal that both want but only one can have, as in *National Treasure*, or while pursuing separate but opposing goals, as in *Heat*.

Vague resolutions won't fly. Someone must win and someone must lose.

## CONFLICT ON TWO LEVELS

In well-written screenplays, conflict plays out on two dramatic levels at the same time.

The first level of conflict is duked out in the external world, the world of sight and sound and physical action. In *Iron Man*, genius engineer Tony Stark (Robert Downey, Jr.) must stop his adversary Obadiah Stane (Jeff Bridges) from selling Stark's advanced weapons to terrorists. Physical conflict.

The second level of conflict is emotional, internal, and personal.

It is turmoil within the hero as he struggles to overcome some psychological roadblock that must be surmounted before he will be able to triumph in pursuit of his physical goal.

This second level of emotional conflict plays out simultaneously with the physical conflict so that the two clashes are parallel and weave together to form one strong screenplay.

In *Groundhog Day*, arrogant weatherman Phil Connors (Bill Murray) finds himself condemned to relive the same horrible day over and over as he attempts to bed the girl he lusts after, Rita (Andie MacDowell). And day after day she rejects him. That is, until Phil learns to grow beyond narcissism and give of himself unselfishly to others. Allowing genuine love to finally enter his heart frees Phil, and he gets the girl and escapes from Groundhog Day at last.

VISIBLE PHYSICAL CONFLICT: Seduce his adversary love interest Rita who refuses all of his advances.

INNER EMOTIONAL CONFLICT: Fight to conquer narcissism and learn to love unselfishly.

In *The Matrix*, computer hacker Neo (Keanu Reeves) joins a band of rebels to fight Agent Smith and the machines who now rule the world. But there's no hope of beating the evil Agent Smith until Neo overcomes self-doubt and grows to accept his true destiny as The One who will lead all surviving humans to victory.

VISIBLE PHYSICAL CONFLICT: Defeat Agent Smith and his army before they kill the rebels and enslave what is left of mankind.

INNER EMOTIONAL CONFLICT: Neo must overcome self-doubt and accept that he is The One able to accomplish impossible deeds.

The first level of physical, external conflict remains mandatory for all screen stories. Gotta have it.

The second level of inner emotional struggle is optional — but highly recommended. We'll explore the inner Character Growth Arc more fully in a later chapter.

In both kinds of conflict not just one but a series of collisions is required. The nature of those repeated smashups must expand as the story advances and conflict grows in ferocity.

Here are the seven basic elements required to make conflict effective for the screen.

### I. The conflict must be strong.

The strength of conflict in any movie will always be a major factor in defining commercial success or the lack of it. Strong conflict develops from three sources within a story:

a. The power of the adversary — he should appear unbeatable;

b. How greatly the hero desires to achieve her goal — she should want victory more than anything in the world;

c. How high the stakes are — stakes need to be nothing less than physical or metaphorical life or death.

In the movie *Breach*, rookie FBI agent Eric O'Neill (Ryan Phillippe) gets assigned as office assistant to veteran agent Robert Hanssen (Chris Cooper). The FBI knows Hanssen has been spying for the Soviets for years, and young hero O'Neill must collect further evidence against his new boss. He copies computer records, tapes conversations with Hanssen, and keeps his adversary boss out of the office so other agents can search Hanssen's files.

The boss spy plans on retiring very soon. So he risks one last "drop" of secret government information for the Russians. Hanssen gets caught red-handed by other FBI agents and the movie ends.

Chris Cooper's stunning performance as the Soviet mole Hanssen may yet save *Breach* from total oblivion.

But there's something fundamentally off about this story. Conflict between the hero and adversary never grows strong enough to create an effective movie.

By the time O'Neill gets assigned as assistant to adversary Hanssen — the point at which this movie begins — Hanssen is no longer a threat to anyone. Scores of FBI agents hover over his every move. This spy has already been removed from the position he held, where Hanssen actually could do damage to the United States, and soon he'll retire anyway. The Bureau only wants O'Neill to scrounge up a few final nails for Hanssen's already closed coffin.

Oh, people shout at each other and get upset in the story, but real stakes don't exist.

The story of *Breach* comes from true events, and like many other such films, the plot suffers for being reality-based. It couldn't be manipulated enough to create the much-needed hero-focused conflict.

Handcuffed by facts, young O'Neill isn't really responsible for causing the climax of his own movie. The hero isn't even present at Hanssen's showdown with FBI agents when the adversary gets arrested. And most of the evidence provided by the hero is redundant.

So core story conflict ends up feeling like the hero isn't very important or at the center of things.

Also, the stakes for young rookie O'Neill are quite low. He works about eight weeks for the FBI, and then when informed that his first case has been closed (since he's not personally present for the climax, he must be told), O'Neill realizes he doesn't much like being an FBI agent after all, so he quits.

What a wuss. The problems in this film are:

a. A weak adversary;

b. A hero who isn't very committed;

c. Stakes that are relatively low.

Conflict here just isn't strong enough to create a captivating movie. *Breach* did not do well at the box office.

If your idea for a new screenplay doesn't contain a powerful collision of two dynamic characters from the earliest "what if" in your head, then keep pounding on the idea until it does.

### 2. Conflict must be seen.

That strong, physical outer battle keeps the plot active and cinematically engaging while at the same time it permits the hero's interior emotional struggle to be brought out into the open through behavior and actions that we can see.

In *Romancing the Stone*, hero romance writer Joan Wilder (Kathleen Turner) lives in loneliness because she longs for a perfect man — "Jessie," who exists only in her books. Then, trying to help her kidnapped sister, Joan is thrown into the Columbian jungle, running for her life alongside sleazy exotic bird smuggler Jack Colton (Michael Douglas) who is everything that's the opposite of Joan's perfect guy. In order to survive — and find happiness — Joan must let go of her fantasy and learn to love a flawed but real man. She grows confident in her survival skills, matures emotionally, and lets go of her romantic notions to find happiness at last with Jack.

The physical plot action-line of this film allows the hero's inner emotional conflict to become visible. If Joan just moped around her New York apartment dreaming about her perfect Jessie for the whole movie, it would be deadly dull. Taking action in the jungles of Columbia to save her sister's life creates a film worth watching.

BOTH outer and inner conflict must be made active and visible.

### 3. Conflict must get nasty.

Screenwriters should abandon all instincts for being nice. At least on paper.

Screenwriting classes are filled with genuinely good souls; honest, warm people who value their families above all else, who live the Golden Rule each day, and meet the world with kindness and compassion. Unfortunately, the stories they create sometimes prove just how nice these students really are. None of their characters treat anybody badly. Nobody tries to stop anyone else from getting what they want.

For a script to succeed, you've got to get mean.

It's your job to figure out the very worst things that can possibly befall your hero, then find the most shocking ways to make those very bad things happen. Not just once or twice but in a dramatically rising manner throughout your whole script.

When asked who the adversary of their story is, many new screenwriting students aren't sure. Or they mention some secondary character who's in no position to stir up any serious trouble for the hero. I've had writers tell me they thought their story didn't need an adversary at all.

Good bloody luck.

When told conflict must be increased and toughened, sometimes a writer will try to fix things by having his powerless adversary burst into a scene and start shouting. Not necessarily about anything in the plot, mind you, just shouting. Then the adversary retreats to the story sidelines until a few scenes later when he strides forward to rant once more. Then withdraws again.

Conflict is not effective if it only starts and stops.

When your plot moves in jerks and fits and feels episodic, assess the strength and commitment of your adversary. Reconceive the story to include a central, powerful adversary who can provide conflict that gets ever nastier throughout.

### 4. Conflict should develop and grow to become more and more challenging for the hero.

The principle of change is never more vital than at the core of story conflict.

The battle must build throughout all the pages of a script. If conflict requires only one scene of real collision between the hero and adversary, and that scene gets put off so it can serve as a climax to the story, you end up with a hero stuck in the middle of the movie for a long stretch with nothing to do.

Did anyone say "passive hero"?

It's quite a common problem and it can be solved forever by using the Hero Goal Sequences® approach to story construction.

No small number of scripts have crossed my desk that offer the following scenario. Loving daughter Phyllis receives a proposal of marriage from grease monkey Ralph, the man of her dreams. But Phyllis knows if her adversary dad hears about an engagement, he'll say no. Dad hates Ralph.

Phyllis worries. Phyllis asks friends what she should do. With another thirty pages of Act Two yet to go, Phyllis writes in her diary and cries, then asks Aunt Sarah what *her* thoughts are. Finally, near the end of Act Two, the daughter musters her courage and confronts dad, tells him she wants to marry Ralph. Dad shouts "over my dead body" several times. The heated climax scene plays out until dad breaks down in tears, expresses his boundless love for his daughter and agrees to the wedding. Dad hugs Phyllis. For Act Three, we watch the daughter's happy wedding.

*One confrontation scene alone cannot create a movie.*

And a story concept built around one scene of genuine conflict leaves nothing for Act Three. A happy wedding isn't an act. It doesn't allow for the powerful dramatic conflict required there, too.

A marriage opposed by parents can be shaped into a fine story. Try *Romeo and Juliet*. But no plot can survive if conceived so that conflict does not develop in growing stages throughout the entire movie.

### 5. Conflict should surprise the audience.

Every story must offer the audience an intriguing conflict with unexpected turns.

This is perhaps the single greatest challenge for screenwriters today because everyone in the audience has already seen thousands of movies. But scripts that claw their way out of the slush pile and into the land of produced films invariably contain some element of the unexpected in their storytelling.

*Juno* presents a story so simple, so obvious, that at first we may expect very little originality from the film. But every character in it proves to be complex and compelling. Sixteen-year-old Juno MacGuff (Ellen Page) quickly begins reacting to her pregnancy in unexpected ways. And who'd have thought the adoptive dad Mark Loring (Jason Bateman) would turn out to be a bigger child than Juno herself? It's a simple story but with unexpected twists.

TIP: Here's an important suggestion that by itself is worth the price of this book. When outlining your screenplay, write down on 3x5 cards, scene by scene, the next most logical thing that could happen in your story. Create a plotline where, after each scene, the next clearly logical thing unfolds. Now line up those cards and tape them to the wall above your computer. A scene spine for your whole movie.

Then — *whatever you do* — DON'T *do that.*

A writer should never, ever accept the easy or obvious plot way out.

Surprise your audience.

### 6. Conflict must be believable.

*The Number 23* is about an Animal Control officer named Walter Sparrow (Jim Carrey) whose wife Agatha (Virginia Madsen) gives him a mysterious journal that she finds in a secondhand bookshop. Walter discovers the book echoes his own life far too closely. He feels a creepy, growing bond with the detective hero in the story named Fingerling (also played by Carrey). The book sparks in Walter an overwhelming obsession with the number 23, which rapidly draws him down a cruel, dark path toward madness.

Eventually this loving family man comes to fear that he's fated to murder his wife just the way it happens in the mysterious red journal. As Walter sinks into desperation, he must also solve a real-life murder mystery that forces him to face terrifying revelations about his own past.

I was captivated by *The Number 23* for a while. Then at some point the plot became so stretched, characters so inconsistent, that I just didn't care anymore. The whole thing became hokum.

Complex plotting often results in conflict believability problems.

This script lost touch with "reality" in the fictional world it created. We are asked to accept that the hero discovers he's a former homicidal maniac who was locked in an insane asylum for years, but got released and forgot all that so now he hunts dogs for a living and nevertheless he's a good husband with a loyal wife and loving son who don't seem to mind he's going nuts while seeking revenge on a stray neighborhood fido after his wife just happens to find an unpublished manuscript in a second hand book store written by the hero himself relating his past life fantasized as a detective who kills his girlfriend so the hero's now worried he'll kill his sweet wife especially after he finds the bones of the first girl he murdered but his wife will stand by her man, all the while the number 23 is supposed to relate to everything but doesn't really.

Come on now.

When characters begin behaving in ways that hold no human truth, when they start doing things that serve no purpose except to advance a tortured plot, the audience feels betrayed. They step outside the movie and become critics.

The night I saw *The Number 23* in a theater — a film that wanted very much to be taken seriously — by the end the audience was roaring with laughter.

Keep conflict believable.

### 7. Conflict must be resolved in a meaningful way.

The race must reach a finish line. Stories can only have real meaning if the hero pursues a final showdown that decides once and for all the main issue of the plot. A hero either triumphs or fails.

Even in serial movies (*The Lord of the Rings, Star Wars, The Matrix*) where the central story question isn't settled until the last installment, each separate episode still requires the resolution of its own main issue.

So conceive your conflict with a finish line built in.

By the end of *Ray*, singer Ray Charles will either overcome his addiction to heroin or he won't.

By the end of *Working Girl*, Tess McGill will either triumph over her evil boss and close her big business deal or she won't.

By the end of *Fargo*, Police Chief Marge Gunderson (Frances McDormand) will either nail the kidnappers or she won't.

A lack of resolution in screen stories leaves audiences emotionally unfulfilled. For true-life biographical films especially, this can present a problem unless the real person died dramatically or reached some other moment of resolution in their life.

*Chaplin* recounts the life and loves of one of the world's most famous comic filmmakers, Charlie Chaplin (Robert Downey, Jr.). But commercially this picture did not do well, and I believe it's because the story is episodic without reaching any larger resolution.

*Chaplin* follows Charlie's quick rise to fame, riches, and creative control over all his films. The movie also dramatizes his many affairs with much younger women. An eventful, incredibly successful life is portrayed. But where's the story and theme resolution?

The concept holding *Chaplin* together involves an interview with Charlie's biographer (Anthony Hopkins) that's conducted at Chaplin's palatial estate in Switzerland during the twilight of the comic's years. As questions are asked by the biographer, the movie flows back and forth in time to various episodes in Chaplin's life.

At the end, the question finally comes up about what the comic star thinks his life has all meant.

Chaplin shrugs and says — I just cheered people up.

Any deeper point of the picture remains unknown. So the theme of *Chaplin* can only be: it's nice when you're born gloriously talented and then get filthy rich.

Compare this to biographical movies that do mean something like *Braveheart* or *Gandhi*, both of which did very well at the box office. The heroes of these films sacrifice their lives at the end for a greater human good. Historically accurate, they also present important themes through powerful story resolutions. And audiences flocked to see them.

Episodes in a life do not by themselves constitute a convincing conflict without some meaningful resolution.

## SUMMING UP

- Conflict is the heart and soul of all screenwriting.

- Conflict develops from three story sources:

  1. The power of the adversary — he should appear unbeatable;
  2. How greatly the hero desires to achieve her goal — she should want victory more than anything;
  3. How high the stakes are — stakes need to be physical or metaphorical life or death.

- In most good movies there are two levels of conflict that play out simultaneously:

  1. A clash in the physical world as a hero struggles against the adversary in ways that can be seen;
  2. Conflict inside the hero where she is forced to overcome some limiting emotional problem that's stopping her from resolving the physical conflict.

- To solve the external physical conflict a hero must first resolve the emotional struggle within.

• The basic elements required to make dramatic conflict effective on the screen are:
  1. The conflict must be strong;
  2. The conflict must be seen;
  3. The conflict must get nasty;
  4. The conflict must develop, grow, and become ever more challenging to the hero;
  5. The conflict must surprise the audience;
  6. The conflict must be believable;
  7. The conflict must be resolved in a meaningful way.

## EXERCISE:

Make up three heroes, and give each a life pursuit. Examples:

  1. Mack Henry — Big-rig trucker.
  2. Gina Ferguson — Reality TV producer.
  3. Ron Bishop — Corporate research & development scientist.

Give each hero a goal that is very important to them. Let's say:

  1. Mack wants to haul his last load before retiring.
  2. Gina wants to make a film about an unjustly imprisoned man in Brazil.
  3. Ron wants to present his research on a new food product.

Next, for each hero invent an adversary to oppose them. Something like:

  1. For Mack: Jessie, a ride-along pal, wants to convince Mack not to retire.
  2. For Gina: Torvold, her egomaniac director who opposes Gina's every wish.
  3. For Ron: Jill, a lab tech, who demands undeserved co-credit for Ron's research.

Now, closely analyze the POWER that each adversary holds over the hero.

> 1. What power does Jessie hold over Mack? (None — Jessie's just a loudmouth)
> 2. What power does Torvold hold over Gina? (None — Gina can fire Torvold)
> 3. What power does Jill hold over Ron? (None — Ron can fire Jill)

If needed, keep inventing new adversaries for each hero until they *fulfill all requirements of an effective opposing force character*. Keep testing the situational POWER that each new possible adversary holds over the hero — until you end up with something along these lines:

> 1. For Mac: Albert, who kidnaps Mack's wife and forces Mack to haul cocaine.
> 2. For Gina: Prison Warden Degron, who schemes to keep the innocent man jailed in order to exploit this prisoner's computer skills.
> 3. For Ron: Alice, the company CEO, who orders Ron "disappeared" when Ron discovers dangerous toxins in the new food product.

Don't stop trying out new adversaries until the *power ratio with the hero looks like this*:

> 1. What power does Hector hold over Mack? (Total power)
> 2. What power does Warden Degron hold over Gina? (Total power)
> 3. What power does Alice hold over Ron? (Total power)

Keep testing and honing each adversary until they become *believably unbeatable*. With each new adversary you try out, the nature of the stories will change. Stay open to that change — and you will ultimately create several strong movie story possibilities.

> *"The truth of any character you create is how he behaves when he doesn't know what to do."*

> ~ Dalton Trumbo

*part two* Creating
Your Characters

*chapter five*

# ELEMENTS OF CHARACTER

——— ⚬ ———

In order to take a hero through the 23 Hero Goal Sequences®, you must first know how all the other characters in your screenplay will function to serve that hero on his journey of discovery. Every speaking character in your story must be there for a reason. Every single one.

They either help or obstruct the hero. Those are the only story jobs available. So you need to cast each character with premeditation about how you intend to use them in the plot.

A story is like a chess game, and every piece on the board has a highly specific function to fulfill. Knights, rooks, bishops, all fit into the pattern of the game in their own unique way. But you can't suddenly thrust Scrabble pieces onto the chessboard and expect them to work, too.

Understanding the concept of character categories is also key to mastering the strength of the 23 Goal Sequence steps.

Once upon a time a scholar to whom we all owe a huge debt, Professor Joseph Campbell, went looking for universal patterns in storytelling. He studied myths in every corner of the globe.

At first glance it might seem that different cultures tell very different kinds of stories. A Japanese Noh play looks nothing like a Broadway musical. But Campbell set out to see if, below the veneer of style, all these extremely different ways for dramatizing the mythology of each society might actually be telling the same stories about the same human truths.

Turns out they do.

In Campbell's book, *The Hero With a Thousand Faces* (Princeton University Press, 1972), he explains the universal mythological character categories as they are used by every culture on Earth. These characters actually reflect different aspects of the human psyche, so knowledge about these archetypes is immensely helpful for storytellers.

Christopher Vogler does a wonderful job of contemporizing and expanding on Professor Campbell's work in *The Writer's Journey* (Third Edition, Michael Wiese Productions, 2007). Chris' book should be required reading for every writer breathing. Also, for a woman's unique perspective on the Hero's Journey add to your reading list Kim Hudson's important *The Virgin's Promise: Writing Stories of Feminine Creative, Spiritual and Sexual Awakening* (Michael Wiese Productions, 2009).

In the character categories under consideration here, I am including Campbell's *Hero, Shadow (Adversary), Mentor,* and *Threshold Guardian (Gate Guardian).*

The Ally character I break into subgroups for more specificity and clarity.

Then to round out, I've added some very useful contemporary screenwriting categories as well.

But remember, *every character you cast in your movie MUST come only from this list of categories.* You need to know exactly the plot function each will serve.

The typical Hollywood movie story makes use of between five and seven main characters. Normally, two of these are the hero and adversary. That leaves you, generally speaking, three to five additional key characters to use for telling a one-hero story well.

Any number of minor characters can also show up to serve lesser functions in support of the main group. But even smaller roles must come from these character categories.

Each screenplay does not have to contain one of every character type. At a minimum you must have a hero and adversary, but after that your goal is to seek the right balance among the other characters you do use.

First, figure out who you want to be the hero. Then start arranging other characters in your story around that individual to provide conflict and subplots. Of course, a movie story can have more than one hero, and I will address that later. For now, for the sake of clearer understanding, I'll refer to the hero in the singular.

Here are the character categories and the functions served by each:

## ■ THE HERO

This character's pursuit of a focused, visible goal originating from urgent high stakes actually creates the story by driving the plot forward.

At the start of the movie your Hero feels somehow unsettled in everyday life… even if he's not totally conscious of this attitude yet. But something's off or out of focus in the way things are going. Then a specific problem plops into his lap.

Now goaded by necessity, the Hero rises reluctantly to defend himself and other people as he pursues a solution to this urgent physical jam, while struggling as well toward a personal sense of inner completion and new balance in life.

Most especially, this Hero is the character who takes the chances and carries the burdens of forwarding your entire story action-line. And only the Hero can make that big showdown finale happen.

Heroes should have personal qualities that are universal and likeable, while at the same time they need to be unique individuals with flaws, shortcomings, and their own personal angst. This goes for stories in all genres.

There are different kinds of Heroes possible. Besides the standard straight-arrow Hero, we have:

### The Anti-Hero

At first glance he might not be admirable, but we quickly

find he's got guts and skill, so he becomes empathetic. Such as: mean mob bosses (*The Sopranos*), professional thieves (*Wise Guys, Heat*), friendly serial killers (*Dexter*), or drunken superheroes (*Hancock*).

### The Tragic Hero

Brave people for whom we feel some empathy but who have uncorrectable flaws of character that bring about their downfall. Like: doomed gangsters (*Scarface*), doomed cops (*The Departed*), or passionate murderers (*Body Heat*).

### The Trickster Hero

Always playfully clowning in order to unmask hypocrisy and stick it to The Man. Such as: puckish surgeons (*M\*A\*S\*H*), irreverent frat boys (*Animal House*), or mischievous newspaper reporters (*Fletch*).

### The Catalyst Hero

Does not personally undergo character growth but brings about growth in others (*The Fugitive, The Spitfire Grill, Bagdad Café*).

## ■ THE ADVERSARY

The Adversary is the one person most utterly determined to stop the Hero from achieving her goal. Qualities defining a strong Adversary are:

### 1. The Adversary opposes the Hero more powerfully than any other character.

Many roles from different character categories can scamper around causing all manner of trouble for the Hero. But each screenplay needs one single, powerful character who's every bit as committed to preventing the Hero from reaching her goal as the Hero is to accomplishing it.

### 2. The Adversary should not be a group of people or an idea, but one individual.

The Adversary provides core conflict in a story and therefore must be present for the climactic showdown with the Hero. This is a necessity, and requires that the Adversary be an actual person.

If a story asks the Hero to fight some faceless group or abstract idea, then that group or idea must be personified as a real, live, single Adversary.

In *The Hudsucker Proxy*, the innocent Hero Norville Barnes (Tim Robbins) is plucked from the mailroom and made president of a company to be manipulated by a greedy Wall Street corporate conspiracy. And that conspiracy is personified by the heartless CEO Adversary Sidney J. Mussburger (Paul Newman).

In *Working Girl*, Hero Tess McGill fights her way up to almost achieve everything she's dreamed of — only to have it torn away from her by her thieving, scheming boss, Katharine Parker (Sigourney Weaver). The movie cannot end until a climactic scene takes place between these two, and all obstacles in the Hero's path— chauvinism, elitism, social privilege, class prejudice— are personified in Tess's singular Adversary, Katharine.

### 3. An effective Adversary looks unbeatable.

The Adversary must appear to be the most powerful character in the story.

In *The Shawshank Redemption*, Warden Norton (Bob Gunton) wields total power over innocent prisoner Hero Andy Dufresne (Tim Robbins). The cruel, corrupt warden Adversary answers to no one. He locks Andy in solitary confinement for months, and he murders the only person who can prove Andy innocent. It looks like there's just no way poor Andy will ever triumph. And it's the warden's seeming invincibility that makes Andy's ultimate victory over him so deliciously sweet.

### 4. The Adversary believes deeply in what he wants, and thinks it's correct to confront and stop the undeserving Hero.

In *Air Force One*, the terrorist commander Ivan Korshunov (Gary Oldman), having hijacked *Air Force One*, tells President James Marshall (Harrison Ford) how Korshunov's wife and child were killed in a revolutionary war in his home country. Now the terrorist is willing to die — and kill the President's wife and daughter, too — in order to avenge his own family and win the conflict still raging back at home. This Adversary remains truly evil, but we sure get why Korshunov is driven to violent actions against the President and why he sees himself as correct in his actions. We understand his motivation.

Adversaries must believe passionately in their own cause.

It also helps to give your Adversary some charming or thoughtful qualities. The impact on any Hero will be much more powerful if that Hero finds his Adversary to be a well-rounded foe.

**5. Psychologically, the Adversary can be the flip side of the Hero herself.**

Dangerous or suppressed qualities within the Hero can be expressed in the character of an Adversary. This way the Hero symbolically ends up fighting some flawed aspect of herself, personified in the Adversary. There is often a scene near the climax of movies where the Adversary points out to the Hero how much they're actually alike. That's what happens in *The Taking of Pelham 123* and *Insomnia*.

**6. An Adversary may use helpers who carry out his will against the Hero.**

In building to a climax many Heroes face legions of bad guys that must be overcome before earning the right to duke it out with the Adversary at last.

In *The Matrix*, Agent Smith commands hundreds of other foot-soldiers he sends off to attack the Hero. But Smith's many operatives are not Neo's one true Adversary. The movie cannot end until Neo and Agent Smith personally face each other and fight to the death.

Smaller, more relationship-driven stories may offer an Adversary who operates without help, like Beth (Mary Tyler Moore), the mother in *Ordinary People*.

Or, as in a few films, the Adversary's influence will be felt and fought by the Hero without any Adversary Agents or even the physical presence of the Adversary until that final confrontation at the end of the story. In *Sideways*, struggling novelist Miles (Paul Giamatti) drinks his way through the vineyards of central California overwhelmed by yearning to get back together with his ex-wife Victoria. Victoria only turns up in the flesh for one climax scene near the end, at sidekick Jack's wedding. But Victoria serves as Miles' Adversary throughout, since his inability to win her back dominates almost every bad decision the Hero makes.

**7. A Hero should not be his own Adversary.**

Any character in the throes of internal self-combat has a lot going on inside, sure. But without an opposing force seen clearly in the outside world, stories containing these Heroes can become off-putting.

*Man on the Moon* presents a bio-pic tale about eccentric comedian Andy Kaufman (Jim Carrey). In this recounting of Kaufman's career, all of the Hero's problems can only be blamed on Kaufman himself. This tale of self-destruction becomes emotionally remote, and the domestic gross for the picture came in well below the break-even point.

When a Hero becomes his own Adversary, the audience does not experience an emotional journey so much as a clinical chronology of *hara-kiri*.

In *Walk the Line*, Hero Johnny Cash (Joaquin Phoenix) fights his inner demons and an instinct for self-destruction just like Andy Kaufman does in *Man on the Moon*. But in *Walk the Line*, Johnny Cash has a clear external Adversary in his father, who has inflicted a lifetime of psychological abuse on Johnny, nearly crushing his soul.

This movie avoids trapping the Hero as his own Adversary and creates a visible, riveting conflict in a film that was a hit with audiences.

**8. A natural disaster isn't an Adversary.**

Getting caught in a violent storm (*Twister*) or lost in the desert (*Flight of the Phoenix*) may provide harrowing adventures and a wonderful arena for conflict. But like every other type of story, man-against-nature movies work best when there's also a human Adversary present.

*The Blair Witch Project* concerns three student filmmakers who get lost in a deep backwoods area and can't find their way out. Being lost in the woods is frightening. But it's the creepy Adversary "witch" they never see who terrorizes them and kills them off one by one.

**9. An Adversary can wear the mask of friendship or romance and not be revealed as the true opposing force until the end — but still remains the Adversary throughout.**

One of the more dramatically intriguing versions of the Adversary character is what Professor Campbell has labeled "The Shapeshifter." This kind of bad person hides from view behind a mask of innocence. The Hero believes that the Shapeshifter will provide a positive force in her life and she has no idea he actually wants to destroy her. A major turning point comes late in these stories when the Shapeshifter's true nature gets revealed.

In *The Usual Suspects*, the lame and cuddly small-time criminal Roger "Verbal" Kint (Kevin Spacey) chatters away to U.S. Customs Detective Dave Kujan (Chazz Palminteri) throughout the movie, telling the tragic tale of a heist gone bad and an ex-cop Hero (Gabriel Byrne) murdered by the vicious, legendary criminal mastermind Keyser Söze. Only in the last few seconds of the film, after Verbal has been released by Kujan and he's limping away down the sidewalk, do we discover that Verbal is actually the legendary Keyser Söze himself. Kujan has just released one of the most insidious and brilliant criminals in the world.

Verbal Kint is a Shapeshifter Adversary.

A Shapeshifter does not change character categories during the story. Shapeshifters just conceal their true opposing nature from the Hero and the audience until it's time for a dramatic Big Reveal later in the story.

**10. The Adversary will not always be a bad person.**

An Adversary is the main opposing force, but he is not necessarily a bad or evil person. Some of the most interesting Adversary characters are good people who fall into opposition with the Hero only because of circumstances.

Zack Mayo (Richard Gere) in *An Officer and a Gentleman* wants to fly jets for the Navy to prove himself better than his low-life sailor father. But drill instructor Gunnery Sergeant Emil Foley (Louis Gossett, Jr.) remains committed to grinding Zack down until he will DOR — Drop On Request — from flight training boot camp. Zack only looks out for himself, and Foley knows in battle such behavior can be deadly. Sergeant Foley isn't a bad man. He's a very good man with a tough job, weeding out recruits who might not back up fellow pilots under fire. Sergeant Foley works to save lives. But for Zack, he's one hard-nosed Adversary.

**11. The Adversary can never become the Hero, but sometimes can dominate the story.**

The Adversary cannot take over the function of Hero in a movie. However, he can sometimes be the star.

A Charismatic Adversary shows up in stories where the plot builds to illuminate the opposition character as the dominant personality. Such roles invariably are played by movie stars and are often misdiagnosed as being the Hero of the film.

In *Primary Colors*, John Travolta plays Governor Jack Stanton, a charming, Bill Clinton-esque presidential candidate driving upwards from small state government to the Oval Office. Stanton dominates the story — but he isn't the Hero of the movie. He's the immoral Adversary to an idealistic junior campaign advisor, Henry Burton (Adrian Lester), who functions as the actual Hero shaping progress for the story, almost below script radar. This movie is about Henry's journey from political idealism to campaign pragmatism, and Governor Stanton, the movie star in the film, stands as Henry's Charismatic Adversary.

**12. When romance becomes the dominant plot, the Hero's object of affection serves as Adversary.**

In love stories and romantic comedies where mate bonding becomes the main plotline, the object of affection character morphs into a central, plot-galvanizing Adversary — as in *Groundhog Day*, (500) *Days of Summer*, and *Leaving Las Vegas*.

If it's a one-Hero love story, as in most romantic comedies, the loved one being chased serves as Love Interest-Adversary only. If it's a two-Hero story focusing on love between the two Heroes themselves, each Hero serves double duty as both one of the Heroes and as the other Hero's Adversary (as in *Pretty Woman*, *The Notebook*, and *The Break-Up*).

### ■ THE LOVE INTEREST

After food and shelter, romantic love ranks as the third strongest human need, and it plays an incredibly important part in bringing depth to screenplays. The presence of a Love Interest character in any story can provide a movie with its primary plot, or with a humanizing, theme-illuminating subplot.

But for a romantic relationship to work in a movie it needs to be about a lot more than just butterfly kisses and Valentine candy.

A Love Interest must fulfill a number of highly specific plot development functions.

### 1. A Love Interest provides major story change.

The principle of change holds true even in the pursuit of sexual conquest, and a romance that works dramatically for a script needs to be about falling in love and then fighting through lots of ups and downs to stay that way.

If we find the Hero already romantically attached when the movie begins, then soon that love affair must shatter.

If the plot starts out with a Hero meeting someone new and getting swept off her feet, before long conflict must arise in that relationship and cause it to fall apart. Girl gets boy, but then girl must lose boy to make it a movie romance. Only then can girl fight the good fight to get boy back.

A fairly common subplot in neophyte scripts I see runs something like this. The Hero meets a cute and clever girl at the library/market/mall and they enjoy chatting; the Hero asks her out to a movie and the date goes well; another date for dinner goes swell, too; at the zoo they find they both love hippopotamuses; he takes new girlfriend home to mom and dad, and the folks just love her to pieces; as the movie draws to a close, the two lovers look forward to a swell future. The end.

This new girlfriend is in no way an effective Love Interest character.

She provides no conflict or confrontation for the Hero. She does not counsel or challenge the Hero as he wrestles with inner pain and character growth. Unfortunately, this new girlfriend doesn't provide any form of change at all, and is therefore dramatically useless.

For screen lovers, hope must crash into despair. Passion into anger. Love into fear. Winning must spiral into losing.

An effective screen romance causes major emotional changes and challenges for the Hero.

### 2. A Love Interest provides sexual tension.

Sexual tension created by the Love Interest draws audiences into a story using universally powerful emotions. Varieties of sexual tension range from the charmingly innocent to the lustfully steamy.

Sexual tension arises when two characters discover an attraction and realize there's the possibility of a sexual relationship between them. This does not mean the Hero must actually go to bed with the Love Interest. Sexual tension wrapped around the mere *possibility* of making love can sustain a whole film.

In *Six Days Seven Nights*, New York magazine editor Robin Monroe (Anne Heche) travels with her fiancé (David Schwimmer)

to the South Seas, and they're flown around by a scruffy is-
land-hopping pilot, Quinn Harris (Harrison Ford). Robin and
Quinn alternate between disinterest and dislike for each other.
This outward indifference masks a deep sexual tension which
draws us in. Through high adventure their love blooms, but it's
not actually consummated during the film.

*Mary Poppins* offers magical nanny Mary Poppins (Julie An-
drews) a great and warm friendship with chimney sweep Bert
(Dick Van Dyke). Mary and Bert sing together, dance together,
undertake wondrous journeys together. Mary and Bert are more
than fond of one another. But seldom has an opposite sex relationship been more devoid of romantic sparks. The complete
lack of sexual tension means Bert does not serve the function
of a Love Interest character. His purpose falls into a different
category, the Sidekick.

If there's no sexual tension, it isn't a romance. Period.

Sexual tension is the most repressed of all human instincts.
It can be explosive and dangerous, or immensely empowering.
It's the foundation of everyone's fantasy life and can be blissful
or destroy people. So it's one of the most powerful dramatic
tools available.

### 3. The Love Interest provides a main plot or subplot of sexual conquest.

Once sexual tension is established for the Hero and a Love
Interest, the campaign for conquest begins. Here's a powerful
plotline in which the Hero will either win the object of desire
or lose it forever. The idea that the Hero must fight for romantic conquest is essential to the dramatic usefulness of the Love
Interest.

In *Hitch*, gossip reporter Sara (Eva Mendes) serves her
character function as the Love Interest-Adversary when Hero
Hitch (Will Smith), the "Date Doctor," wins her, loses her,
then wins her back again in pursuit of sexual conquest.

If we find the Hero in a story already happily married before the movie begins, and he stays that way throughout the story, the Hero's spouse is NOT a Love Interest character. The conquest is already over. It's only possible to build a genuine romance plot thread between a wife and husband if that marriage falls apart early in the movie. Divorce must be imminent, or recently finalized.

Then the campaign for sexual *re-conquest* can begin.

When movie stories require the girlfriend or wife of the Hero to be kidnapped and held for ransom, or held to force the Hero into something he doesn't want to do, a romance subplot is not present. Trying to save the life of someone the Hero loves serves as a goal, not a romantic conquest plotline.

In the movie *Miami Vice*, Detective Tubbs' (Jamie Foxx) main squeeze Trudy (Naomie Harris) gets kidnapped by the evil drug cartel, and both Crocket (Colin Farrell) and Tubbs race to save her life. Although we've seen Trudy lathering up in a steamy shower scene with Detective Tubbs, Trudy is *not* a Love Interest character because no campaign for sexual conquest remains in question. They already sleep together. They're in love and stay that way.

An actual win-then-lose Love Interest subplot develops in *Miami Vice* between Crocket and the drug cartel's business manager, Isabella (Li Gong). At first the relationship appears impossible, because Isabella works for the cartel and sleeps with the mob boss. But ultimately love triumphs between Crocket and Isabella, gets consummated, then is lost in a bittersweet parting. Cops and crooks can't end up together. But Isabella serves as a true "forbidden" Love Interest character because she tests Crocket's moral commitment to justice.

**4. A Love Interest forces the Hero to look inward and pursue character growth.**

Here's another critical concept for good screenwriting that will be fully addressed later when we take a closer look at the

Character Growth Arc. For now, we'll just say that a Love Interest serves as a window into the soul of the Hero.

Emotional intimacy with the Hero places the Love Interest in a privileged position to question, confront, and push the Hero toward dealing with his personal inner demons.

In a manner of speaking, a Love Interest plays the role of psychiatrist to the Hero. That's why a Love Interest must challenge the Hero as well as support him. Kisses then slaps. Help then confrontation. Constant change.

As *L.A. Confidential* Hero Bud White (Russell Crowe) shares pillow talk with his Love Interest Lynn Bracken (Kim Basinger), he confesses his key motivation in life. He tells Lynn about how, when he was a boy, his father tied him to a radiator, then beat his mother to death as young Bud watched helplessly. This explains Bud's compulsion to save women in jeopardy, and it's the emotional wound he must overcome. A Hero like Bud White can't tell this sort of stuff to just anyone. Only in an intimate romantic relationship could this critical revelation come out.

Bud also confesses to Lynn his lack of self-confidence — he doesn't think he's smart enough to solve the Night Owl Café murder case. Lynn lovingly encourages him. "You were smart enough to find me. You're smart enough." Nice.

A few scenes later, though, Lynn is caught having sex with Bud's arch rival on the force, Lieutenant Ed Exley (Guy Pearce). See? Emotional support, then a kick where it really hurts.

**5. Not every movie has room for a Love Interest, but romance remains the best subplot available.**

Whereas the presence of the Hero and Adversary remain an absolute requirement for every feature screenplay, the presence of a Love Interest character does not. Many fine films have been made without a romance in them at all: *The Hurt Locker, The Shawshank Redemption, Unforgiven, Apocalypse Now, Iron-Man, Jaws,* and *The Dark Knight* all do not have Love Interest characters.

But a screen romance relationship can be the source of

strong emotion for an audience. Love stories get our blood pumping and we enjoy living them vicariously. So if a romance main plot or subplot is a natural extension of the story you wish to tell, then by all means include one.

### ■ THE MENTOR

We come into this world already knowing how to breathe and eat. Beyond that, pretty much everything has got to be learned.

Many different people teach us. Kindly strangers, junkie muggers, that kid on the street corner who made betting on Three Card Monty look like such a sure thing.

Brilliant teachers, clueless teachers, teachers who don't even know they're teaching, all leave their mark upon us.

Teachers in screen stories are called Mentors.

A Mentor conveys to each Hero important skills and knowledge that must be mastered before the Hero faces an Adversary in the showdown to come. Whether a physical or psychological battle lies ahead, Heroes must prepare, and for that they need help.

Here are the key traits of a Mentor character:

**1. A Mentor can be any person of any age as long as they pass on important knowledge or skills to the Hero.**

Most often we think of Mentors as older people.

In *Inception*, Miles (Michael Caine) is a wise older professor who once taught the Hero, Cobb (Leonardo DiCaprio), everything he knows, and who now offers more insightful assistance. *The Matrix* offers Hero Neo an older, sage Mentor in Morpheus (Laurence Fishburne), father figure supreme.

But even though motherly or fatherly behavior is common for a Mentor, teachers can still come in many other shapes and ages. There's Jiminy Cricket in *Pinocchio*, where a singing bug serves as Mentor to a wooden boy with a penchant for lying. How old can a cricket in a top hat be? And Pinocchio's already got a father, Geppetto. Still, Jiminy stands as one of the classic Mentors of all time.

In *Léon: The Professional*, middle-aged hit man Léon (Jean Reno) takes 12-year-old orphan Mathilda (Natalie Portman) under his wing to protect her. But it's Mathilda who serves as Mentor to Léon, teaching him the real value of life. Here, the Mentor character is a child.

## 2. Often the Mentor dies.

This usually happens only if the Mentor is an older person, so that their demise will not feel completely outside the natural order of things. Sad, yes. Tragic, no.

The death of a Mentor serves three functions. First, having trained the Hero and having passed along special tools and wisdom for the ultimate battle ahead, the Mentor's death forces a lead character to stand completely alone and prove himself as the Hero. There's no longer anyone to fall back on for help.

Second, the passing of the Mentor offers up a symbolic death in the metaphor of story just before the ritual rebirth of the Hero. The lead character emerges from the loss of the Mentor a transformed person, now all grown up and able to overcome the worst any Adversary can throw at her. The Mentor's death is a rite of passage.

Third, death of a Mentor often comes as Unfair Injury to the Hero. This provides even stronger emotional motivation for victory. A climactic showdown becomes time to win one for the lost Mentor.

In *Urban Cowboy*, blue-collar Hero Bud Davis (John Travolta) learns the Way of the World and the Truth of the Human Heart from loveable Mentor Uncle Bob (Barry Corbin). When Bob dies, Bud redoubles his efforts to beat the mechanical bull and best his Adversary Wes (Scott Glenn) so he can win back Love Interest wife Sissy (Debra Winger).

## 3. There can be more than one teaching character serving as Mentor in a story.

For some Heroes there's just so much to learn it takes a committee.

In *Wall Street*, young hotshot stockbroker Bud Fox learns from two Mentors, his dad Carl Fox (Martin Sheen) and his boss Lou Mannheim (Hal Holbrook). Bud's delighted to think Wall Street tycoon Gordon Gekko (Michael Douglas) might become his third Mentor, but Gekko turns out to be Bud's Adversary, a Shapeshifter hiding out behind the mask of a Mentor.

Luke Skywalker in *Star Wars* has Obi-Wan Kenobi for his Mentor, but he's also got Han Solo.

**4. A Mentor often gives the Hero an important or life-saving gift.**

Usually the gifts are only presented after the Hero earns them, through some form of self-sacrifice or commitment to the story goal. The gifts can be tools for the journey ahead, or objects with secret powers, or special knowledge that will turn out to be lifesaving.

In *Kung Fu Panda*, it's the Magic Scroll of Power; in *The Lord of the Rings* it's the ring; in *Last Action Hero* it's a magic movie ticket; in *Inception* it's an introduction to a brilliant dream constructing "architect," Ariadne (Ellen Page).

**5. Mentors can be dishonest or immoral, unchaste or bawdy, failures or reprobates.**

Some Mentors attempt to lure Heroes down the wrong path. Such negative teachers provide examples for the Hero of how not to do things.

Mentors can also come in the form of hardened cynics or losers who have blown their own chance at success, like failed baseball player turned coach Jimmy Dugan (Tom Hanks) in *A League of Their Own*. The Mentor may start out as a reprobate, then reform and rise to fulfill the Hero's need for wise council. Or they may be wisecracking pains in the butt, like the obnoxious insurance salesman Ned (Stephen Tobolowsky) in *Groundhog Day*.

A committed Hero can learn from them all.

One senior law partner in *The Firm*, Avery Tolar (Gene Hackman), takes new associate attorney Mitch McDeere (Tom Cruise) under his wing to teach him the soulless but profitable ways of working for a law firm that's secretly run by the mafia. Avery serves as a negative Mentor who teaches Mitch how not to live his life.

In *Moll Flanders*, Mentor character Hibble (Morgan Freeman) works as a servant in a 19th century London brothel. Bouncer and enforcer, he's an unsavory guy. But Hibble offers kindness to Hero Moll Flanders (Robin Wright Penn) when she sells herself to the brothel to avoid starvation. He lends strength and helps Moll through some of the worst times imaginable. Hibble works most of his life in a whorehouse, but he rises to redemption by helping and mentoring the Hero.

## ■ THE SIDEKICK

A Sidekick character provides another important window into the heart of the Hero.

Sidekicks join the Hero for all or most of the story journey. Along for the ride, they tend to accept willingly a secondary, subservient position in service to the Hero. But they are frequently big personalities who insist on being heard, and most often function as the Hero's non-romantic conscience.

A Sidekick has no trouble speaking his mind — or giving a piece of it to the Hero.

A Sidekick can teach, but lives to serve the boss, not instruct the Hero in any obvious way. Sidekicks usually don't hold respected positions or carry the bona fides of most Mentors. They come from more humble, service-oriented walks of life. But the Sidekick character challenges motivations, keeps Heroes honest, forces the Hero's inner conflict to the surface where it can be examined — not unlike a Love Interest, but without the sexual tension.

Here are the primary attributes of a successful Sidekick:

**I. The Sidekick commits to the same goal as the Hero, but isn't the prime mover of the story.**

A Sidekick shares lots of screen time with the Hero and often shares the Hero's physical risks in pursuing the goal. But the Sidekick does not originate the quest or become the source of any major story choices in pursuit of that goal. A Sidekick character knows his place.

The Sidekick brings dramatic variety to a story. He offers another level of interest and sympathy, and hopefully some laughs. But the Sidekick leaves all story-advancing thought and energy to the Hero.

Sancho Panza serves Don Quixote. Donkey serves Shrek. Forgetful Dory serves clownfish Marlin as he searches for his son, Nemo.

### 2. A Sidekick isn't as skilled as the Hero.

Since a Sidekick doesn't want to overshadow the Hero in any way, her skill levels are usually pretty good, but never quite as good as the Hero. She sometimes possesses a skill the Hero doesn't have, but nothing so wonderful as to steal glory from the central character.

Tinker Bell can fly. Tinker Bell can spread pixie dust that allows others to fly. But she can't lead an attack on the pirates like Peter Pan, or fight like him, or play games with the Lost Boys like him. In Never Land we know who's boss.

### 3. A Sidekick remains completely loyal and trustworthy.

R2-D2 remains eternally loyal to Luke Skywalker. Oda Mae Brown (Whoopi Goldberg) from *Ghost* takes many risks to help out her friend and most demanding spirit contact Sam Wheat (Patrick Swayze), to whom she is completely loyal.

A Sidekick will never, ever turn against the Hero.

### 4. Sidekicks don't die.

Sidekicks represent mythological continuity. They are the Hero's P.R. person. Killing off the Sidekick would mean destroying the Hero's thematic message for the future of society. It just isn't done.

And if a Hero can't save his own Sidekick, he's not worthy to be star of the story.

Sometimes a Hero dies at the end of the movie, and he needs his Sidekick alive to go forth and tell the Hero's tale. The Sidekick character keeps the Hero's myth alive to ensure that their sacrifice wasn't in vain.

In *Gladiator*, Hero Maximus (Russell Crowe) wants only to return home to his wife and child, but evil Emperor Commodus orders Maximus' family killed. The Hero becomes a slave gladiator who eventually triumphs over Commodus in the Coliseum, and in death Maximus saves Rome and at last returns to his family. But then his gladiator Sidekick Juba (Djimon Hounsou) honors Maximus with a symbolic burying of small carved effigies of Maximus and his wife and son in the blood-soaked earth of the Coliseum. Finally Juba sets off for Africa, thereby living out the Hero's dream for real by returning to the arms of his own family. Loving and loyal, it's clear Juba will pass on the story of Hero Maximus to the next generation.

EXCEPTION: The only time a Sidekick can die is if the story is a formal tragedy, as in *King Lear* (the Fool) or *Scarface* (Manny), where the Hero is fatally flawed and therefore destroyed in the end.

### 5. Sidekicks do not experience character growth.

Should you discover while working on your script that there's a Character Growth Arc developing inside your Sidekick, it means that character isn't a Sidekick any longer. She has been elevated to the status of a co-Hero and perhaps it's time to reshape your story structure to accommodate two leads.

Sidekicks exist only to serve their Heroes, and allowing them a Character Growth Arc of their own steals thunder away from the Hero.

How disloyal is that?

### 6. Sidekicks often question the Hero's motivations and offer conflict as well as counsel.

Though they cannot experience character growth on their own, Sidekicks are readily available to help the Hero wrestle with thematic inner conflict. Sidekicks also offer wise counsel, just like Mentors. And they don't let the Hero dodge any painful introspection. In return for absolute loyalty a Sidekick demands honesty from her Hero.

The Sidekick is in a privileged position to know the Hero's inner life and to see up close the Hero's weaknesses as well as his strengths.

In the moody, smart movie *Insomnia*, Detective Will Dormer (Al Pacino) flies into a remote Alaskan town with his partner Detective Hap Eckhart (Martin Donovan), on loan from a big city police department to help with a local case, the murder of a teenage girl. Detective Dormer suffers from insomnia, and here in the land of the midnight sun he cannot sleep at all. (Dormer's name derives from the French word *dormir*, meaning "to sleep," his deepest wish.)

A young local cop, Detective Ellie Burr (Hilary Swank), thinks he's a rock star among detectives. Ellie eagerly becomes Dormer's non-comedic Sidekick.

Hero Dormer sets a trap for the killer (Robin Williams), but in dense fog Dormer accidentally fires on Detective Eckhart and kills his partner. Ellie's assigned to investigate this fatal officer shooting.

So she tags along with Dormer, peppering him with questions. Ellie Burr becomes a real thorn in his side. (Her name is Burr, after all.)

By now Detective Dormer's so sleep-deprived he no longer knows if shooting his partner was an accident or not. It turns out that back home Eckhart was about to rat out Dormer for planting evidence on a dead criminal. So truth be told, it's quite convenient for Dormer that Eckhart is now silent.

Dormer tampers with evidence to distance himself from his partner's accidental death.

By the end, after Dormer kills the murderer and lays dying

himself, Ellie holds in her hand hard proof of Dormer's own wrongdoing. In her loyalty to the Hero, Ellie moves to destroy the evidence.

And with his last breath, Dormer stops her. He tells Ellie, "Don't lose your way."

The dying Hero keeps his Sidekick ethically pure. It's a powerful variation on the Hero/Sidekick relationship. This Hero dies, but his Sidekick will go forth to keep her flawed Hero's mythology alive — and she will become the moral cop Dormer failed to be.

**7. A same-sex Sidekick often echoes the Hero's romance with a comedic romance of his/her own.**

The use of two sets of lovers in a story heavy on romance is a plot form as old as the ancient Greeks. The secondary romance of a Sidekick will almost always be comedic, because if played straight it tends to draw focus and thematic importance away from the Hero's own love relationship.

In *When Harry Met Sally* there are two Heroes, Harry (Billy Crystal) and Sally (Meg Ryan), and each has their own Sidekick: Harry's got Jess (Bruno Kirby) and Sally's got Marie (Carrie Fisher). Both Sidekicks experience separate comedic love problems early on, but when the Sidekicks finally meet each other, it leads to marriage. No heavy or time-consuming subplot, of course, because that might distract from our focus on Harry and Sally. The Sidekicks' romance serves only as comedic echo to that of the Heroes.

If the secondary romance subplot is tragic, like in *An Officer and a Gentleman* and *Sayonara*, then often the secondary character involved is NOT a Sidekick, but either a negative Mentor, as in *An Officer and a Gentleman*, or a classic Mentor, as in *Sayonara*.

## ■ THE GATE GUARDIAN

Heroes must be tested. Over and over.

The journey to wholeness and victory for the Hero must be fraught with unexpected obstacles, setbacks, disasters, and formidable opposition characters who jump up and yell "Stop! You can't go any further!"

Here, the Gate Guardian can be immensely useful. Gate Guardians exist to force a Hero into proving his worthiness before moving on.

The power of this character category comes from the fact it reflects somebody we all live with — that voice inside our own heads telling us not to try. When you undertake something difficult, something that requires huge effort and new skills — say, like writing a full-length feature screenplay — don't you occasionally hear a low whispering in your ear that says, "Are you nuts?! You can't do this! Why waste time trying? Stop right now and save yourself the grief."

We are all tested by our own internal Gate Guardians. And only a worthy Hero finds the courage to surmount that voice.

There's real beauty in this character because first a Gate Guardian stops and opposes, slams a gate shut in the Hero's face. But after the Hero finds a clever way around that obstacle, the Gate Guardian transforms into an ally.

This later switch to the Hero's side makes the Gate Guardian unique among supporting characters.

During an audition at the Rose Theatre in *Shakespeare in Love*, "Thomas Kent" reads from Shakespeare's new play, and Will Shakespeare (Joseph Fiennes) thinks he's found the perfect actor to play Romeo. But Thomas Kent is actually Viola De Lesseps (Gwyneth Paltrow) dressed in men's clothes, and she runs away. The Hero chases Viola back to her huge ancestral home, where Viola disappears inside. Will bangs on the kitchen door to get in. When it opens, Viola's formidable Nurse (Imelda Staunton) stands blocking Will's way, glowering back out at him.

No way will she let him inside. Nurse brushes off Will's entreaties and swings the heavy door closed in his face. By her action, this Gate Guardian informs Will flat out that he's not worthy to enter Viola's aristocratic world.

But does it stop him? No! Our Hero rises to the test and figures out another way to get inside the castle, passes himself off as a musician come to play at a ball.

Later in the story, Nurse proves her true Gate Guardian mettle and she becomes a full-fledged ally. When Will and Viola at last make love in Viola's room, it's Nurse who parks her chair in front of the closed bedchamber door to protect the lovers' privacy.

Nurse first stops the Hero, then assists him.

## ■ OTHER ALLY CHARACTERS:

There are characters that serve specific plot purposes as allies but require far less screen time than, say, a Sidekick or Love Interest.

In any movie you can usually find a number of roles from these other Ally categories because it's very rare that a Hero will fight the good fight completely alone.

But these Allies must serve as sources of conflict for the Hero, too. Even friends stir up trouble. They're not just window dressing, but key elements useful for building dramatic tension.

And not all of these other Allies mean to be helpful. Not all are cheerfully willing. Sometimes a character must be pushed into helping out.

Here are the main subcategories of lesser Ally characters:

### I. Comparison Ally

This person starts the story as a friend or co-worker or acquaintance of the Hero, basically in the exact same circumstance as the Hero. Same job, income level, lifestyle, and pursuing a similar general goal.

Usually the Comparison Ally is a same-sex pal to the Hero, but not always.

At the start the Comparison Ally is a mirror image of the Hero, an identical twin to be used later for tracking the Hero's growth in the story. A Comparison Ally stays put, while the Hero ventures onward and upward, developing and changing.

The Comparison Ally can also be used as a confidant; someone else the Hero can talk to.

But most importantly, the Comparison Ally character visually makes clear to the audience how much the Hero is changing.

At the start of *Pretty Woman*, Hero Vivian Ward (Julia Roberts) lives in a dumpy apartment with friend and fellow streetwalker Kit De Luca (Laura San Giacomo). They look and sound alike. But then Vivian meets Edward Lewis (Richard Gere) and develops as a person.

Toward the climax of *Pretty Woman*, pal Kit shows up at the posh Beverly Hills hotel where Viv has been staying and Kit remains the crude, gum-chewing streetwalker she's always been. But Viv now dresses elegantly. She's poised, well spoken, versed in the social graces and she could pass as an important member of any posh country club. We can compare and see just how profoundly the Hero has changed.

Kit isn't a Sidekick. She's not around that much, and she's not interested at all in Viv's inner character growth. She's a Comparison Ally, a visual point of reference that makes the depth of Vivian's transformation crystal clear for the audience.

### 2. Comic Ally

This character usually falls short of being a major player in the story and serves more of a cameo secondary role.

Any Ally can tell a joke or two, but the Comic Ally possesses real attitude, a skewed view of the world that makes them inherently funny even without jokes. They assist the Hero while providing some comic relief.

In *Pulp Fiction*, Anti-Hero hitman Vincent Vega (John Travolta) receives orders to babysit his gangster boss's wife, Mia Wallace (Uma Thurman). When Mia accidentally overdoses on Vincent's drug stash, he rushes Mia to the home of his friendly neighborhood dope dealer, Lance (Eric Stoltz), and demands help. Lance wants nothing to do with a flat-lining customer. But Vincent will not be turned away. So the drug dealer pulls out a huge syringe full of adrenaline and tells Vincent it must be stabbed directly into Mia's heart.

Adding to the chaos, Lance's spaced-out, overly pierced wife Jody (Rosanna Arquette) jabbers on hysterically. Lance and Jody do not willingly assist the Hero, but they help Vincent nonetheless. It's a gruesomely funny scene and Lance and Jody reek of attitude, serving as twisted Comic Allies.

### 3. Helper-Follower Ally

The story world of a script can get so large that a Hero needs skilled help beyond what the Mentor or Sidekick can provide.

In *Ocean's Eleven*, the heist requires many technical trades beyond the expertise of Danny Ocean (George Clooney) the Hero, and Rusty Ryan (Brad Pitt) the Sidekick. So they gather Helper-Follower Allies including Reuben (Elliott Gould), Frank (Bernie Mac), Saul (Carl Reiner), Basher Tarr (Don Cheadle), and Yen (Shaobo Qin).

In *Outbreak*, epidemiologist Colonel Sam Daniels (Dustin Hoffman) gets mere hours to create a vaccine that will save the world and his Love Interest ex-wife. He's aided in the lab by a loyal Helper-Follower Ally, Major Salt (Cuba Gooding, Jr.).

Sometimes the Helper-Followers come as a married or romantically committed couple (opposite-sex or same-sex), two for the price of one. *White Palace* presents a Helper-Ally couple Neil (Jason Alexander) and Rachel (Rachel Chagall) who try to match-make for young widower Hero Max (James Spader). The Hero sees their efforts as meddling, but the couple's attempt qualifies as Helper-Follower activity. Allies provide conflict, too.

Helper-Follower Allies can be neighbors (*Romancing the Stone*), nuns (*Sister Act*), family members (*The Notebook*), servants (*Chinatown*), oppressed citizens (*V for Vendetta*), prison guards (*The Green Mile*), carnival performers (*Fur*), African villagers (*Out of Africa*), or many, many others.

### 4. Hopeful Savior Ally

A Hopeful Savior Ally holds out the promise of assistance or rescue for a Hero in deep trouble. Then, shockingly, the Hopeful Savior Ally gets killed.

It's a major principle of good screenwriting that *the Hero must save herself.* A Hero must solve her own problems. She cannot be saved by the cavalry or by coincidence or some outside force or stranger arriving in the nick of time. So even though the death of the Hopeful Savior Ally shocks us — they nearly always die — still, deep down, the audience recognizes this problem can only be solved by the Hero.

The film *Collateral* finds cabdriver Hero Max kidnapped by hitman Vincent (Tom Cruise), then forced to drive Vincent around while he assassinates people. In a parallel plotline, Detective Fanning (Mark Ruffalo) investigates the first killing and suspects there's something bigger afoot here. We're rooting for Fanning to figure it all out and reach Max in time to save him.

After a shootout sequence in a big night club, the detective pulls Max outside, away from Vincent, and it appears Fanning has saved the cabdriver.

At the curb Max feels overwhelming relief — then Detective Fanning drops down dead, shot by Vincent. Max ends up once more in the clutches of a most deadly Adversary.

And another Hopeful Savior Ally bites the dust.

### 5. Cheerleader Ally

Sometimes Heroes need pep talks. The Cheerleader Ally can remind both Hero and audience that the struggle has been undertaken for a greater public good than just the personal needs of the Hero. Cheerleader Allies usually aren't major players, but they keep the Hero on track toward his goal.

The Cheerleader Ally can also function as a Greek chorus, standing in for the rest of us to extend our encouragement and good wishes to the Hero.

In Disney's *Lady and the Tramp*, scruffy mongrel dog Tramp leads classy cocker spaniel Lady down an alley to the back door of an Italian restaurant. Tony, chef and owner, provides the pups with a full romantic spread; table and tablecloth, spaghetti, meatballs, and a robust love-sappy serenade. Tony encourages the dogs' romance as a Cheerleader Ally.

In *Must Love Dogs*, single thirty-something Sarah (Diane Lane) advertises online for Mr. Right. She mostly meets Mr. Pathetic. At her local market deli counter, Sarah, day after day, orders yet another single chicken breast for dinner, thereby admitting to the Deli Guy that she's always eating alone. The Deli Guy (Kirk Trutner), cheerful and happily married himself, offers Sarah unsolicited advice and encouragement about hanging in there. He's so endlessly upbeat that Sarah gets ticked off at him.

At the end of the movie, however, Sarah shows up at the deli counter one last time, but now with Mr. Right (John Cusack) by her side. She proudly orders two chicken breasts at last and The Deli Guy shares in her moment of romantic victory.

This Deli Guy is a Cheerleader Ally.

### 6. Endangered Innocent Ally

These are the poor helpless captive souls at risk of being executed if the Hero doesn't save them.

The Endangered Innocent Ally serves as the story goal, that person at risk who must be found and/or retrieved. This can be a man, woman, child, or group. In *Man On Fire* it's a child. In *Firewall* it's a wife and child. In *Dog Day Afternoon* it's a whole group of bank employees.

Sometimes the story of the Endangered Innocent gets expanded to become a subplot action-line. This happens with the little lost clownfish Nemo in *Finding Nemo*, and the kidnapped schoolgirl in *Along Came a Spider*. Most often, though, just enough subplot is used to remind the audience what deep trouble the Endangered Innocent remains in, and how time is running out for the Hero to save her. (As in *Con Air*, *Panic Room*, *Die Hard*, and *Fargo*.)

# ■ OPPOSITION CHARACTERS

The Hero must contend with opposing forces every minute of every good movie in order to make attaining the story goal fulfilling for the audience.

And in addition to agents who do the Adversary's direct bidding, stories sometimes also need characters to oppose the Hero separately from the Adversary in their own subplots.

Any character who works consistently against the goal of the Hero, whether that person is intrinsically good or bad, serves as an Opposition Character.

There are three general types:

## I. Adversary Agent

In some movie genres the plot frequently consists of the Hero plowing his way up through the ranks of Adversary Agent henchmen before finally facing the head honcho at the climax.

In *A History of Violence*, Hero Tom Stall (Viggo Mortensen) must face a shootout with psychopath Carl Fogarty (Ed Harris) and his two thugs before Tom advances up the ladder and earns the right to square off with his mobster brother Richie Cusack (William Hurt) who's the true Adversary. Fogarty and his killers serve as Adversary Agents working for Richie.

In *The Aviator*, Senator Owen Brewster (Alan Alda) holds Senate hearings with plans to destroy Howard Hughes (Leonardo DiCaprio) by publicly denouncing him as a war profiteer. The plan backfires when Howard Hughes proves before the world that Senator Brewster himself operates from deep within the pocket of Juan Trippe (Alec Baldwin), President of Pan American Airways and the real off-stage Adversary pulling Brewster's strings. Senator Brewster serves as an Adversary Agent for Juan Trippe.

## 2. Independent Troublemaker

All screenwriters must swear a blood oath to make the lives of their Heroes as miserable as possible. In some plots this means opposition must come at the Hero from more than one direction.

Since there can be only one Adversary, other formidable enemies not associated with the Adversary should be considered Independent Troublemakers. These can be major subplot characters, or minor ones.

These characters provide another arena in which the Hero can prove himself. But they cannot be allowed to overpower or overshadow the main storyline which leads relentlessly toward the emotional climactic showdown with the actual Adversary.

Even in a secondary position of story focus, though, Independent Troublemakers should still provide their own beginning-middle-end subplot story structure.

In *Batman Begins*, not only must Bruce Wayne (Christian Bale) fight his evil Adversary Henri Ducard (Liam Neeson), he must also contend with business back-stabber Earle (Rutger Hauer), who has torn away control of Wayne Industries. The main storyline pits Batman against Ducard. But an unjust corporate takeover subplot also plays out with Independent Troublemaker Earle.

In the classic comedy *Some Like It Hot*, musician co-Heroes Joe (Tony Curtis) and Jerry (Jack Lemmon) witness the Saint Valentine's Day Massacre, then cut out on the lam from Adversary gangster Spats Colombo (George Raft) who wants these witnesses dead. Joe and Jerry don wigs and dresses and join an all-girl band to throw Spats off their trail. The band leader, Sweet Sue (Joan Shawlee), runs a tight ship and cracks the whip over her girls. She hounds Joe and Jerry relentlessly. Sweet Sue isn't the Adversary, she's an Independent Troublemaker serving as the main opposition force in the romance subplots of *Some Like It Hot*.

### 3. Adversary Minions

At the end of many action movies the landscape is strewn with the corpses of dead Minions.

Minions are lower-level functionaries. In *The Bourne Identity*, Hero Jason Bourne (Matt Damon), alone and suffering from amnesia, must outsmart all of the Operation Treadstone Minions who staff the computers and monitors and surveillance vans, and who take their orders from Adversary Alexander Conklin (Chris Cooper).

An Adversary Minion may have a few lines of dialogue, or none at all. But whatever Minion characters believe they are doing, they are always in the wrong. That's why they die in such large numbers.

## ■ ATMOSPHERE CHARACTERS

There are often people in a screenplay present simply to make the world of the story real. The man who runs the newsstand. The chipper waitress who drops a sassy quip with the check. The hotel desk clerk, the cab driver, the surly babysitter. They are usually neutral toward the Hero.

Atmosphere Characters are not so much people as they are props.

When any of these characters actually takes sides for or against the Hero, of course, they are not an Atmosphere Character any more but become some kind of helper or enemy. Atmosphere Characters can be pleasant, grouchy, or indifferent, but they don't take sides. They are the extras that populate each movie world to make it believable and create verisimilitude.

A character in one category cannot change categories midstream in the story to suddenly serve a different plot purpose. Once a Sidekick, always a Sidekick. Once the Hero, always the Hero. Once a Gate Guardian, always a Gate Guardian.

If deep in Act Two your Love Interest suddenly morphs into an Adversary Agent, that means he was always an Adversary Agent and just temporarily disguised himself as a Love Interest.

Even if an opposition character undergoes a change of heart about their motives, it doesn't mean they've switched categories.

In the action movie *The Rock*, a despondent and unhinged Brigadier General Hummel (Ed Harris) commands his henchmen in seizing Alcatraz Island and taking some tourists hostage. The general demands a huge ransom, threatening to fire chemical weapons from Alcatraz into San Francisco. Co-Heroes Dr. Stanley Goodspeed (Nicolas Cage) and John Patrick Mason (Sean Connery) sneak onto Alcatraz and set out to stop Hummel.

During the climax sequence Hummel finds out no ransom will be paid and jet fighters are on their way to destroy Alcatraz. Hummel's bluff has been called — and he isn't actually prepared to kill tens of thousands of innocent people. He orders his Adversary Agents to stand down and not fire the weapons of mass destruction. But his angry agents mutiny, shoot Hummel and charge off to fire the rockets anyway. Now Adversary Hummel dies trying to help the co-Heroes stop his own evil agents. But that doesn't make Hummel any less the Adversary. He sets in motion actions that still threaten to kill half of San Francisco, and even though he comes to his senses just before death, he's still very much the Adversary.

A co-Hero, a Love Interest, a Sidekick, or any Ally can offer advice to the Hero, just like a Mentor. But that doesn't make them a Mentor if the main story function they serve comes from a category other than Mentor.

Even the Adversary can offer genuine wisdom from time to time without changing his opposition stripes. Occasional wisdom makes an Adversary more multifaceted and interesting, as long as it doesn't tip him into another character category.

Key characters never change categories.

## SUMMING UP

**Most movies contain five to seven main characters. A Hero is required, and an Adversary. That leaves three to five more key characters you can employ from the rest of the character categories list to fill out a primary cast.**

## • THE HERO
**The person whose goal, originating from urgent high stakes, drives the story forward. All other characters function as either helpers or enemies to the Hero.**

• THE ADVERSARY

This is the main opposition character for the Hero. Defining characteristics include:

1. The Adversary more powerfully opposes the Hero than any other character;

2. The Adversary should be one individual, not a group of people or an idea;

3. The Adversary appears to be unbeatable;

4. The Adversary sees himself as the Hero;

5. An Adversary can be the psychological flip side of the Hero herself;

6. The Adversary often has helpers who carry out his will against the Hero;

7. A Hero should not be her own Adversary;

8. Natural disasters cannot serve as the Adversary;

9. The Adversary can wear the mask of friendship or romance and not be revealed as the true opposing force until closer to the end;

10. The Adversary will not always be a bad person;

11. The Adversary can never become the Hero, but sometimes can dominate the plot;

12. When a love story becomes the main plotline, the Love Interest Character also serves as Adversary.

• THE LOVE INTEREST

To serve as a true Love Interest character the role must fulfill highly specific plot development needs. These include:

1. The Love Interest provides major story change, bringing both joy and conflict to the Hero;

2. A Love Interest provides sexual tension;

3. The Love Interest offers a main plot or subplot of sexual conquest;

4. A Love Interest forces the Hero to look inward and pursue character growth;

5. Not every story has room for a Love Interest, but romance remains the best subplot available for enriching your story.

## • THE MENTOR

A Mentor conveys to the Hero worldly wisdom and expertise that must be mastered before the Hero faces the Adversary in a final showdown. The main qualities of the Mentor are:

1. The Mentor can be any person of any age, provided they pass on key skills or information to the Hero;

2. The Mentor often dies;

3. There can be more than one teaching character serving as Mentor in a story;

4. The Mentor often gives the Hero an important or life-saving gift of a powerful object or vital information;

5. Mentors can be dishonest or immoral, unchaste or bawdy, failures or reprobates.

## • THE SIDEKICK

Sidekicks fight shoulder to shoulder with the Hero, challenge the Hero's motivations, keep the Hero honest, force the Hero's inner conflict to the surface where it can be examined, and often provide comic relief. The primary attributes of a successful Sidekick are:

1. The Sidekick commits to the same goal as the Hero, but isn't the prime mover of the story;

2. The Sidekick isn't as skilled as the Hero, and often holds a lesser social status;

3. The Sidekick is completely loyal and trustworthy;

4. Sidekicks cannot die (unless the tale is a tragedy);

5. Sidekicks do not experience character growth;

6. Sidekicks often question the Hero's motivations and offer personal counsel as well as conflict;

7. A same-sex Sidekick often echoes the Hero's romance with a comedic romance of his own.

## • THE GATE GUARDIAN

Gate Guardians force a Hero to prove his worthiness before moving on. At first, Gate Guardians stop and oppose, then they become ally and helper to the Hero.

## • OTHER ALLY CHARACTERS

Ally Characters support the Hero:

### Comparison Ally

Starts in the same social and economic position as the Hero then stays there, so Hero growth can be clearly seen by comparison later on.

### Comic Ally

Possesses attitude and a skewed world view that makes him inherently funny even without jokes. He assists the Hero while providing comic relief.

### Helper-Follower Ally

Offers special talents, skills, or assistance the Hero cannot provide herself.

### Hopeful Savior Ally

An outsider who rushes to rescue the Hero, then dies just before saving him.

Cheerleader Ally
A lesser character who functions as a Greek Chorus and stands in for the audience to extend encouragement and good wishes to the Hero.

Endangered Innocent Ally
Serves as the Hero's story goal, that person at risk who must be found and/or retrieved.

## • OPPOSITION CHARACTERS
An Adversary rarely works alone. There are three general types of opposition characters:

Adversary Agent
A significant character who works for, and takes orders from, the Adversary.

Independent Troublemaker
An enemy of the Hero not associated with the Adversary who provides another subplot arena in which the Hero can prove himself.

Adversary Minion
A minor plot functionary with few or no lines of dialogue who marches to the command of the Adversary, Adversary Agent, or Independent Troublemaker.

## • ATMOSPHERE CHARACTERS
Atmosphere Characters make the world of the story feel real. These background roles are minor, usually five lines of dialogue or fewer, and they serve more as props than people, not taking a position either for or against the Hero.

**EXERCISE:**

Watch a successful American movie that won the Academy Award for Best Picture. It must contain a single, clearly defined Hero (i.e., no multiple-hero films like *Crash* or *The English Patient*).

Now assign every major and major-supporting character to a character category:

Hero
Adversary
Sidekick
Love Interest
Mentor
Gate Guardian
Helper-Follower Ally
Comparison Ally
Comic Ally
Hopeful Savior Ally
Endangered Innocent Ally
Cheerleader Ally
Adversary Agent
Independent Troublemaker

Do you see a consistent use of character categories in the film?

CONSIDER:

- If you think a character doesn't fit any category, re-read the category requirements and try again. The category function of each character in the story is not necessarily obvious.

- You will most likely NOT find every category represented.

- Remember, Mentors can teach the Hero the wrong way to live as well as the right way.

- Be careful when categorizing a character who has a sexual relationship with the Hero. *Sleeping with the Hero does not automatically create a Love Interest character.*

*chapter six*

# DIALOGUE THAT SHINES

———— ⟨∞⟩ ————

One of the many benefits of using Hero Goal Sequences® is that these 23 progressive Hero actions keep the writer focused on telling a driving, riveting story without ever letting it lag. Hero Goal Sequences® limit your page count in each section, which helps you to spot and trim those windy, overwritten dialogue scenes.

Many storytellers take up screenwriting because they have a knack for good dialogue. But an ear for how characters speak can be both a gift and a handicap — because one way film professionals spot amateurs is by the excessive number of six-, seven-, or eight-page dialogue scenes that appear in a script. When movie characters talk so much it usually means the writer is pasting wallpaper over holes in a weak story.

Here's a simple truth that took me years to learn: *Dialogue isn't story.*

Dialogue serves as one of many important tools used to help build a captivating screenplay. But with a less than scintillating story, even some of the greatest dialogue ever written remains just so much chatter.

In a movie, talk does not reveal the totality of character — behavior does.

What characters choose to do and how they do it *demonstrates* who they are far more tellingly than anything they say. Words only convey intent when placed in the emotional context of behavior.

Go see *WALL-E* and you will meet a Hero who speaks barely three discernable words in the whole picture. For the first half-hour WALL-E says nothing at all. Still, a fully round-ed, loveable, brave yet lonely little robot Hero longing to give his heart away gets portrayed through his actions and choices alone.

Screen story is about people wanting things and the lengths they go through to get them. Every line that each person speaks should be considered an attempt by one character to squeeze what they want out of another. I mean that literally. *Every single line.*

And if you're not so great with dialogue, don't worry. I've known writers in Hollywood who have done very well indeed without any particular gift for writing dialogue. There's a whole sub-category of screenwriters, sometimes among the better paid in the business, who are brought in during the final weeks of preproduction on a film to "punch up" the dialogue. But that screenplay was purchased, rewritten, and greenlighted for production long before any dialogue got punched.

Dialogue alone never sells a screenplay. Story does.

Professional writers know that if a specific dialogue se-quence lacks conflict, or if it doesn't advance the plot as a whole, if it slows down a scene even for a moment or the words are brilliant but badly timed, that dialogue must be cut.

There are a few top filmmakers like Quentin Tarantino who are famous for long scenes full of brilliant repartee. But turn down the volume and watch the crackling life-or-death conflict going on just under the talk. Often Tarantino's dialogue has a deceptively calm, ironic tone used to help build excruci-ating tension just below the surface, such as in the extended French basement bar scene in *Inglourious Basterds* where a Nazi SS officer casually plays cards with some American spies. Here, as characters just make small-talk, the writer-director winds ten-sion so tight the audience can hardly sit still anticipating the explosive scene climax to come.

But only very rarely will long dialogue scenes work in a movie.

So here is a list of what dialogue *should* and *shouldn't* accomplish in your script:

**I. Dialogue should advance dramatic conflict that takes place in the here and now.**

Every scene must advance the conflict on some level.

No exceptions. That means dialogue should always be an expression of whatever dramatic tug of war is going on right now, in the present tense, on each page of a script.

In quiet scenes as well, there's a battle taking place.

Your scene should be conceived in a way that requires everyone in it to want something, and each character must attempt to talk the other characters into giving them what they want... right *now*.

Even the very earliest scenes in a film must take place in the present moment. They cannot just be speeches to set up backstory.

The following is the first dialogue scene in a script. It takes place on page two, after an Action Hook in which the Hero does not appear:

EXT. SANTA MARTA — ESTABLISHING — MORNING

Small Central California coast town. Tile roofs and stucco.

Weaving through morning town center traffic chugs an old motorcycle. A 16-year-old young man steers, a woman in her thirties holds on behind.

> FRAN (VOICE OVER)
> No muggings, no murders. Just plain friendly folks who smile all-1-1 day.

> SPENCE (V.O.)
> Sounds creepy.

A beat.

> FRAN (V.O.)
> My God, Spence... what are
> we *doing* here?

The camera moves in to meet SPENCE KOFCHEK
driving the motorbike, intense, deeply
feeling eyes.

Clinging to his waist rides mom, FRAN,
disheveled, no ring.

EXT. FIRST THRIFT BANK — DAY

Spence swerves up to the curb in front of
a small-town bank, stops. But Fran won't
get off. She buries her face in his back.

> SPENCE
> Hey. You're late your first day.

> FRAN
> Oh-h-h. My father doesn't want us
> here. In his house, in his town...

> SPENCE
> It's only been a week, mom.

She sighs, stares at the bank through
strained eyes.

> FRAN
> I swore I'd never come crawling back.

> SPENCE
> Home towns are cool.

Fran reluctantly climbs off the motorcycle.

> SPENCE (CONT'D)
> I mean, look around. No gangs, no
> graffiti, more freaking fresh air
> than you can stand.

He revs the engine. Fran lays her hand on the handlebar, reluctant to see him go.

>                    FRAN
>         Make nice at school.

>                    SPENCE
>         Don't I always?

>                    FRAN
>         Yeah, right. How do I look?

>                    SPENCE
>         A real babe.

He winks, squeezes out a smile.

>                    SPENCE (CONT'D)
>         Knock 'em dead. Gotta go.

Spence kicks it into gear and, pulling the handlebar away from her, roars on down the street.

Fran takes a breath, watches him go.

Rooted in the here and now, this scene is about conflicting desires between a teenager and his mother even the very first time we meet them. Spence's action is to escape from his needy mom. Fran's action is to slow down his departure and gain more emotional support.

Fran wants reassurance. Spence loves her but feels trapped. He just wants to get gone. Conflict in the present tense.

Even in an opening set-up scene.

## 2. Dialogue should hum with dramatic tension.

One of the important ways conflict reveals itself in a script is through the underlying tension in dialogue. Even the simplest scenes in a movie need desire and anxiety running inside the spoken words.

In *The Jacket*, ex-G.I. Hero Jack (Adrien Brody) finds himself incarcerated unjustly in a madhouse. One cruel doctor (Kris Kristofferson) shoots Jack up with drugs and locks him in a morgue refrigerator compartment for long periods as "treatment." Alone in the claustrophobic blackness, instead of going truly insane Jack discovers that for short periods he can project himself forward through time.

In the future he meets a troubled but deeply feeling young woman, Jackie (Keira Knightley).

During a scene in Jackie's apartment they move toward making love. Urgency drives them. Jack doesn't know how long he might be able to stay with her. He could disappear back into the past at any moment, so each word, each touch might be their last.

JACK

Now I'm running out of time.

JACKIE

I don't care. I didn't ask for
you... but now... you just have to
come back.

JACK

It's not like that. I don't have
control over it.

JACKIE

Well — get control.

After making love, Jackie wakes up to an empty bed. Is Jack just in the next room or gone forever? She breathes in his scent on the pillow.

The longing and fear of loss echoed in their simple, short dialogue reveals genuine love and sustains a powerful dramatic tension just under the surface of these few simple lines.

**3. Generally, dialogue should verbalize only one thought at a time.**

Think of spoken dialogue as a baseball thrown in a game of catch. It's caught by the other player, then gripped and fired back. The more thoughts crammed into one speech — the more balls thrown all at the same time — the more difficult it becomes to catch any one ball and throw it back. The game grinds to a halt.

Scenes with many ideas crammed into a few lines of dialogue become unfocused and hard to follow.

A speech I will paraphrase from one newcomer's script goes something like this. After a medieval battle with swords and spears, a Helper-Follower messenger runs up to the Hero:

```
            HOWARD
    The enemy withdrew, sir, but
    damage is bad. Campton and Smyth
    are dead and your closest friend,
    Sir Alaster, lies badly wounded
    near the river. The bastards will
    be back, that's for sure. The men
    are hungry, shall I tell the cooks?
```

What's this scene about? Mourning the dead? Helping a wounded friend? Wolfing down a square meal?

The words contain the conflict and tension of war, but this monologue flies scattershot in all directions at once. What idea should the character being addressed answer first?

A line of dialogue serves as a form of pursuit. Each spoken sentence is an attack, withdrawal, feint, subterfuge, or quest after something, and a response is required. Generally, a speech should contain only one idea that will force a clear response and help drive the story forward.

**4. Good dialogue frequently conveys subtext.**

Subtext refers to any meaning contained in a line of dialogue that isn't actually stated in the words. Audiences love sub-textual dialogue because they enjoy figuring things out for themselves.

A screenwriter should lead her audience to understand the meaning of a line without flatly stating it.

When Don Corleone (Marlon Brando) in *The Godfather* says "I'll make him an offer he can't refuse," we all smile knowingly. There's nothing in the Don's words about killing people, but we clearly understand the violent *subtext*.

Not every line written can have subtext, of course, but too much "on the nose" dialogue should be avoided. First drafts are frequently heavy with lines that say exactly what the writer means. Consider any blunt, obvious dialogue you may write in early script versions as the first outline for subtext to come. Then find more interesting ways to say it without actually saying it.

Think how much less impactful *The Godfather* would have been if the Don had said, "I'm gonna go threaten to kill a guy so he'll do what I want."

### 5. Describe the physical action.

Writing scenes where people talk to each other doesn't absolve us from the responsibility of telling stories visually. Always keep the physical action in the scene vivid and in motion even as people converse.

On every page of dialogue add descriptive lines about what the characters are doing. A scene focusing on a marital spat, let's say, becomes far more interesting if the wife silently irons her husband's shirts at the same time, pressing hard, precise creases in the sleeves with a heavy hot iron as hubby loudly demands a divorce.

Even when the actions are small, if they relate to the emotional content and conflict in the scene, include those descriptions.

Does the Hero pace in an agitated manner while speaking calm lines? Does the Adversary glance out a window as if impatient for reinforcements? Include it.

Let's say a husband and wife walk into a living room, he from an inner bedroom, she through the front door:

                    HE
          Hi, honey, how was your day at work?

                    SHE
          Oh, the usual. You know. What's
          for dinner?

                    HE
          I thought we could go out.

                    SHE
          Okay, fine.

So what's the conflict here? As far as we know from these four lines there isn't any. We assume he's happy, more or less. She's happy, more or less. No bigger issues lurking. Yawn.

With a more completely described context on the page, however, these very same words might carry a powerful subtext of betrayal, and perhaps even violence. All good dialogue requires describing actions to establish the underlying conflict that gives the words emotional meaning.

Try this:

INT. LIVING ROOM — NIGHT
A click at the front door and SHE enters,
still fussing with her hair.

HE shuffles in from the bedroom wearing
the uniform of the unemployed: T-shirt,
dirty jeans, and a beer gripped hard in
one hand.

                    HE
          Hi, honey.
               (looks her over)
          How was your day at work?

                    SHE
        Oh, the usual. You know.

She clears her throat, throws him a forced
smile. Smoothes some wrinkles from her
blouse.

                SHE (CONT'D)
        What's for dinner?

He sips his beer, still eyeing her.

                    HE
        I thought we could go out.

She sighs. Lowers her gaze, makes a bee-
line for the bathroom. Sweeps right past
him.

                    SHE
                (snippy)
        Okay, fine.

As she passes, he inhales her deeply.
Catches an unfamiliar scent.
It hits him.
His face drains of all color.

    This time, with the scene more fully described these simple words of dialogue possess an emotional context that advances dramatic action.

    This is not to say every line of dialogue requires description. Just add a few well-chosen details of behavior in order to open a window on a character's emotional state in every scene. *No screenplay page should ever contain only dialogue.*

    And when a scene ends, avoid always cutting to the next scene heading (slugline) right after the last line of dialogue. Describe the exit — how the Hero grabs those divorce papers from the table and storms from the room.

Most scenes need a *tag*, some short physical description at the end that brings visual focus back where it should be, usually on the Hero's reaction to what just happened. It pushes the story forward into the next scene.

If from time to time you do choose to end a scene on a line of dialogue, let it be a "button," the strongest or most clever line in the scene.

In Lawrence Kasdan's film noir *Body Heat*, after love making, lawyer Ned Racine and his married girlfriend Matty Walker (Kathleen Turner) talk about how sweet it would be for them if some accident befell Matty's wealthy husband Edmund. The lovers immediately pull back from the idea. That's never going to happen they say, it's dangerous to even think such things, nothing will befall Edmund at all.

The lovers' own fear of the thought reveals their subtext. And a final line of dialogue from the Hero buttons the moment:

```
RACINE
The only thing wrong with your
husband right now... is us.
```

Without a direct word about it, Ned Racine and Matty Walker have just decided to murder her husband.

It's a powerful scene-ending "button" line without any further description needed in Kasdan's terrific screenplay.

**6. Dialogue should come out of the lives, joys, and pain of unique characters.**

While writing the second or third draft of a script, arrange an evening when you can have your dialogue read aloud to you, preferably before a small audience of friends. Ask actors or people you know to volunteer to do the reading.

Do *not* read any parts yourself.

Just sit and listen.

Say nothing. *Defend nothing.*

Shut up and listen.

If your dialogue comes out sounding like all the characters speak and think in the same way, then there's more work to be done.

From the Hero on down to the smallest walk-on role, every character should speak with a voice that's uniquely her own.

Spend enough time with your characters to truly understand who they are, where they come from, their educational background, socio-economic position, emotional state, ambitions, life history, and all the other qualities that make up the personalities of real people.

Is your Hero used to living with the ease money provides, or resigned to struggling along without it? Did she get an education? If so, where? If not, what is it she's always secretly longed to study?

Investigate idiosyncrasies, regional speech patterns, colloquialisms. At the exact moment your script requires a character to speak, is he happy, scared, depressed, distracted, in love, in hate? Most importantly, what's his current *attitude* toward what is going on?

Every character who speaks, while trying to get what they desire, reflects an attitude toward what's happening around them. Capture a character's state of mind about what's going on in the story and you make a huge leap toward clearly defining that character.

If people in your script use some type of professional vocabulary — like doctors, scientists, cops, journalists, telephone linemen, and just about every other profession — take the time to get their vocabulary right. Do the research.

Respect your characters. Honor their life experience by taking the time to learn who they are, what they've done, and the unique way they speak.

### 7. Avoid small talk.

In real life people say "please" and "thank you" a lot. They fill uncomfortable silences with endless small talk. Real conversations meander from topic to topic with lots of repetition and "you knows" thrown in.

Dialogue, on the other hand, serves a targeted story purpose and creates the *illusion* of reality. What characters say should be condensed and purposeful. Many of the conventions of everyday speech should be eliminated. Like "please" and "thank you."

Have you noticed in movies how at the end of phone calls people seldom say goodbye? They just hang up.

Dialogue takes up precious space in a screenplay. There's only room for lines that mean something.

Introductions such as "James, meet Penelope — Penelope, meet James" should be avoided. If two important characters need to meet for the first time, do it in a unique way that reveals character.

The Hollywood term "meet cute" means that lives should cross in clever and unexpected ways involving action and behavior, not merely through formal rote spoken introductions.

Good dialogue usually avoids the formalities of niceness or politeness, skips over common pleasantries and gets right to the juicy, dramatic stuff. That's what people come to the movie theater to see.

Also eliminate from dialogue the excess baggage of repeating character names. New screenwriters often start lines of dialogue with the name of the person addressed:

"Henrietta, we must start packing for our trip."

"Charles, I'm aware of that."

"Henrietta, did you remember to stop the mail?"

In casual conversation people who know each other seldom address each other by name.

So keep the illusion of reality alive in dialogue by avoiding it.

### 8. Dialogue should be brief.

On average, one or two short sentences are plenty for a line of dialogue.

Avoid long speeches unless they come at climactic moments and resolve major plot threads. Big speeches tend to stop stories cold.

One person in a scene gushing monologues at another person doesn't allow for any true contest of wills. And long speeches usually want to explain things. The audience doesn't want to be told, they want to see and experience it for themselves.

Keep it concise and active. Dialogue must thrust, defend, parry. Shorter is better.

### 9. Character must be demonstrated, not described.

A Hero can't just tell his Sidekick what a brutal killer the Adversary is. An audience needs to experience the Adversary in action. It's difficult or impossible to build strong dramatic tension around mere statements.

At the beginning of *The Departed*, gleefully evil mob boss Frank Costello (Jack Nicholson) tells the audience in Voice Over his cynical philosophy of life. We get that Frank is a successful mafia-style criminal. But it's not until we actually watch Frank murder an innocent young woman in cold blood as she pleads for her life, then comment "She fell funny," that we truly understand the soulless, terrifying nature of this psychopath.

### 10. Avoid history lessons.

*Exposition* is dialogue that explains events that have taken place in backstory before the scene begins.

Expository dialogue lets us know how a character arrived at his current lot in life and how the traumatic emotional wound he suffered once upon a time now stands in the way of his pursuing much-needed character growth.

But for some writers, telling the audience about the past can become a substitute for drama in the present.

Most of the exposition that writers feel is absolutely crucial to understanding a story is, in truth, unnecessary. Audiences are smart. They catch on quickly with just a few clues.

And they don't like being informed twice. So cut that scene where the Hero dashes over to her best friend's house to tell, blow by blow, everything the audience just saw happen in the scene before.

A good screenwriter slips in information about the past almost unnoticed as characters clash in the foreground.

*Signs* begins with a shot of a farmhouse backyard at dawn; empty picnic table, empty swing set, acres of lush green corn growing tall. In his bedroom, Graham Hess (Mel Gibson) wakes with a start. Alone in the double bed, hyper alert, he listens intensely. Nothing. On the nightstand there's a family photo showing Graham as happy father with his lovely wife and kids. In the photo he wears a minister's collar.

Graham gets up and walks into the hall, almost enters his children's bedroom to check, but doesn't want to wake them. He picks up the kids' dropped socks from the floor. We notice a faded spot on the hall wallpaper outlining where a crucifix must have recently been taken down. Then while brushing his teeth Graham finally hears from outside a distant scream. He rushes back to the children's room and throws open the door — the kids are gone. Suddenly terrified, he leaps down the stairs.

Look how much we have learned about this Hero with not one word of exposition spoken.

He's a deeply caring father, and his house is meticulously ordered and clean, obsessively so. He's haunted somehow, sleeping very lightly. And he sleeps alone. For some reason his lovely wife in the photo no longer sleeps in his bed and we can tell from the favored placement of his family photo that their separation was not voluntary. Also we know he's a man of the cloth, but a crucifix has recently been removed from his wall. Something's wrong here. The plentiful, healthy crops surrounding Graham's home show he's a good steward of the earth and a hard worker.

All of this gets communicated without any dialogue. We learn it through behavior and environment, not talk.

A lesser writer might have included some scene where Graham and his brother sit down over morning coffee to talk about what life has been like these past rotten months since Graham's wife died in that horrible car crash where she was cut in two and Graham got depressed and walked away from the ministry because now he figures God doesn't exist and his kids are exhibiting post-traumatic stress disorders.

I've read plenty of scenes in other scripts just like this.

Sometimes at the midpoint in a screen story or toward the end of Act Two, a character will offer a "killer reveal" — a longish monologue about the past. But these scenes are about character growth recognition, not merely exposition.

During the midpoint sequence of *Hitch*, the "Love Doctor" Hero Hitch sprawls on the couch of gossip reporter Sara as he recovers from a severe food allergy he got the night before. In this quiet moment Sara tells Hitch a story about when she was ten, the time she and her sister went ice skating on a pond. Her sister fell through the ice and Sara looked on helplessly as her father worked to pull her sister out of the water and attempt mouth to mouth resuscitation. This traumatic experience made Sara extremely self-protective and emotionally closed. She learned to run from any emotional tie that might someday lead to pain. That's why she keeps Hitch at emotional arm's length, to avoid ever getting so badly traumatized again.

This monologue does not merely explain Sara's history. Here she opens her heart to Hitch and reveals through subtext how much she wants to love him, while confessing her obstacle. This speech is about Sara's inner emotional conflict and her vulnerability in the present.

So after you complete a first draft of your screenplay, read through it and mark every line containing exposition/explanation — then cut 90% of those lines. Rewrite the scenes to show us instead.

## 11. Don't preach.

When you have something thematic to say in a screenplay, rather than just blurt it out in a series of speeches you must build a dramatized argument as to why your theme is correct.

Good writers tell stories that *convince* us their ideas are true. They win audiences over by demonstrating how a sympathetic Hero discovers these very truths through personal struggle.

In *A Beautiful Mind*, math genius John Nash (Russell Crowe) starts out as a college student believing that his nimble mind alone will bring him the world recognition he so craves. But his mind lets him down and he goes insane. Instead of the hoped-for recognition, John receives pity and derision. It's the loving commitment from his wife Alicia (Jennifer Connelly) that finally leads John to understand that his longing for world recognition was misguided. Only Alicia's love for him, and John's for her, really matters.

By the time recognition finally does come to John in the form of a Nobel Prize, his life is in balance at last and standing before the world he can say to Alicia, "You are all my reasons." This Hero has learned that what he valued at the beginning of the story was meaningless. What really counts is love.

There's no preaching or speechifying in this movie. We watch the Hero discover the meaning of life through his intensely dramatic struggle to overcome mental illness.

In movies we learn by observing the trials, mistakes, failures and triumphs of our surrogate Heroes. First convince your audience's heart. Their heads will follow.

And keep off the soapbox.

## SUMMING UP

• Dialogue alone is not story.

• Too much dialogue, or weak dialogue, can blur dramatic focus and dilute conflict.

• The most important considerations when writing movie dialogue are:

1. Dialogue should advance conflict that's going on in the present moment;

2. Dialogue should hum with dramatic tension;

3. A line of dialogue should generally express only one thought;

4. Good dialogue frequently conveys subtext;

5. Scenes should contain more than just dialogue, they must also describe the physical action;

6. Dialogue should come out of the lives, joys, and pain of unique characters;

7. Avoid small talk or pleasantries unless it accomplishes a larger purpose;

8. Lines of dialogue should generally be short;

9. Character must be demonstrated, not just described;

10. Avoid history lessons;

11. Dialogue isn't a license to preach.

**EXERCISE:**

Using the following parameters, in proper format write a screen-play scene where a woman and man end their relationship.

- The scene can be set anywhere.
- The scene can have any number of characters in it.

BUT:

- The whole scene cannot be longer than *four pages*.
- No line of dialogue can be longer than *three words*.
- No single word of dialogue can be longer than *two syllables*.

THEN:

- Ask some friends to also write such scenes.
- Invite them all over to your place to read their scenes aloud and discuss them; suggested price of admission, one bag of chips and a quart of beer.

"If you can build stories — it doesn't matter a damn how you write them."

~ Somerset Maugham

*part three* Building Story Structure

*chapter seven*

# BASIC SCREEN STORY STRUCTURE

———— ⚬✕⚬ ————

Chicken first? Or was it, in truth, the egg?

Most biologists would say neither.

They tell us the earliest living cells formed quite accidentally as carbon and oxygen swirled together beside a cozy, warm volcanic vent at the bottom of the sea, long before Mother Nature got around to developing fowl and ovum.

So to ask "chicken or egg?" poses the wrong question.

And an old debate in screenwriting asks: what's more important, character or plot? But this query also raises a false question.

Because in visual storytelling it's impossible to separate effective plot from character. We can't declare either one more important. They're two aspects of the same thing.

A good story plot provides action through which character is revealed. Character exists only as the cumulative meaning of a well-structured plot.

So when we discuss screen story structure and Hero Goal Sequences®, we are considering the basic cinematic ways in which the very soul of a character gets revealed to an audience. Building effective plot structure *means* creating powerful characters.

## MOVIES VS. NOVELS

Some writers dive passionately into this old debate of character versus plot — almost always on the side of character, although Aristotle favored plot — and argue their case using concepts of storytelling they learned from reading novels.

But how story communicates in a novel and how it communicates in a movie can be very different.

Movies are a visual medium. All story information gets objectively communicated through images and actions that can be viewed, ogled, stared at. Films create stories out of an ever-flowing river of objective, visual change.

Novels on the other hand are neither visual nor objective. Stories intended exclusively to be read offer a completely different approach as they transmit information through language alone.

Any tale told in a novel can only be experienced sentence by sentence. It must focus on one thing at a time: the description of a sunset, how someone lifts their coffee cup, or what a particular character feels at that moment. Then the writer moves on to describe the next single detail.

Each visualization called to mind from words in a book can only be experienced in a completely *subjective* manner — meaning that what one reader sees in their mind's eye will differ a bit from what another person imagines as each fills in details and adds individual interpretation unique to personal experience.

But when we go to the movies we all see exactly the same thing. There it is right in front of us, all pieces of visual composition chosen by the writer and director with no room for individual interpretation at all.

Movies are also unique as an art form because of the huge amount of visual information thrust upon a viewer all at once. Unlike one-thing-at-a-time novels, films flood our senses with many kinds of story elements simultaneously. The location, lighting, camera angle, music, movement of characters, background, foreground, emotions, pace, editing, dialogue — all hit us in an instant. All moving, morphing, changing second by second. Movies grip our emotions in part by overwhelming our senses with a tidal wave of objective information.

A novel communicates through the literary conceit called *interior monologue*. One character or narrator speaks to us about what they remember, or about what they observe. Even in a third-person voice — when the narrator of a novel sounds like some sort of god figure describing things from a privileged viewpoint in the sky — the form of storytelling is still interior monologue. It's a tale conveyed through a narrator who has a subjective viewpoint and who jumps from inside the emotions of one character to inside the next, informing us how they all feel. The reader must trust the narrator's interpretation.

And many Heroes in novels undergo a great deal of emotion without actually doing very much.

In movies we can only know what characters feel from story clues picked up visually. We see how people behave, what choices they make, watch their expressions, hear what they say while taking action.

So in film, what people *do* represents who they *are*.

Novels are often long. A person can spend weeks reading a book as the author wanders from one character to the next, taking as much time as she wishes for story side trips.

But motion pictures simply don't have the luxury of limitless time and scattered focus. Movies are not paced to be enjoyed in a series of small reading bursts at bedtime, but in a single two-hour sitting. Keeping a story focused remains essential in film, where everything, even subplots, must advance the Hero's journey. There can be no waste.

So plot structure — the visual ordering of events to elicit the strongest emotional reaction from an audience — becomes the single most important component of a screenplay.

And over time we are seeing many popular novelists adopting prose styles that more closely echo the immediacy of screen story.

## SCREEN STORY STRUCTURE

Before we explore how Hero Goal Sequences® will create a powerful linking chain of story events to ensure that your screenplay will wow audiences, we first need to look at the traditional story structure that these Goal Sequences overlay.

There are ten structural tent poles that hold up every effective screen story:

### I. ACT ONE

Movies that work emotionally for audiences are composed of three acts. The human mind naturally seeks a beginning, middle, and end to interpret the meaning of any story.

For feature-length screenplays the beginning, or the Act One introduction and set-up section, usually runs between 25 and 35 pages. At approximately one minute of film for each page of script, that's 25 to 35 minutes of movie for the first act.

Of course, the page count per act in any screenplay can vary depending on the tale told. Act One of *Titanic* runs 42 minutes, an incredibly long first act. But *Titanic* screens for three and a quarter hours overall. Act One of *Collateral*, on the other hand, runs barely 19 minutes, because that first act plays out mostly inside one taxi cab. So to avoid claustrophobia, this thriller needs to jack up the stakes and blast into Act Two conflict as soon as possible.

Act One presents a Hero living his everyday life in his ordinary world, and then introduces a general, physical story goal to that Hero. It ends with Stunning Surprise #1, which throws the Hero unexpectedly into the next act and suddenly transforms this general goal into a highly specific one. We'll get into more detail with that in a moment.

### 2. ACT TWO

Act Two is the true heart of any movie and certainly the most challenging to write. This is where the Hero travels from emotional immaturity and isolation to emotional maturity and connection. For a standard-length feature film, Act Two typically runs 60 to 80 pages/minutes, and often represents 60% or even 70% of the whole movie.

Here the Hero pursues a very specific, visible goal in the face of strong opposition from a determined Adversary.

Act Two ends with Stunning Surprise #2, which unexpectedly throws the Hero into Act Three. More in a moment.

### 3. ACT THREE

Act Three, the resolution act, can run anywhere from 7 to 20 minutes depending on the genre of the film. A third act longer than 20 pages usually spells trouble and should be avoided. *The Matrix*, with a longer than usual second act, balances running time with an Act Three resolution lasting less than 8 minutes.

### 4. INCITING INCIDENT

The Inciting Incident provides a plot event which usually takes place near the beginning of a film and really sets in motion a Hero's involvement in the story. This is the event that introduces a Hero's general, visible goal for the rest of Act One. Depending on story requirements, though, the Inciting Incident can happen *any time* in Act One. Most commonly it's within the first one to seven minutes.

In *The Bourne Identity*, the Inciting Incident takes place at the very start of the film when fishermen pull the body of Jason Bourne from the Mediterranean sea. Although Bourne has been shot, he gasps and begins to breathe again, returning to the world as a man with no memory. The entire rest of the movie then follows Jason Bourne as he fights to regain his memory and survive the evils of Operation Treadstone.

In *Gladiator*, the Inciting Incident takes place much later, 34 minutes into Act One and only five minutes from the end of the act. The evil Commodus kills his own father, wise Emperor Marcus Arelius, then Commodus informs Maximus that the Emperor is dead and demands the Hero general's loyalty. This is the Inciting Incident for *Gladiator*. Finding out about this vicious murder sets Maximus on a collision course with Commodus.

The Inciting Incident can take place any time in the first act, but it must happen in Act One. No later. As a general rule, sooner is better. The longer you wait to officially launch your story with the Inciting Incident, the harder it becomes to hold audience interest.

It's helpful to think of an Inciting Incident as *the event which begins this story and no other.*

For instance, the Inciting Incident of *E.T.: The Extra-Terrestrial* is NOT when E.T. gets left behind by his spaceship. At that point E.T.'s story could still go in any number of directions. He might wander into a landfill dump instead of Elliott's backyard and launch a completely different adventure... not to mention the fact that E.T. isn't even the Hero of this movie. He is the Mentor, and *primary story structure moments must involve the Hero.* So the Inciting Incident of "this story and no other" is when Elliott (Henry Thomas), the Hero, and E.T. first run into each other in the brush. They scream — both terrified as their lives intersect. Here Elliott meets his extraordinary adventure to come and the boy's personal struggle to protect E.T. really begins.

The Inciting Incident of *The Lord of the Rings: The Fellowship of the Ring* takes place when Bilbo Baggins first entrusts Frodo with the all-powerful ring. Everything else follows from this event.

And in *Pretty Woman*, it's when millionaire Edward Lewis asks street prostitute Vivian Ward up to his penthouse hotel suite for the night.

Vivian and Edward meet on the street when Edward asks her for directions to his Beverly Hills Hotel. But once Vivian gets him there he says goodnight and Vivian walks to a bus stop. Their drive to the hotel together is NOT the Inciting Incident. If Edward just says thanks and heads up to his room alone, this story stops cold. But Edward glances back and sees Vivian waiting for the bus, and he then makes a decision that will change both of their lives forever. Only when Edward asks Vivian up to his penthouse does the relationship truly begin.

## 5. STUNNING SURPRISE #1

The ending of Act One requires the arrival of some event or dramatic reversal that creates a moment of shock for the Hero and drops a curtain on the first act — while immediately raising it again on the second act.

This takes place about 25 to 35 pages into a screenplay and it's one of the most important story turns in your movie. It announces the arrival of a huge change in the Hero's life.

Sometimes called the first major turning point, or Crossing the First Threshold — I choose to name this essential story moment Stunning Surprise #1 because that's the effect it should have on both your Hero and the audience.

I've heard this act-ending shocker described as something that comes out of the blue, changes everything, and the Hero's life will never be the same again.

Stunning Surprise #1 in *Gladiator* comes during Maximus' arrest, when the Hero asks Quintus to look after his family — but then is told Maximus' wife and child are to be executed. In *Contact*, it's when scientist Ellie Arroway (Jodie Foster) first stumbles across an intelligent message being broadcast to Earth from deep space.

These are the requirements for an effective Stunning Surprise #1:

**a.) Stunning Surprise #1 must happen to no one but the Hero.**

The purpose of this moment is to create a life-changing emotional impact on the Hero. So the Hero MUST be present for us to see her react. It cannot happen to the Adversary or Love Interest or Mentor or any other character, only to the Hero.

If your story contains more than one Hero, Stunning Surprise #1 must happen to them all — either *simultaneously* or *serially*. In *Open Range*, after the two Heroes, Boss Spearman (Robert Duvall) and Charlie Waite (Kevin Costner), gain a small bloodless victory over some bad guys, they return in triumph to their cattle camp… and are shocked to find dear friend Mose murdered, as well as Spearman's ward Button barely alive. Now their disagreement with the local kingpin rancher has suddenly become a battle to the death. The two Heroes discover this Stunning Surprise #1 *simultaneously*.

But in *L.A. Confidential*, Ed Exley stumbles alone into the scene of horrific slaughter at the Night Owl Café, a life changing moment for him. Then in the very next scene Bud White, the other Hero, learns separately about the Night Owl murders when he finds his partner Dick Stensland lying dead on a gurney in the morgue. This discovery will change Bud's life forever, too. And these two Heroes discover their Stunning Surprise #1 *serially*.

### b.) Stunning Surprise #1 takes place in an instant.

Stunning Surprise #1 is not a scene or a sequence of events that unfold over time. It's a single punch to the jaw. It can be big or small, negative or positive — but it arrives abruptly.

For *Thelma & Louise*, Stunning Surprise #1 takes place in the parking lot of a honky-tonk roadhouse bar where Louise (Susan Sarandon) grabs a pistol from her glove compartment and points it at the sleazy brute trying to rape her friend Thelma (Geena Davis). The would-be rapist is forced to let hysterical Thelma go. All danger has past. But the guy says something to Louise so crude, so insultingly sexist that even though Thelma is now out of danger, Louise snaps. Stunning Surprise #1: she shoots the man dead. Now Thelma and Louise enter Act Two as fugitives on the run, a whole new world for both of them. And it has happened in an instant.

### c.) Stunning Surprise #1 must truly shock and surprise the Hero.

Stunning Surprise #1 must be completely unexpected. In the two-Hero movie *Mr. & Mrs. Smith*, John (Brad Pitt) and then Jane (Angelina Jolie) are both stunned speechless at the end of Act One as each finds out *serially*, one after the other, that they are married to a competing contract assassin.

Stunning Surprise #1 can be as big as a whole planet blowing up or as tiny as a shared glance. Sometimes in love stories the life-changing shock can be as small as the moment when a woman looks deep into the eyes of a man she has always hated and she's suddenly stunned to see this might actually be Mr. True-Love-Forever.

**d.) Stunning Surprise #1 must fundamentally change the Hero's circumstances.**

With the arrival of Stunning Surprise #1 the Hero finds that his former life is over — in the sense that things will never feel or look quite the same to him again. Act One can be described as the Hero's ordinary world yesterday, the place where a Hero has lived and worked most of his life until now. Stunning Surprise #1 throws that Hero into the special world of Act Two, where an extraordinary once-in-a-lifetime journey will now commence.

In *Training Day*, Hero rookie cop Jake (Ethan Hawke) joins a narcotics investigation unit and hits the streets to learn the ropes from his new partner and boss, Detective Alonzo (Denzel Washington). Alonzo shows Jake around town, introduces him to the smell of the 'hood. Jake thinks he's learning from the best narco cop in the city.

When Jake sees a schoolgirl being assaulted in an alley, he rushes over to fight the two perps and handcuff them. Detective Alonzo saunters up, abuses the suspects, then robs them of their drugs and cash. Next, *Alonzo cuts the suspects loose*. This is Stunning Surprise #1 for Jake. Alonzo has just revealed himself to be no role model, but the hardest, meanest bad guy on the streets. The Hero's circumstances have suddenly changed from hopeful police rookie to something like a kidnap victim who can either join Alonzo as a criminal or get killed by him. A whole new world.

**e.) Stunning Surprise #1 changes the Hero's destiny.**

Whatever the Hero thought was going to happen to her in life, whatever predictable path she had anticipated up to now... suddenly that's out the window. Now the Hero finds herself in a new ballgame with a completely unknown future. Only in this sort of bewildering and uncertain world are Heroes afforded the chance to prove themselves and grow.

*Elizabeth*, a movie about the early years of Queen Elizabeth the First, takes place in sixteenth century England, where young

Elizabeth Tudor (Cate Blanchett) wants only to pursue romance with Robert Dudley (Joseph Fiennes) while keeping a very low profile.

Then Queen Mary dies unexpectedly and *Kapow!* — Stunning Surprise #1: at twenty-five years of age, plucked from obscurity, Elizabeth is handed the royal ring as she becomes the Queen of England. Her anticipated life of love and children with Lord Dudley abruptly ends. Elizabeth now has no idea what will become of her.

**f.) It tells the audience what the movie action-line will be.**

Since Stunning Surprise #1 provides a Hero with his focused goal, it's also the event that announces to the audience exactly what action-line the movie will pursue.

In *E.T.*, once Elliott's got E.T. safely up in his bedroom, the boy treats the creature like a puppy dog, tells his brother and sister he wants to keep E.T. as his pet.

But E.T. demonstrates to Elliott where his home is by sending balls of Play Doh floating into the air and spinning like orbiting planets, using only the power of his mind. In awe, Elliott suddenly realizes that E.T. is no pet — he's the most advanced creature anyone will ever meet.

So with Stunning Surprise #1 in *E.T.*, Elliott's world of carefree childhood ends. The boy's commitment now becomes a rescue mission to get E.T. home. This will be the movie action-line.

Keep your eyes peeled for Stunning Surprise #1 in every good movie you see. Often it includes a close-up shot of the Hero looking amazed, mouth open in shock. Good directors punch up the moment.

Spotting this key event should become second nature for screenwriters. It arrives in many shapes and sizes but all versions accomplish the exact same dramatic purposes.

## 6. THE MIDPOINT

Smack in the middle of all great movies there's a unique gathering of scenes that provides several important storytelling functions. Unlike the Stunning Surprise, a Midpoint is not one moment of shock, but a string of two, three, or more scenes that together can last up to eight minutes.

You can find a few good Midpoints that are only one scene long, but it's rare.

Act Two is effectively broken into two halves by the Midpoint Sequence. The Midpoint offers the Hero a way station, a time for reflection and a chance to rededicate himself to achieving the goal on a do-or-die basis.

A good Midpoint will contain some or all of the following attributes:

**a.) In mood, style, and pace, the Midpoint feels different from the rest of the screenplay and may contain a montage with music bridging some passage of time.**

Halfway through *Finding Nemo*, clownfish Hero Marlin needs to travel across a huge ocean quickly to reach his son. So he finds his way to the East Australian Current and rockets off. On this sweeping voyage, Marlin gets tutored by a surfer-dude sea turtle, Crush, who passes on parenting skills to the Hero about giving "little dudes" enough freedom to find their own way. As they all romp and play, music soaring over a montage, these Midpoint scenes transport Marlin across thousands of miles of ocean in mere minutes of screen time with a mood and tone unlike anything else in the film.

**b.) Usually the Midpoint serves as a dramatic "Point of No Return."**

In many film stories, for the first half of Act Two the Hero energetically pursues victory over the Adversary, but there's a sense that if the Hero suddenly decided to dump the whole thing and go home, she still could. Then something happens at the Midpoint that eliminates all possibility of turning back.

In *Thelma & Louise,* for the first half of Act Two these friends hide out by traveling on back roads as they struggle to raise money for an escape to Mexico. But if Louise changed her mind about escape at this point, she could still turn herself in. Sure, she'd face manslaughter charges and might get one to three years in prison. But eventually she could carry on with her old life.

Then in a Midpoint scene Thelma robs a small-town grocery store at gunpoint. Now their fates are sealed. When the women add armed robbery to manslaughter, getting straight with the law no longer remains an option. They've crossed the Point of No Return.

By the Midpoint in *Groundhog Day,* obnoxious weatherman Phil Conners has tried everything he can think of to break the spell condemning him to relive this one awful day over and over. He's pursued every selfish advantage from seduction to theft and he still can't get sweet TV producer Rita into his bed. So Phil kidnaps the groundhog, steals a van, and roars off a high quarry cliff to kill himself. Kaboom. Peace at last? No, Phil wakes up in his country inn bed as always, still doomed to relive the same day of failing to seduce Rita. In a montage covered by music, Phil attempts suicide a dozen different ways, but always gets the same result; he awakens to face Groundhog Day yet again. Point of No Return. Phil now knows for certain there's no escape route, even in death. He can only push forward and figure out how to make eternal life in Groundhog Day worth living.

**c.) Often it's during the Midpoint that a Hero's conflict with the Adversary becomes personal.**

Here the Hero and Adversary may face each other eyeball to eyeball for the first time.

In *Men In Black,* it's during the Midpoint that Agent J (Will Smith) and Agent K catch up with "the Bug," a dangerous space alien wearing the ill-fitting skin of a human, and square off with him personally for the first time.

In *Spider-Man,* Peter Parker (Tobey Maguire) saves Mary Jane Watson (Kirsten Dunst) from falling off a crumbling balcony and makes his first major romantic impact on her, then also fights the Green Goblin for the first time face to face during the Midpoint.

**d.) In love stories and romantic comedies it's commonly at the Midpoint where the lovers kiss or make love for the first time — literally or metaphorically — or it's here that same-sex buddies overcome differences and work together as a true team for the first time.**

These key romantic moments signal a Point of No Return in love stories where deeply felt bonds are formed or promised at the Midpoint.

It's during the Midpoint Sequence of *Shakespeare in Love* that Will Shakespeare and Viola first make love, the sequence filmed as a montage covered with music.

In *Titanic*, two Points of No Return are crossed during back-to-back Midpoint scenes: the ship hits an iceberg, and Rose and Jack make love for the first (and only) time in a car down in the cargo hold.

When two same-sex Heroes are thrown together to under-take some mutual task, their "buddy" relationship follows the same arc as a romance. They start off hating each other. Then Buddy-Heroes gradually learn to respect one another and at the Midpoint — since kissing is out — the plot gives them a chance to function as a true team for the first time. This is what hap-pens at the Midpoint of *48 Hours* when cop Jack (Nick Nolte) and con Reggie (Eddie Murphy) finally overcome mutual spite in order to walk into a bar together and masterfully brace a whole room full of dope-dealing thugs.

**e.) The Midpoint often includes an unmasking, either literally or metaphorically.**

An unmasking may be used as a step toward making conflict more personal or to reveal the Hero's true inner self.

In *Shrek*, during the Midpoint scenes the lovable ogre saves Princess Fiona and Donkey from a fire-breathing dragon while wearing a helmet that covers his face. Once they're safe, Princess

Fiona insists "Sir Shrek" remove his helmet so she can look upon her savior. Shrek doesn't want to reveal how ugly he is, but Fiona demands he take it off. So Shrek slips off his helmet, and for one sweet, vulnerable moment he grins in hope that his appearance won't matter to her. Donkey laughs and makes a joke out of it. Shrek joins in the laughter and retreats quickly back into his self-defensive "I don't care what anyone thinks" mode. But for a fleeting moment he has unmasked his true vulnerable self to the woman of his dreams. A perfect Midpoint moment.

**f.) The Midpoint almost always contains the second crucial step in character growth.**

The important issue of character growth will be fully investigated in Chapter Eight. But in summary: the first step in character growth takes place early in the first half of Act Two, when the Hero EXPRESSES, or names, his inner emotional conflict. He brings it to the surface as a problem that must be dealt with. The second step comes during the Midpoint when for the first time a Hero directly takes action to BATTLE this inner emotional suffering which is holding him back. This makes the Midpoint thematically very important. More in a moment.

**g.) A "ticking clock" countdown often begins at the Midpoint.**

Running out of time creates rising dramatic tension. Every successful film uses some form of ticking clock, either literal or figurative.

In *Titanic* the ship hits an iceberg at the Midpoint and a tense countdown starts running through the two hours and fifteen minutes left before that ship will sink.

Many adventure movies contain an actual clock ticking off the minutes and seconds before the end of the world. During a Midpoint scene of *Men In Black*, the Arquillian space battleship sends a message to MIB headquarters that if the Arquillians don't get their galaxy back real soon, the human planet will be vaporized. At headquarters, on a big wall screen, a digital clock actually starts counting down the seconds left before Mother Earth goes bye-bye.

Time can start running out earlier in a movie, like in *My Best Friend's Wedding*, where the clock begins ticking at the Inciting Incident in Act One as Hero Julianne Potter (Julia Roberts) learns she's only got 48 hours to steal back her former boyfriend before he gets married to another woman.

But more commonly a final countdown gets launched at the Midpoint to raise tension and drive the stakes ever higher in the second half of Act Two.

**h.) Often there is a literal or metaphorical death and rebirth moment at the Midpoint as a ritual rite of passage for the Hero.**

For adolescents in cultures all over the world it's part of an entrance into adulthood that they undergo some ritual "death" and "resurrection" to cast off childhood forever so they can join the grown-ups of the tribe. Some native peoples send their pubescent girls off to undergo a first menstruation alone in a ceremonial hut, then they return to the village as an adult woman. Some boys in Australia are sent off on a spiritual "walkabout" through the wilderness so they may return as a man. The child must symbolically die before an adult can be born.

During the Midpoint of *Star Wars*, Luke Skywalker and his cohorts find themselves trapped in a waterlogged, oversized trash compacter in the Death Star while a huge snake-like creature swims around them. The dragon snake wraps around Luke and yanks him down under the water. Urgent seconds pass, far beyond what anyone could endure without breathing. Seems it's curtains for adolescent Skywalker. Then at long last he bursts up gasping for air, reborn. Luke has survived the fatal grasp of the dragon snake and is now resurrected as a man who no longer fears the power of the phallus beast. Luke has returned to life as an adult male who owns one himself.

Often these symbolic rebirth moments are variations on a baptism, either by water or by fire.

In *Shrek*, the Midpoint Sequence begins with an escape from a fire-breathing dragon. The Hero outwits the beast and chains it in the castle, but Shrek and friends must still scramble across a rope bridge. The dragon blasts the bridge with flame and ropes break on the castle side, dropping them all down closer to the boiling lava in the moat. But Shrek climbs up the still-burning bridge and saves the princess and Donkey. He tumbles into a new world beyond the fairytale castle and now rises to face the princess as a full-grown man gazing upon a full-grown woman. And the bridge leading back to Shrek's immature past has been burned forever. A Point of No Return.

Self-isolated Shrek passes through a baptism of fire and gets reborn as a man capable of loving and being loved.

## 7. ACT TWO CLIMAX

Depending on the genre of your film, an Act Two climax can be a big action sequence that roars on for an extended period, or a simple confrontation between two or three people. Here, toward the end of the second act, the forces of conflict rise to the highest level so far, as the time limit approaches zero hour just before the Hero discovers Stunning Surprise #2. This is NOT the climax of the whole movie — that will come in Act Three. This is the crescendo leading to a big finish for Act Two that most often demonstrates how the Hero has grown as a person.

A feature film has two climaxes; one near the end of Act Two that does NOT resolve the central conflict, and then the final Hero/Adversary showdown in Act Three that does. This crescendo in Act Two gives every impression of being the big deciding clash... but then that sneaky, unforeseen Stunning Surprise #2 pops up and throws the Hero for a loop, suddenly changing the rules of the game.

In the Act Two climax, energy must rise. The Hero's plan, cobbled together and pursued throughout the second act, looks like it's finally paying off. By now the Hero has completed the hard slogging work of character growth so he's fully self-aware and up to the task at hand. All systems go. And now the real fireworks, be they physical or emotional, cut loose.

In the Act Two climax of *The Truman Show*, Truman Burbank (Jim Carrey) overcomes his childhood terror of water at last and sets out in a small sailboat to escape the island where he has been trapped all his life as the unknowing star of a reality TV show. Adversary Christof (Ed Harris), the director of this TV hit, sits in his control booth high in the sky and creates a violent storm at sea, trying to stop Truman so he'll remain in his caged island set. Truman presses onward toward escape. The storm grows worse and the Hero yells skyward, "You'll have to kill me!" Christof capsizes the sailboat in an Act Two climax where Truman nearly does die. But Truman awakens in the boat the next morning, still alive, weather now calm. He feels victorious — but only in the world he understands.

Truman sails forth once more, about to discover a Stunning Surprise #2 — reaching the outer wall of the TV island set — which will launch the true Act Three finale showdown between Truman and his Adversary Christof.

## 8. STUNNING SURPRISE #2

Around page 95, at the end of Act Two, another Stunning Surprise springs up that serves many of the same dramatic purposes as Stunning Surprise #1, but with a twist.

This second shock also comes out of the blue and changes everything. It signals the end of Act Two and the beginning of Act Three.

But most frequently the primary additional punch of Stunning Surprise #2 is that it completely destroys the Hero's plan for victory and announces that sweeping improvisation will now be required for the Hero to have any chance of besting the Adversary.

Stunning Surprise #2 (S.S. #2 for short) is often called The Hero's Darkest Hour because at this point all hope for victory seems lost.

At the start of Act Two, right after the big shock of Stunning Surprise #1, a Hero flounders around trying to figure out a plan of action. Once the plan for victory gets formed, a Hero then pursues it doggedly in the face of all opposition for the rest of the second act.

Toward the end of Act Two it looks like the Hero's plan just might work. There's hope on the horizon. Then, *Zap!* — Stunning Surprise #2 shows up to decimate the plan, and the Hero gets drop-kicked into Act Three with few of his old resources left.

In *The Shawshank Redemption*, S.S. #2 comes after prison lifer Andy Dufresne, high on hope that he's found a fellow prisoner witness who can prove him innocent, gets thrown into solitary confinement by the warden.

Then cruel Warden Norton shows up at Andy's cell to tell him that Andy's key witness has just been shot dead for "attempted escape" (S.S. #2). The one witness who could spring Andy has been murdered by the Adversary. Now it seems all hope for the Hero's release has been lost.

This is the most common form of Stunning Surprise #2, when the Hero's best plan for victory gets completely destroyed.

In *3:10 to Yuma*, small-time rancher Dan Evans (Christian Bale), desperate for cash, signs on as a deputy to help a Pinkerton operative and his men escort the notorious outlaw Ben Wade (Russell Crowe) to Yuma, where the 3:10 train will transport Wade to the hangman.

After many struggles they reach Yuma a couple of hours before the train arrives. It looks like Hero Evans just might finish the job, collect his pay, and return to his family.

But then killer Wade's large gang of vicious gunmen rides into town and the gang pays local men to join them and swell their numbers even more. Stunning Surprise #2 — the head Pinkerton man tells Evans he won't die for this job. The Pinkerton man and his other deputies will not help Evans take Wade to the station after all, since it's become a suicide mission.

Evans is now completely alone. In order to save his family's ranch the Hero will have to shoot through dozens of killers all by himself to get Wade on that train. So ends Act Two, at the Hero's darkest hour.

There are some marvelous variations possible on this usual "all hope is lost" ending for Act Two. An upbeat surprise twist can work well also *as long as it does not resolve the main conflict of the story* and as long as it springs major change upon the Hero.

In *E.T.*, during the final scenes of Act Two poor Elliott must watch E.T. die. The space creature's death is NOT Stunning Surprise #2, because it is expected. It causes no shock or change in the situation. Alone and looking down on E.T.'s frozen corpse, Elliott offers his tearful goodbye, then slouches toward the exit. Childhood lost forever. Imagination dead forever.

But as Elliott shuffles past the wilted potted plant, ever so slightly the withered bloom perks up. Wide-eyed Elliott scrambles over to watch with thrilled wonder as the flower rises fully back to life.

It means E.T. isn't dead after all! Gloom instantly flips to unbridled joy.

This is Stunning Surprise #2 in *E.T.*, and although it's filled with hope, this moment does not resolve the basic question of the plot — whether E.T. will make it home or not. But E.T.'s wonderful resurrection fuels Elliott's final desire for a last desperate, improvised do-or-die push to get E.T. on the next spaceship home.

In this case, at the Hero's darkest possible moment hope suddenly comes gushing back.

But in both versions of S.S. #2, negative or positive, we see a huge reversal engendering surprise.

Stunning Surprise #2 must involve the biggest sudden reversal in your movie. Change so fundamental it alters the Hero's circumstances and throws her into the next act shorn of all support systems.

In romances, romantic comedies, and buddy movies, Stunning Surprise #2 serves to separate the Hero from her lover or buddy so that the relationship can be tested: the lovers break up, or the buddies are forced to split apart. That's the S.S. #2 plot turn in *As Good As It Gets*, *48 Hours*, *There's Something About Mary*, *Romancing the Stone*, *Maid in Manhattan*, *Midnight Run*, *Mamma Mia!*, *Wedding Crashers*, *Runaway Bride*, *Knocked Up*, *Notting Hill*, and many, many others.

## 9. THE OBLIGATORY SCENE

The second and final showdown climax of every film takes place in Act Three, and it's called the Obligatory Scene.

Obligatory means you gotta do it; either this scene gets included, or your movie will fail commercially (as *Breach* did). This is the moment when the Hero and Adversary go at each other to resolve the central conflict of the story once and for all.

Act Three of *Gladiator* finds Maximus chained in a cell. Evil Emperor Commodus embraces Maximus and knifes him in the back of the neck, inflicting a slow-killing wound to weaken Maximus for their fight to come. Now seriously disadvantaged, Maximus must enter the arena and fight the emperor to the death. With his last breath, Maximus finds the strength to rise and slay the emperor, thus saving all of Rome. This is a classic Obligatory Scene. The central conflict in *Gladiator* gets resolved here. Adversary dead, Hero dead, but Rome saved.

In *Sideways*, Miles' ex-wife Victoria serves as his Adversary. Miles' self-pity over losing her and thinking they will someday get back together dominates the man in every wrong life choice he makes.

By the time of Jack's wedding in Act Three, Miles has matured past his narcissism and the stage is set for a simple but powerful Obligatory Scene. Outside the church Miles finally stands before his Adversary, ex-wife Victoria. She introduces Miles to her new husband. Here, the most painful news possible gets dropped on the Hero — Victoria is pregnant. Miles in Act

One would have freaked out, said awful things, gotten drunk and caused a scene. But by Act Three our Hero has learned to give love as well as expect it from others. Even though deeply wounded, Miles takes his pain like a man and honors both Victoria and her new husband with respectful, caring words. Miles "wins" this confrontation because, as painful as it is, he finally overcomes his compulsive clinging to the past and he lets Victoria go. He's at last proven himself worthy of new love and a new future.

The Obligatory Scenes in romances and romantic comedies often involve a chase. The Hero lover pursues the lost object of affection to make a final, desperate declaration of lifelong commitment.

Such moments are Obligatory Scenes because the Love Interest characters in stories with romance as the primary plot serve double duty as the Adversary, too, like in *Hitch, Notting Hill,* and *Runaway Bride.* (Note: if the romance is only a subplot, not the primary plot, then the Love Interest is NOT the Adversary — as in *The Firm* and *Bringing Down The House* — and the Obligatory Scene will pit the Hero against the primary plot Adversary.)

The chase-and-retrieve moment in a romance plot becomes the final resolution because it's the showdown between Hero and Love Interest-Adversary that answers the core question of who wins love or who loses it.

But first, a chase.

Even though the main conflict stands resolved after the Obligatory Scene, the movie isn't over yet. There's one more very important step left to take.

### 10. DENOUEMENT

It's a French word (pronounced *dey-noo-mah*) meaning an untying. This description comes originally from Aristotle. The Denouement unties all remaining plot and character threads at the very end of a movie, after the central conflict has been settled.

The audience now needs some time to relish the Hero's victory (or defeat, as in the panorama of gore at the end of *Scarface*) and to ponder what this story resolution means to society as a whole. If the movie has succeeded in offering a powerful emotional ride, the audience will also need a moment to collect themselves before returning to reality.

The Denouement should not go on for very long. But it can never be skipped. It usually runs two or three short scenes, and in some cases only one scene is necessary.

In *Die Hard*, high atop the Nakatomi Tower office building, Hero John McClane fights criminal mastermind Hans Gruber (Alan Rickman) until the Adversary falls to his death. Obligatory Scene over. But several relationship threads need to be wrapped up in the Denouement. Limping from the building, McClane reunites with his estranged wife Holly, and it's clear they will now stay together. Then McClane meets Sergeant Powell, the sympathetic cop who encouraged the Hero over the phone throughout, and their relationship is resolved with a warm handshake. Holly punches rotten reporter Richard Thornburg in the face, resolving that relationship. A couple more small character subplots get capped off and this Denouement ends as credits roll to cheery Christmas music.

Without these wrap-ups, however, *Die Hard* would not be nearly as emotionally satisfying.

In *Star Wars*, the Denouement takes the form of an elaborate royal award ceremony, where a grateful rebel army, now free of the evil Galactic Empire, hangs medals on our Heroes as thousands cheer. It allows Luke, Han, Chewbacca, and Princess Leia to savor the importance of their victory to society and drink in the joy it has brought to innumerable planets.

Award ceremonies are often used as the Denouement of action, drama, and romance films. Either formally at an official event as in *L.A. Confidential*, or informally as in *Love Actually*, *Norma Rae*, *The Rocker*, and other movies where groups of strangers spontaneously applaud for the Hero at their moment of triumph.

Smaller films often use a quieter Denouement.

In *Sideways*, after the Obligatory Scene with Victoria at Jack's wedding, Miles ditches the reception to throw himself a solitary "graduation" party. Alone in a burger joint, Miles pops open his very best bottle of wine, a vintage he has saved for years, awaiting the perfect special occasion. He drinks it now out of a paper cup, by himself, in bittersweet acceptance of his loss.

Thus Miles formally bids farewell to Victoria and his past. He's all grown up and ready at last to fall in love for real. In the concluding scene Miles races back to Buellton, strides up the stairs to Maya's apartment door and knocks. Maya becomes the Hero's reward for character growth.

Movie over. Cut to black.

So these are the basic ten universal components of story structure. Soon I'll show you how the 23 Hero Goal Sequences® template fits perfectly over these story bones to guide you through all of those big blank spaces in between.

## SUMMING UP

• Building effective story structure is essential to creating powerful characters. Screen story structure is the basic cinematic way that the truth of character gets conveyed to an audience.

• Movies and novels tell stories in different ways:

1. Movies communicate objectively through what we see and hear — novels communicate subjectively through interior monologue;

2. Movies convey character through observed behavior — novels convey character through descriptions of thoughts and feelings;

3. Movies impart vast amounts of objective story information instantaneously — novels impart one detail of subjective story information at a time;

4. Movie stories must stay focused — novel stories can wander into side trips;

5. In movies, story structure is critical — in novels, physical plot can be a bit less important;

6. Movies are limited by running time — novels can take as long as they like.

- Successful movie story structure consists of ten basic components:

   1. ACT ONE — the story setup section;

   2. ACT TWO — the rising conflict development section;

   3. ACT THREE — the plot resolution section;

   4. INCITING INCIDENT — the moment in Act One where this specific story and no other begins;

   5. STUNNING SURPRISE #1 — the surprise event that ends Act One and begins Act Two, throwing the Hero into a new world;

   6. MIDPOINT — characteristics that may be included during this important group of scenes are:

      a.) In mood and style the Midpoint is different from the rest of the picture and frequently has a transitional montage covered with music;

      b.) The Midpoint scenes serve as an emotional or physical Point of No Return;

      c.) A Hero's conflict with the Adversary becomes personal;

      d.) In love stories and romantic comedies it's often at the Midpoint where the lovers kiss or make love, literally or metaphorically, for the first time, or where same-sex buddies work together as a true team for the first time;

      e.) The Midpoint can include an unmasking that's either metaphorical or literal;

f.) The Midpoint scenes most often contain the second crucial step in character growth;

g.) A "ticking clock" countdown often begins at the Midpoint to increase suspense;

h.) Often there is a literal or metaphorical death and rebirth moment at the Midpoint — as a ritual rite of passage for the Hero.

7. ACT TWO CLIMAX — where dramatic action rises to a crescendo and the Hero's expected victory appears to be near;

8. STUNNING SURPRISE #2 — surprise dramatic reversal that ends Act Two by destroying the Hero's plan for victory while launching Act Three (occasionally it can be a reversal to the positive);

9. OBLIGATORY SCENE — third-act final showdown between Hero and Adversary that resolves the main plot question once and for all;

10. DENOUEMENT — wraps up all plot loose ends and relationships.

**EXERCISE:**

Get the DVD of a successful Hollywood single-Hero movie, in whatever genre you might favor — action-adventure, romance, horror, sci-fi, etc. — *that you have seen before.* Watch the movie again.

As you view it this time, study the movie plot progression. Write story structure notes. You will probably need to fast-forward and fast-back a number of times in order to:

*Find all ten key tent poles of basic screen story structure in the film.*

Keep a wristwatch handy — it will help you to locate the major sign posts of S.S. #1 (about 25 to 35 minutes in), Midpoint (roughly halfway through the film), and S.S. #2 (about 90 to 100 minutes in).

MAKE NOTE OF:

1.  Act One (how long, and story content)

2.  Act Two (how long, and story content)

3.  Act Three (how long, and story content)

4.  Inciting Incident (how far in, and content)

5.  Stunning Surprise #1 (how far in, and content)

6.  Midpoint Sequence (how many Midpoint plot elements are present, and duration)

7.  Act Two Climax (duration and content)

8.  Stunning Surprise #2 (how far in, and content)

9.  Obligatory Scene (duration and story resolution content)

10. Denouement (duration and wrap-up content)

- *Do not expect to get everything exactly right.*

- *Just because you can't yet locate a particular story element doesn't mean it isn't there.*

- Now try it again with another movie.

- By training yourself to spot these structure points you will take a huge leap forward as a storyteller.

*chapter eight*

# The Character Growth Arc

——— ⚬ ———

Character growth is basic to good screenwriting. It's often discussed — but seldom genuinely understood.

Many new writers assume it's something mysterious and immensely complex. That's how I felt starting out as a playwright at UCLA.

For me, the very name "Character Growth Arc" called to mind Freud and Jung and psychoanalysis and the vast inner workings of human personality. Surely it must be a subject too intricate for tackling any other way except through intuitive creativity. Just do your best to write deep characters, then pray that your muse will take care of the rest.

Because trying to *plan* character growth causes migraines.

Well, save the aspirin. Here's good news.

Once a writer genuinely understands story structure, adding character growth becomes a relatively simple task.

## STEPS OF THE CHARACTER GROWTH ARC

Here's how you do it.

Begin in Act One by creating a Hero who has experienced a deep emotional TRAUMA. Just one single personal injury to the heart, no more. A specific past event so hurtful to your Hero that it has had the effect of isolating him emotionally, causing some blind spot and defensiveness in his relationships with other people.

Be very specific here. This past TRAUMA has created a source of great emotional pain, so the Hero's SHIELD of emotional self-protection raised to defend against any more suffering in the future now prohibits him from connecting on a personal level with others.

In *Signs*, Reverend Graham Hess's beloved wife Colleen went out for a walk one evening and accidentally got hit by a car that cut her in half (Hero's TRAUMA).

Devastated, Hess lost all faith in a caring God, resigned as pastor of his church, and became an atheist (his SHIELD).

In *The Silence of the Lambs*, Clarice Starling (Jodie Foster) tells Hannibal Lecter (Anthony Hopkins) that when she was a child on her uncle's farm she tried desperately to save lambs from slaughter, but failed. Ever since, she's been haunted by dreams of screaming, terrified lambs and the sudden awful silence that falls when they are butchered (her TRAUMA).

So Clarice became an FBI agent driven to defend the helpless (her SHIELD).

Back in his college days, Hitch was a geeky, clumsy guy who fell madly in love with stunning Mandy. But uncool Hitch got his heart broken when he found Mandy with another man, and she dumped Hitch for being too needy (his TRAUMA).

So Hitch turned himself into an ultra-suave, invulnerable lady's man who sells lessons to nerds about winning the woman of their dreams (his SHIELD).

Now, having stuck your Hero in a world of emotional misery in the first act, in the second act add the three following scenes.

Each of these character growth scenes should take place at a specific moment in the story:

a.) Character growth scene #1 takes place during the first half of Act Two;

b.) Character growth scene #2 takes place during the Midpoint Sequence, and…

c.) Character growth scene #3 takes place during the second half of Act Two.

In these scenes, at these three specific locations in the second act, your Hero will:

Scene One: *EXPRESS*
Scene Two: *BATTLE*
Scene Three: *OVERCOME*

...his inner emotional conflict and finally lay down his emotional SHIELD.

Add these three scenes to your script and Hollywood will hail you a master. Leave them out, and chances of breaking into the big time become more remote.

Lets look at these three steps/scenes more closely.

## GROWTH ARC — STEP ONE

In Act One we meet a Hero who lives life under the cloud of an as yet unnamed emotional problem that's causing him to isolate himself from other people. We don't yet know anything specific about the past, emotionally scarring event that caused the problem. That will be revealed later in the story. For now, the Hero himself isn't even aware he has a problem, although he does recognize there's some malaise deep inside keeping him from experiencing any real fulfillment in life.

The general nature of this inner discontent gets demonstrated to the audience through the Hero's behavior and attitudes. *It's never spoken of directly during the first act.* The Hero is convinced he's coping just fine, thank you very much, and thinks there's no need for change.

Then the Hero gets called upon to pursue some sort of general external goal.

What the Hero doesn't yet know is that he can never achieve the real world goal required of him by the plot unless he first throws away his self-protective emotional SHIELD.

After entering the special world of Act Two and launching a vigorous pursuit for what has now become a highly specific physical real-world goal, our Hero begins to feel the full leaden weight of this emotional encumbrance he carries within. But still, he can't quite put a name to it.

- *The FIRST STEP of character growth requires the Hero to EXPRESS — consciously or unconsciously — the nature of the emotional baggage that's holding him back.*

This usually happens fairly early in the first half of Act Two. Some physical event must challenge the Hero and cause the fact that he's hiding behind a shield to rise to the surface and be stated in dialogue.

This shield revelation statement is often ironic and not yet fully self-aware. But either in a literal or figurative way, the Hero at last expresses his problem. It gets verbalized and now is out in the open for the Hero to hear and discover.

In *Pretty Woman*, by the start of Act Two billionaire Edward Lewis has hired prostitute Vivian Ward to be his "beck-and-call girl" for the week and to stay with him in his Beverly Hills penthouse hotel suite. Edward gives Vivian a large wad of cash and tells her to go buy some nice clothes.

When Vivian walks into an upscale Beverly Hills women's store wearing her street hooker togs, she receives condescending sneers from a saleswoman who tells Vivian, "You're obviously in the wrong place. Please leave." Crushed, feeling too worthless to raise a word in her own defense, Vivian slinks off.

Back at the hotel, the manager pulls her into his office for a stern admonition about hooking. Near tears, Vivian pulls out Edward's large wad of useless greenbacks and shows them to the hotel manager (her Mentor).

"I have to buy a dress for tonight. I have all this money... and nobody will help me." Thereby Vivian EXPRESSES her inner suffering. Money is useless without self-respect. Vivian's mother used to call her a bum magnet, and Vivian believed her (her TRAUMA). If a person thinks she is worthless, the world will always agree and treat her like dirt. Having lots of money to spend won't change that.

Vivian is forced to recognize her problem. From here Vivian begins her inner journey toward higher self-regard.

Also in *Pretty Woman*, a two-Hero movie, Edward Lewis goes through his own Character Growth Arc as well. Edward's moment to EXPRESS inner pain comes a couple of scenes later when he tells Vivian, "We're such similar creatures. We both screw people for money." On the outside Edward is a wealthy and powerful man. But inside he feels deep dissatisfaction with the destructive way he makes his fortune, by buying companies, and then selling off their assets. Each company he kills is an act of revenge against his deceased father who abandoned him as a boy, leaving Edward's mother to die in poverty (his TRAUMA). But destroying things is chipping away at Edward's soul. Here he consciously identifies his need for growth.

Hero Miles in *Sideways* drives out to a lovely spot overlooking a vineyard with best friend Jack. Miles waxes nostalgic about how he picnicked with his ex-wife Victoria — the loss of whom was his TRAUMA — on this very spot.

Jack breaks it to Miles that Victoria just got remarried. Miles is devastated. "Is she bringing him to the wedding? I'll be a pariah! I'll be *persona non grata*! Everyone will be waiting to see if I get drunk and make a scene." Miles sinks pouting into his car and whines, "I'd like to go home now."

Here, quite early in Act Two, Miles EXPRESSES and names his inner pain. He doesn't say "let's go back to the motel." He says, "I'd like to go home now."

Miles has always felt he and Victoria would someday get back together. More than anything he wants to go home to Victoria. But that door has closed forever. Notice how Miles' thoughts are only about himself, about what other people will think of him, about his infantile semi-threat of making a scene at Jack's wedding. He's not yet ready to offer genuine unselfish love to any woman.

Miles grabs an open wine bottle and runs from the car seeking "poor me" oblivion.

Now it's out in the open. Miles must choose between self-centered obsession with his past, or character growth.

## GROWTH ARC — STEP TWO

After the Hero EXPRESSES her emotional problem and thereby identifies it, the story drives onward to the Midpoint where the Hero must lay down her defensive shield and take action against that core emotional conflict.

> • *The SECOND STEP of character growth requires the Hero to finally BATTLE this self-isolating, wounded condition — but this attempt will not succeed.*

The old inner suffering soon returns as painful as ever.

The Hero once again lifts up her defensive SHIELD against the emotional slings and arrows of the world. However, she has now experienced an honest attempt to live without one, and has glimpsed what might be accomplished if she could just lay down this heavy, cumbersome thing forever.

The first inner BATTLE takes place during the Midpoint scenes because it represents an emotional Point of No Return. Although he is unsuccessful this time, the Hero realizes that the hard work of inner growth will be required to achieve real-world victory over the Adversary.

Remember that this inner BATTLE must be visualized through the Hero taking a revealing physical action.

Approaching the Midpoint of *Collateral*, hitman Vincent demands that he and cabdriver Max go visit Max's mother in the hospital because Vincent doesn't want anything about Max's routine to appear out of the ordinary. As hospital patient mom chats pleasantly with Vincent, ignorant of who the hitman really is, mom unthinkingly belittles Max.

The scene speaks volumes about how Max was raised as a child to distrust his own abilities (his TRAUMA). The story jabs a sharp stick into Max's wounded heart, where his SHIELD has become the use of fantasy escapism to cover cowardly inaction.

If you don't try anything — like actually starting up Island Limos, for instance — you don't have to risk failure.

But Max desperately wants to get Vincent away from his mother. So finally Max grabs the hitman's briefcase and runs. In a burst of courage Max throws down his SHIELD of inaction and makes a break for it.

As the Adversary runs after him, Max BATTLES his inner conflict during this Midpoint scene by scrambling to a freeway overpass, then throwing Vincent's briefcase into the traffic below. Papers scatter as an eighteen-wheeler smashes the hitman's computer.

When Vincent races up, Max freezes again. He's once more immobilized by terror. Max lifts his self-protective SHIELD of inaction anew and once again becomes Vincent's limp captive.

But for a few glorious seconds Max found the guts to take action against the fears of a lifetime.

Notice that Max risks his life here on behalf of other people; his mother, and the two remaining hit-list victims whose unknown names are in the briefcase. This is what makes him a true Hero. He's not just trying to save his own neck, Max is trying to save the lives of other people, too.

Max has not yet beaten the demon of his fantasy-shrouded cowardice. That would be too easy. But he's finally done BATTLE with it right where he should, during the Midpoint Sequence.

## GROWTH ARC — STEP THREE

As the second half of Act Two progresses, the Hero warms up to other people. He's made good friends during his main plot-line struggle, and by now the Hero has committed to a do-or-die attitude in pursuing the goal. Emotion runs high in the Hero and his Allies. Preparations are almost complete for a final assault on the Adversary, and success may be at hand.

Then a second plot opportunity presents itself for the Hero to unlock his heart.

• *The THIRD STEP of character growth arrives just before the Act Two climax. By finally taking action to resolve the intensifying conflict in a new, more emotionally enlightened way, the Hero lays down his shield and OVERCOMES his inner defensiveness, proving that he has changed.*

In this step the Hero tastes true emotional freedom at last. The Hero now pursues an honest, emotionally unguarded approach to achieving his goal. This positive change from within creates hope for victory.

Toward the end of Act Two in *Collateral*, a chaotic and bloody shootout erupts in a nightclub. Cabby Max is almost saved by Detective Fanning, but Vincent kills the cop, grabs Max and pushes him back in the cab.

Again Max must drive Vincent off to his next hit.

Finally it's absolutely clear to Max. No rescue will come. So for the first time he finds the guts to directly confront the psychopath in his backseat by openly questioning what might be missing inside such a man.

"You are way low, my brother," Max says, courage growing. Vincent and Max go at each other verbally. Vincent calls Max out for wasting his life in a cab, "You can't even call that girl!" Max retorts, "That's one thing I gotta thank you for, bro, because until now I never looked at it."

And Max stomps on the gas. In seconds he's flying through the late night streets of downtown L.A. while Vincent screams at him to slow down. "Go ahead, shoot me," Max taunts, "you want to kill us both?"

At last Max finds the courage to boldly confront Vincent in this Act Two climax. He OVERCOMES his fear of taking action. Max begins his gutsy duel to the death with Vincent.

Max achieves inner emotional victory in preparation for physical victory. He's no longer the loveable loser of Act One. Character growth has transformed this Hero and now he's proven it by risking his life in a calculated way that will finally let him break free of the Adversary.

In *Pretty Woman*, during the second half of Act Two Edward takes Vivian out on a date. First, he places around her neck jewelry worth a quarter of a million dollars — teaching Vivian how much she's really worth as a person. Then he flies her by private jet to an opera house in San Francisco.

Since Edward's mother was a music teacher, this date is rather like taking Vivian home to meet mom. Deeply moved by the opera production, Vivian passes Edward's love of music test with flying colors.

That night in bed Vivian and Edward make real love at last. She kisses him fully on the mouth, something she had said before was too personal.

Then, drifting off, believing Edward asleep, Vivian says softly, "I love you." Here she OVERCOMES her oppressive lack of self-worth. This ex-streetwalker has now gained the self-respect to sincerely declare her love for a man far, far above her station in life. She at last feels worthy to love a billionaire and be loved back by him.

Edward is not asleep, he has heard her. He looks anew at this extraordinary woman who has grown to discover her deep value as a person. A woman now capable of saving Edward's own soul, too.

At the start of Act Three, after this third step in character growth of OVERCOMING the inner emotional battle, often there's a moment of emotional retreat where the Hero tries to lift his old heavy shield back into place once more. He tries — but discovers that his defensive mechanism isn't really effective now.

At the start of Act Three in *Shrek*, upset about handing Princess Fiona over to Lord Farquaad, the loveable ogre withdraws emotionally back into his I'm-still-building-a-wall-around-my-swamp-so-leave-me-alone mode, and he tells Donkey to get lost. But that shield doesn't really work now. Even a grumpy Shrek can't deny it. He recognizes he has changed inside, and soon enough Shrek and Donkey climb aboard the dragon together, flying off to rescue Fiona.

Finally achieving the maturity of character growth teaches the Hero that there's no need to return to the folly of emotional childhood. In Act Three the Hero experiences completion as an emotionally liberated person.

But remember, *you must demonstrate emotional growth without damaging Hero sympathy*. A Hero so self-shielded at the beginning that the audience doesn't like him will usually fail at the box office. Think *Waterworld* and *Ghost Town*.

Powerful plots are engineered in ways that force the Hero's key emotional problem into the open, then stir up as much painful emotional turmoil for the Hero as possible. You must find your Hero's deepest trauma, then use your story to jab a taser at it, forcing the Hero onward toward an arc of personal growth.

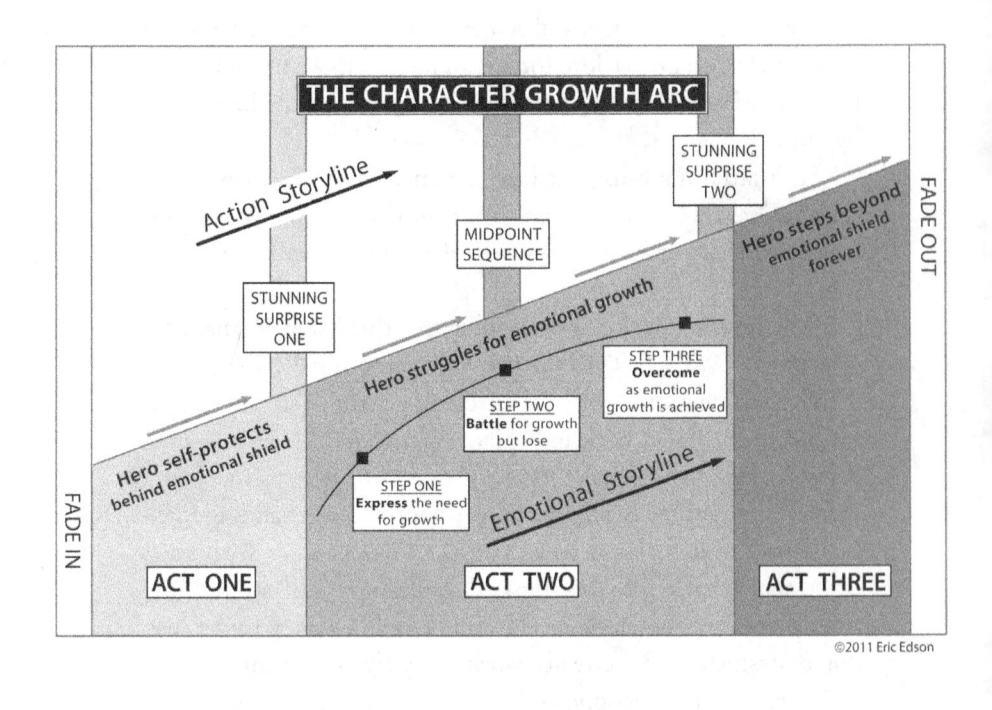

©2011 Eric Edson

## SUMMING UP

- Once a writer genuinely understands screen story structure, adding character growth becomes a relatively straightforward task.

- Create a Hero who has experienced an emotionally devastating event in the past — his TRAUMA — and who now self-protects with an isolating SHIELD of attitude that keeps the world at emotional arms length so the Hero won't have to feel such pain again.

- Add the following three scenes at specific places in the script, and so give the Hero an opportunity to lay down his SHIELD forever:

    1. During the first half of Act Two the Hero must EXPRESS in dialogue — consciously or unconsciously — the nature of the emotional suffering that's holding her back;

    2. During the Midpoint scenes the Hero actively does BATTLE to lay down her self-protective emotional shield but loses this first try at combat with inner conflict;

    3. Late in the second half of Act Two, the Hero finally OVERCOMES and conquers this isolating emotional defense system.

- The Hero may relapse into defensive emotional suffering at the beginning of Act Three but soon realizes character growth is permanent — that he has become a changed, more mature person who can finally accomplish the goal of the story plot.

**EXERCISE:**

The films *Contact, The Truman Show,* and *On the Waterfront* all contain strong Character Growth Arcs. Get your hands on one of these movies.

Watch the film and locate the following character growth elements, writing them down.

In Act One:
What's the Hero's TRAUMA? (The past event that caused this Hero great emotional pain.)

What's the Hero's SHIELD? (The self-protective mechanism used to avoid more pain.)

In Act Two:
Describe the scene where the Hero EXPRESSES or HEARS EXPRESSED his need for inner growth.

Describe the Midpoint scene when the Hero BATTLES inner conflict and first tries to lay down his SHIELD.

Describe how the Hero finally OVERCOMES inner conflict toward the end of the act and lays down her SHIELD forever.

In Act Three:
How does the Hero now *physically demonstrate character growth* to show us his inner world has changed permanently?

When you're ready, try another one of the three movies listed above. You will see similar story structure tools being used as each Character Growth Arc evolves.

> *"Never, never rest contented with any idea, always be certain a new one is still possible."*
>
> ~ Pearl Bailey

*part four* The Power of Hero Goal Sequences®

*chapter nine*

# THE 23 STORY LINKS IN EVERY GREAT MOVIE

———— ⌘ ————

Learning basic structure is incredibly important. No film has *ever* succeeded commercially without incorporating all ten of the story structure components outlined in Chapter Seven.

But what if you've got the fundamentals of structure down cold and still find yourself completely lost deep in the jungle of your second act?

Really mastering screenwriting requires an understanding of visual storytelling that goes far beyond the basics.

Back when I took university graduate seminars in playwriting, those classes were little more than emotional support groups conducted under the assumption that nothing about dramatic writing could really be taught. Either your "writer's intuition" would create good work or it wouldn't. Students were pretty much left to flounder on their own.

Some writers prefer this Cosmic Mystery *it-comes-to-you-or-it-doesn't* approach. A tiny handful of scribes in the world actually thrive on it.

But most of us mere mortals do not.

You become a good screenwriter through hard work, study, and practice. And constructing an effective storyline has always been the toughest challenge.

To make a point, let's count script pages.

Say you're outlining your next screenplay and you've got a powerful Inciting Incident you expect will grab an audience's attention, and it will run about three pages. Then Stunning

Surprise #1 done right should be good for two or three more pages, quick and shocking. Most Midpoints clock in at around five or six pages, then later, the Act Two climax roars on for, say, another five. Your powerful Stunning Surprise #2 can be penciled in for three more pages. If you've got a hot Obligatory Scene that'll really cook, add five more. Then you plan to wrap it all up and leave 'em weeping with a strong three-page Denouement.

That's a total of 28 pages. In a movie script that needs to be about 115 pages long.

So what will your Hero do during those other 87 pages?

Working as a screenwriter and studying a whole lot of movies through the years, I've discovered a pattern in successful film storytelling that overlays the ten components of basic structure and offers a much more complete, writer-friendly paradigm. Simply put, *all screenplays that work for audiences can be broken down to between 20 and 23 distinct sections.* These chain links of story that I call HERO GOAL SEQUENCES® are linear, progressive, and flow logically, one into the next, to create a seamless and powerful rising dramatic tension.

The single most common failing of new original screenplays is the lack of enough sheer story to sustain audience interest. Often writers who are quite capable of creating strong plot threads simply stop weaving those threads too soon, and their film scripts feel thin or unengaging.

And that's when the eight-page dialogue scenes, or the repetitive, tangential, or irrelevant story events start to appear.

Hero Goal Sequences® solve these problems by telling you in advance exactly how much story your screenplay will require, and where all the smaller plot twists and turns should take place.

Successful screen storytelling is built around the concept of relentless change, pushing us forward in every scene, every single line. Using the Goal Sequences template allows a writer to map this change accurately up front for an entire motion picture.

When I first began noticing this story pattern in films, I was stunned. Because genre didn't matter. Mood and tone didn't matter. Nor did length, or scope, or budget, or setting. Studio, director, screenwriter, star — none of it altered in any way the number of Hero Goal Sequences® — no fewer than 20 and no more than 23 — to be found in films that were successful.

After closely analyzing several hundred American feature films from as far back as 1927, I gave up trying to prove myself wrong. Clearly, this sequencing pattern speaks directly to the way in which the human mind processes story.

## DEFINITION

Distilled to its essence, the Goal Sequence concept lays out like this:

A HERO GOAL SEQUENCE® consists of three to seven pages of screenplay — usually two to four scenes — wherein the Hero pursues one short-term physical goal as a step toward achieving ultimate victory in the story. Then the Hero discovers some form of new information I call Fresh News that brings the current goal to an end and presents a new short-term physical goal — thereby launching the next Hero Goal Sequence®.

The discovery of Fresh News plot information by the Hero at the end of each Goal Sequence always resolves the current short-term goal. It also provides the Hero with his next goal, or occasionally sends him on a short search to find it. This unbroken chain of Fresh News discoveries — each one driving dramatic intensity up another notch — is the key element that links together an entire screen story from beginning to end.

Determining the length of a Hero Goal Sequence® and the number of scenes involved in each one requires some flexibility. Some may have only a single scene; some can contain as many as five or more. Some, on rare occasion, are less than two minutes. Others can be more than nine minutes if the overall running time of the movie is unusually long.

There's a single Hero Goal Sequence® in *Titanic* that lasts more than 21 minutes. There's one in *Shrek* that lasts only one minute twenty-two seconds. In most cases the numbers are two to four scenes lasting a total of three to seven pages.

This is how Hero Goal Sequences® will drive a story forward: if your Hero must pursue a new short-term physical goal (*NOT merely an emotional one*) every three to seven pages, your story will never languish or veer off onto some tangent. Your screenplay will be tight, clear, and focused. And if every action any Hero undertakes is in the pursuit of some current, urgent end, passive Heroes automatically will transform into active ones.

Hero Goal Sequences® also ensure originality and prevent your screenplay from becoming redundant because each sequence must contain a new action in pursuit of a short-term goal that has not been seen in the story before.

The Hero's big, overall story goal remains the same throughout, of course, whether it's finding true love, beating a powerful Adversary, or saving the world. But each short-term smaller goal in pursuit of that ultimate big plot objective must be unique in some way. A Goal Sequence might be similar to one that has gone before... but any time a comparable goal is pursued, some strong new element must be added.

Now here's the really remarkable thing about Hero Goal Sequences®: *the number of Goal Sequences in Act One and Act Two remains constant.* Both *Titanic* and *Shrek* contain the exact same number of Hero Goal Sequences® in their first two acts. The only difference is that those in *Titanic* are longer.

Act One *always* consists of six Hero Goal Sequences®, with Stunning Surprise #1 occurring in Goal Sequence number six.

The first half of Act Two contains another six Hero Goal Sequences®. No more, no less. And the Midpoint scenes *always* unfold during Goal Sequence number twelve.

In the second half of Act Two there are six more Hero Goal Sequences® and Stunning Surprise #2 must *always* arrive during Goal Sequence number eighteen.

Act Three typically contains three Goal Sequences — most often resulting in a total of 21 for a screenplay. This number can sometimes vary by one or two, but only in Act Three. And there are never *ever* less than two, or more than five, Hero Goal Sequences® in the third act of any successful film.

So: minimum 20, maximum 23, for every feature film.

Less than two sequences in Act Three won't work because at a minimum, the story components of Obligatory Scene and Denouement are always required and each needs a separate Goal Sequence of its own. *Erin Brockovich, Rain Man, The Matrix*, and *Stranger Than Fiction* all contain a mere two Hero Goal Sequences® in the third act.

Because many action-adventure films and thrillers can be thin on character growth, they frequently use only two Goal Sequences in Act Three, too. Once the Adversary gets defeated, the action is over and these stories need to wrap up quickly.

The maximum number of Goal Sequences in Act Three is five, yes, but using this many can stretch the patience of an audience. There are, however, some successful movies with five, including my personal favorite romantic comedy, *As Good As It Gets*.

This Hero Goal Sequences® paradigm can be used effectively only when writing feature length motion pictures 85 to 200 minutes long. Shorter films and individual television episodes require a more abbreviated structure. Or, as with some TV series, the story arc can last an entire season, providing way too much plot to be contained in 23 Hero Goal Sequences®.

Often film school students try to take the script from their short film project and expand it into a feature-length screenplay. Most such attempts are destined to fail because there just isn't enough story to be found in a short film to fill the required 20 to 23 Hero Goal Sequences®. Short film writers must rethink and expand their entire concept, then develop a complete set of Goal Sequences for the new story in order for it to work on the bigger, more demanding feature film canvas.

The Goal Sequences approach is also enormously helpful when adapting novels into screenplays. This writing task usually requires leaving a lot of story material behind because novels tend to run long. With Hero Goal Sequences® you know exactly how much material to keep in the script version. Or you can spot the story holes in the book with Goal Sequencing, and so learn how much plot still needs to be invented.

When writing a novel it can also be incredibly effective to outline your story from the start by using Goal Sequences if you are looking to create an experience for your reader that's powerfully filmic.

## COUNTING NON-HERO SCENES
## IN GOAL SEQUENCES

We know that every single scene in a movie must be, at its core, about the Hero, whether that Hero is present in a scene or not.

But this raises an important question. Most films contain a few scenes that do not have the Hero in them. They cut away to some subplot character or to the Adversary. So when constructing Goal Sequences, how should scenes be counted which do not involve watching the Hero's direct, physical action-line?

The answer is, *don't count them at all.*

These subplot cutaways from the Hero often explore some aspect of the Adversary to reveal how unbeatable he or she is. (Darth Vader lording it over his troops in *Star Wars*, Cruella De Vil planning her worst against *101 Dalmations*.) Or they cut to the Love Interest character to demonstrate what jeopardy she's in, or how she is experiencing emotional pain, too. (Waitress Carol fretting about her son's allergies in *As Good As It Gets*, wife Abby risking her life for estranged lawyer hubby Mitch in *The Firm*.)

Subplot cutaway scenes can also involve a Sidekick or Ally or Mentor, or even a lesser enemy character. But the definition of Hero Goal Sequences® always remains the same. A sequence does not end until on-screen focus returns to the Hero as she or he pursues some short-term goal resulting in the discovery of Fresh News.

All story surprises, shocks, turns, and apparent Fresh News moments that seem to appear in subplot scenes without the Hero present *cannot count in the main storyline* because the Hero isn't there to experience them.

In *Finding Nemo* there are several major scenes that cut away from clownfish Marlin, the Hero, as he battles across the whole Pacific Ocean to save his son. We also watch little Nemo, trapped in a dentist's fish tank, as he struggles to grow more self-confident under the guidance of angelfish Gill. At one point Nemo almost gets killed during an escape attempt when he tries to jam a pebble in the tank filter pump. A harrowing, exciting scene. But son Nemo's adventures with his new friends in the dentist's office are only the extended subplot moments of an Endangered Innocent Ally character. These are just cutaway scenes without the Hero. Only primary plot scenes directly involving Marlin count toward Goal Sequence structure. What Nemo experiences can have no emotional impact on Marlin because the Hero isn't aware of it yet, therefore Nemo's scenes can't contribute to the Goal Sequences of the primary storyline.

Hero Goal Sequences® must make room for subplot or cutaway scenes where the Hero does not appear, so frequently the actual Goal Sequence becomes a shorter one in order to accommodate. But the 23 Sequences themselves are always constructed around Hero actions in the primary plot.

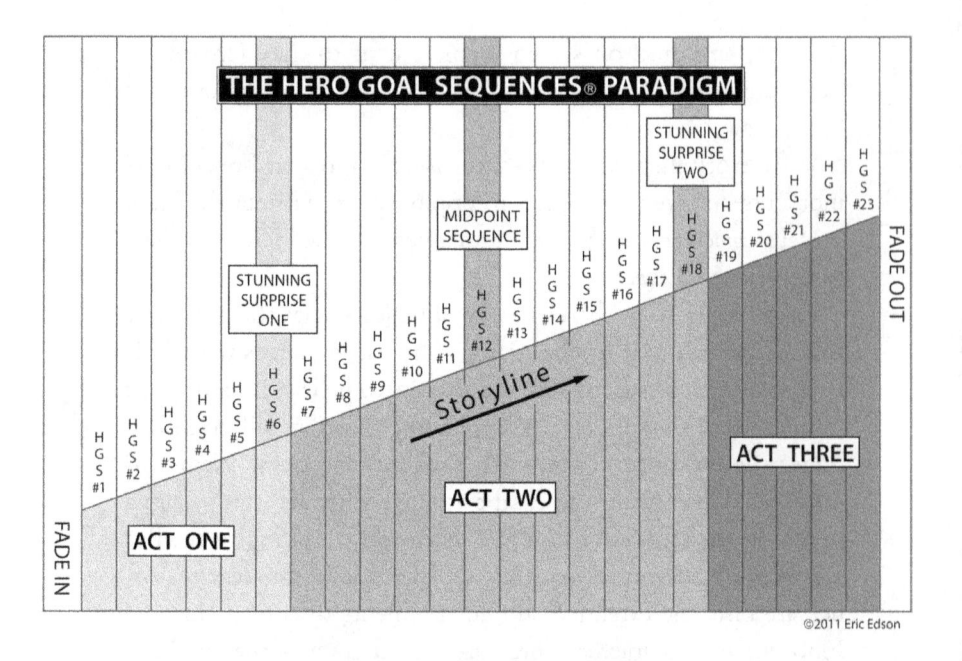

## COUNTING GOAL SEQUENCES
## WITH MULTIPLE HEROES

Emotionally riveting movies are built by following the goals and passions of either a single or multiple Heroes. The number of Heroes present in your story must be decided during the concept stage, before you begin structuring your story and applying the principles of Hero Goal Sequences®. The more Heroes, the more complex storytelling becomes.

In a movie with two Heroes, a Goal Sequence does not end until both Heroes experience Fresh News either simultaneously or serially. *If two characters function fully as genuine Heroes in one movie, the Hero Goal Sequences® paradigm must apply to both.*

With three or more Heroes in a screenplay, unless all Heroes are part of a group that is always together to share each Fresh News moment, Goal Sequencing becomes even more complex. Plotting turns unwieldy and key dramatic moments must be cut. Such motion pictures don't have time to fully explore the journey of any single Hero. They become, in essence, short-story anthologies.

Some wonderful movies have been created by cutting back and forth to scenes following three or more Heroes. But many of these films have a hard time at the box office. Paul Thomas Anderson's multiple-Hero *Magnolia* remains a favorite of mine, but it did not break even on its initial theatrical release. *Syriana*, with multiple Heroes, did not do so well, nor did *200 Cigarettes* or *Dancing at the Blue Iguana* or *Babel*.

Determining how many Heroes a film contains can sometimes be tricky. At first glance *As Good As It Gets* may appear to have three Heroes. In addition to obnoxious romance writer Melvin Udall, a great deal of screen time gets spent on sweet waitress Carol and gay artist neighbor Simon. Three Heroes?

No. This is a one-Hero movie. Responsibility for all Goal Sequence actions and all Fresh News revelations falls to obsessive-compulsive putdown-meister Melvin Udall. Neighbor Simon serves Melvin's primary plotline as a Mentor character. Waitress Carol serves wonderfully as a fully drawn, complex Love Interest character. Only Melvin advances this story by pursuing Carol, she never pursues him. Carol is the Hero's reward for character growth at the end like a Love Interest-Adversary should be. But the Hero's journey, ultimate victory, and lessons learned all belong to Melvin.

Just because there are many characters front and center in a screenplay does not necessarily mean the story contains multiple Heroes. And spotting the real Hero at all may not always be as straightforward as you might think.

In the moody and powerful film *Leaving Las Vegas*, it may seem obvious that hard-drinking dead-ender Ben Sanderson, played by Oscar winner Nicolas Cage, is the Hero. Except he isn't. Ben serves as the Love Interest-Adversary to Sera (Elisabeth Shue), who is the real Hero of this film. Despite a long opening sequence that establishes the Adversary first, all sequence energy, Fresh News discoveries, character growth, and plot reversals originate with Sera. Ben is a Charismatic Adversary character.

Remember that clearly identifying who the Hero is in your story won't always be simple, but it's essential to do it. You must make a clear choice of Hero before you can set out to build a screen story that works.

And when writing original screenplays it's far easier to outline your story with Hero Goal Sequences® *before* writing the first draft. After scenes are written in script form it can become difficult for a neophyte writer to let go of those scenes if they don't mesh with the requirements of Goal Sequencing. The tail ends up wagging the dog and you can lose sight of story priorities.

## SUMMING UP

- All successful screenplays can be broken down into 20 to 23 Hero Goal Sequences®.

- In a Hero Goal Sequence® the Hero pursues a single, short-term physical goal as one step toward achieving ultimate victory in the main overall goal of the story.

- A Goal Sequence continues until the Hero discovers some Fresh News information that brings pursuit of the current short-term goal to an end and creates a new goal, or sends the Hero on a short search for a new goal, thereby launching the next Hero Goal Sequence®.

- A Hero Goal Sequence® usually consists of three to seven pages of screenplay, or two to four scenes.

- Act One always consists of six Hero Goal Sequences®.

- Stunning Surprise #1 must always arrive in Goal Sequence number six.

- The first half of Act Two contains another six Hero Goal Sequences®.

- The Midpoint always arrives during Goal Sequence number twelve.

- In the second half of Act Two there are six more Hero Goal Sequences®.

- Stunning Surprise #2 always takes place during Goal Sequence number eighteen.

- Two to five Hero Goal Sequences® are present in the third act, including (at a minimum) the Obligatory Scene and the Denouement.

- The paradigm of Hero Goal Sequences® applies only to feature-length films, not short films or episodes of television series.

- When scenes in which the Hero does not appear are included in a Goal Sequence, the sequence cannot end until the story returns to the Hero and we see him acquire the Fresh News information.

- The number of Heroes in a screenplay story must be determined before applying the Goal Sequencing paradigm because each Hero needs to be given their own full contingent of Hero Goal Sequences®.

- If a story contains two or more Heroes, Fresh News moments must occur for each of them either simultaneously or in immediate succession.

- When developing the story for a script, employing Hero Goal Sequences® in the outline stage before writing the first draft is the most effective way to ensure success.

**EXERCISE:**

Get a DVD of the film *The Proposal.* View the first 35 minutes.

It's a one-Hero story about Margaret (Sandra Bullock). Her assistant Andrew (Ryan Reynolds) serves as her Love Interest.

Since this is a romantic comedy, there are two parallel plotlines involving the Hero. In the try-not-to-get-deported plotline, Margaret's Adversary is INS Agent Gilbertson. In the romance plotline, Andrew serves as *both* Margaret's Love Interest and her Adversary.

NOW:
Using your remote control to scan back and forth in the film, make notes describing the six Hero Goal Sequences® in Act One of *The Proposal.* Write down the focused, physical HERO GOAL for each sequence, then the sequence-ending FRESH NEWS that concludes the current goal and creates the next one.

You'll find some hints below.

I'll give you the first sequence to get you started.

- For HGS #1 the HERO GOAL is — *Pursue another day of being great at her job.* FRESH NEWS arrives when Andrew informs Margaret that — *Her top boss wants to see her right away.* With credits, this sequence runs 9 min.

- So… in HGS #2 the HERO GOAL becomes — *See her boss and hit him up for another raise.* But that goal changes drastically when… what's the next FRESH NEWS? (It has to do with Andrew entering the room.) This sequence runs 4 min. (It ends when Margaret leaves her boss' office.)

- Then in HGS #3, what's Margaret's new HERO GOAL? (It has to do with paperwork.) What FRESH NEWS changes things? (Has to do with a need to travel.) Sequence runs 6 min. 28 sec.

- For HGS #4, what's the HERO GOAL? (Getting ready to do something.) FRESH NEWS for HGS #4? (Andrew gets plucky.) This runs 2 min. 24 sec.

- In HGS #5, what's the HERO GOAL? (On the move toward where and what?) And FRESH NEWS? (An underestimation is revealed.) This runs 3 min. 22 sec.

- What's the HERO GOAL in HGS #6? (Has to do with getting someplace.)

Remember, this time FRESH NEWS is also STUNNING SURPRISE ONE (has to do with what Margaret sees when she arrives) that throws the Hero into new circumstances. This one runs 3 min. 46 sec. — and creates a total Act One running time of 29 min.

TAKE YOUR BEST SHOT. You are looking for the single physical Hero Goal that drives each sequence of scenes forward *until some kind of story-changing Fresh News appears to alter that goal.*

REMEMBER — there can be other story surprises along the way in any single HGS, but if those plot turns do not change the Hero's current motivating physical goal, those story moments DO NOT qualify as Fresh News.

- Do not expect to nail them all! Getting just one or two right is an excellent start at truly seeing into screen story structure.

After you take a stab at it, you'll find the answers at the end of Chapter Ten.

*chapter ten*

# SHAPING ACT ONE: HERO GOAL SEQUENCES® 1~6

———— ⊘⊘ ————

A list of every action that must appear minute by minute in each and every screenplay doesn't exist. Thank heavens. Movies would be pretty dull if it did.

Sure, an Obligatory Scene will always be required in Act Three. But it can take place in Sequence nineteen, twenty, or twenty-one, just as long as it shows up somewhere before the Denouement in the third act.

An Inciting Incident must occur as well, but exactly where in Act One depends on the individual needs of each story.

However.

Thousands of years of human expectation arising from our enjoyment of the storytelling ritual does allow us to get fairly specific about what happens GENERALLY in most Hero Goal Sequences®. We can pretty much predict, within a few pages, what common story elements can be expected to appear at what point in any successful screenplay.

For the sake of demonstrating how Hero Goal Sequences® work across all genres, I will take my examples from a number of very different film story categories: drama, science-fiction, fantasy, action, romance, comedy, original screenplays, and adaptations.

As I lay out the more specific content for each of the Hero Goals in order, for some of you it may begin to feel a wee bit clinical. But I will do my best to keep it filmic as we revisit some wonderful sequences from great movies.

And this I promise.

Hand pressed firmly over heart.

These next five chapters hold revelations that could turn you into a truly superb screenwriter. Or novelist. Or producer, director, agent, professor, script analyst, or…

You owe it to yourself to charge onward.

Tally-ho!

## HERO GOAL SEQUENCE₍®₎ ONE

Each appearance of Fresh News information signaling the close of a Goal Sequence should build audience anticipation for the sequence to follow. But the dramatic impact of Fresh News for Goal Sequence #1 in your story can at times feel small. The movie is just getting started, though, and you've got a long way to go.

In Hero Goal Sequence₍®₎ One (HGS #1) a writer should:

*a.) Offer the audience some short glimpse of the Hero's current, everyday life;*

Establish the ordinary world in which a particular Hero lives and works in the hours leading up to the moment when he runs into the Inciting Incident and the story really begins. In *My Best Friend's Wedding*, we first meet Hero Julianne Potter going about her daily business as a food critic. In *Unforgiven*, we first meet William Munny doing chores and going about his business of running a small ranch out on the Great Plains.

Action movies begin with an Action Hook first that gets the story started with a bang, then slow down to show the Hero in his more sedate everyday life second.

*b.) Give the audience reasons to like the Hero immediately, even if the character is an Anti-Hero in a script that explores the darker side of human nature;*

Use the Hero sympathy tools. In *L.A. Confidential*, we first meet Officer Bud White on Christmas Eve as he checks up on a parolee wife abuser. Bud finds the convict at it again, beating his wife. So the Hero lures the parolee outside, knocks him senseless, wraps him up in Christmas lights, and saves the con's wife from further abuse. We immediately see Bud demonstrate that he is brave, cleaver, skilled, and a champion of women oppressed by men… even if he is a tad violent about it. We like him right away.

c.) *Give the audience it's first glimpse of the Hero's emotional SHIELD;*
This usually is not a revelation of the actual TRAUMA (the past event that caused the emotional wound which necessitates use of the SHIELD) or of the pain itself. It's just a demonstration of the Hero's shield. This self-defensive reaction by the Hero hints at inner disquiet and for now that's enough. Like when Bud White goes out of his way to beat up a wife beater and so demonstrates his shield, a compulsion to protect women.

d.) *Establish your lead while he's in pursuit of a short-term goal, even just going to work, so we meet the Hero in motion where some Unfair Injury or danger can strike;*
These tools aid identification and allow us to meet the Hero while she's dealing with active problems. Like at the start of *Erin Brockovich*, where Erin works hard in an unsuccessful job interview, then leaves in defeat only to find a parking ticket on her windshield. And just as Erin pulls away from the curb… her car gets smashed by a reckless Jaguar. Unfair Injury strikes three times as the Hero pursues her active goal of hunting for a job.

e.) *The Hero is not happy with the world as he finds it;*
It's demonstrated that the Hero knows there's something wrong or unjust going on in his ordinary world. In HGS #1 of *Erin Brockovich* we immediately see how Erin struggles against the unfairness in her everyday life. In HGS #1 of *Fight Club* the Narrator finds his world so out of whack he's got chronic insomnia.

EXAMPLE: Hero Goal Sequence® #1 of *The Matrix*.

**Opening Subplot Action Hook:** This film begins by introducing the Adversary character Agent Smith as he sends his minions to kill the future Love Interest character Trinity. They chase her across rooftops and down alleys, and Trinity barely escapes. This Action Hook runs five minutes before we actually meet Hero hacker Neo, asleep at his computer.

So in *The Matrix* the actual HGS #1 needs to be fairly short to allow for this long beginning hook in which the Hero does not appear.

**Hero Goal #1:** *Neo wakes up to see that his computer is suddenly sending him strange text messages, and the Hero wants to find out what it means.*

In Neo's small apartment his computer suddenly displays anonymous phrases: "The Matrix has you..." and "Follow the White Rabbit..." He's puzzled.

There's a knock at his door. Party people have come looking to score something — and we find out Neo runs a black market business creating and selling "head trip" software that offers distraction from real-world meaninglessness.

**Fresh News for HGS #1:** *A White Rabbit does show up at Neo's front door in the form of a tattoo on the shoulder of a party girl.*

Curiosity now piqued, Neo follows the White Rabbit into the night.

So in HGS #1 of *The Matrix* we find:

An opening subplot Action Hook which displays the power of the Adversary, then;

a.) *Neo's ordinary world is introduced — he's a hacker at the fringes of society selling illegal computer programs to rich party animals;*

b.) *We're given reasons to like Neo — he's smart, skilled at what he does, and brave;*

c.) *He has a personal SHIELD — the computer programs he creates are used to escape the existential angst of his world;*

*d.) He's placed in danger by selling black market programs and by the implications of the Action Hook;*

*e.) The Hero is not happy with his world as he finds it.*

When an Action Hook establishes the Adversary first, without the Hero, the overall problem of the plot is introduced before meeting the Hero who will attempt to fix that problem. *Jaws* starts this way, too, as does *Outbreak*, and even *Doubt*.

Just remember that *Hero Goal Sequence*₍₎ *#1 cannot be complete with only an Action Hook if that hook excludes the Hero.* We must also then meet the Hero and see some shorter goal pursued by him, leading to the arrival of Fresh News.

EXAMPLE: HGS #1 of *Collateral.*

**Opening Subplot Action Hook:** We start with a quick introduction of the bad guy, hitman Vincent, as he arrives at an L.A. airport. He receives his next assassination assignment. This scene drips with menace and serves as a low-key Adversary-up-to-no-good kickoff.

**Hero Goal #1:** *Max wants to get his cab spotlessly clean and ready for work.*

In a taxicab dispatch garage we meet Hero Max while he gets ready to begin his usual working night as a cab driver. The double intro of Adversary and Hero back to back implies a major clash soon to come between them and it sets the tone for this psychological thriller.

We see cabby Max as smart and industrious. He keeps a meticulously clean vehicle and he's clearly good at what he does. Max tucks the photo of a remote South Seas island into his car visor so it's available for his frequent nightly escapes into fantasy.

Only after his cab has been perfectly prepared does Max drive off to serve his clients as the best cab driver in town.

Then Max must start his shift by putting up with a bickering couple in his backseat. The squabblers ignore him and disrespect him as they argue. No matter how well he has prepared, Max isn't appreciated for the true professional he is.

**Fresh News for HGS #1:** *Max lives as an invisible man in his own world.*

Fresh News for a HGS #1 is the only place where the new information revealed doesn't have to be a surprise to the Hero himself because he is still living in the ordinary world that he knows all too well. Here Fresh News can sometimes provide revelatory information to the audience, but not the Hero, and it's usually about the Hero's emotional life involving Unfair Injury.

So *Collateral* begins with:

A short Subplot Hook introducing the sinister nature of the Adversary, followed by;

*a.) A glimpse into the Hero's ordinary life and the isolated way he goes about his work;*

*b.) Lots of reasons to like Max — he's smart, tidy, pleasant, and skilled at what he does;*

*c.) Presentation of his SHIELD — Max favors escapist fantasies with a photo of a tropical island placed on his visor;*

*d.) No matter how well Max goes about his job, Unfair Injury strikes when he's disrespected in his own cab;*

*e.) Max clearly knows there's something wrong in his isolated world.*

## HERO GOAL SEQUENCE® TWO

Now it's time to get your central story rolling.

The Inciting Incident can take place anytime in the first act, but commonly you'll find it in Goal Sequence #2. The storyline needs to feel like it has direction and motion as soon as possible.

Before a Hero begins the journey toward character growth you must demonstrate that there's some deep emotional pain inside him. This pain is what causes the Hero to protect himself against any further emotional involvements, and that suffering usually surfaces here.

So in HGS #2:

*a.) The central conflict is introduced in a general way and story-driving action begins;*

We first clearly see the Hero's main plot conflict now, but painted with a broad brush. The Hero's more focused and specific mission won't actually begin until the start of Act Two.

In *E.T.*, Elliott first figures out in HGS #2 that there's something extraordinary roaming around his neighborhood. The boy meets E.T. in the bushes and wants to help the creature hide from scientists — Elliott's general goal. But it won't be until Act Two that Elliott's general goal becomes specifically to get E.T. "home."

In *Titanic* it's in HGS #2 that Old Rose, after arriving aboard a salvage vessel exploring the sunken ocean liner, begins her tale to the crew about the mysterious contents they've retrieved from a stateroom safe. The movie fades back to 1912 and Rose at seventeen arrives at a dock to board the doomed ship. We see immediately that Rose isn't in love with her controlling fiancé (the Adversary) and the general conflict of this film begins when Old Rose narrates, "To everyone else it was the ship of dreams. But to me it was a slave ship." However, Rose will not specifically fight to choose Jack over her fiancé until Act Two.

*b.) The Inciting Incident most often occurs here, serving as the story catalyst event;*

The upcoming examples from *Rain Man* and *Erin Brockovich* both have their Inciting Incident in Hero Goal Sequence® #2.

*c.) The first hint of the Hero's specific emotional pain — that permanent suffering which resulted from her past TRAUMATIC event — frequently appears here.*

In Hero Goal Sequence® #1 the Hero's SHIELD gets revealed — *how* she protects herself. Here in Sequence #2 the viewer's understanding of the shield deepens with a hint at the inner pain which required creation of this shield in the first place.

This is not to say the specific past TRAUMA that caused the Hero's emotional suffering is revealed. Only a flash of the resulting pain should be seen.

EXAMPLE: HGS# 2 of *Rain Man*.

**Hero Goal #2:** *Exotic car importer Charlie Babbitt wants to drive to Palm Springs with girlfriend Susanna for a weekend getaway.*

While driving off to escape from the pressures of a failing car import business (set up in HGS #1), Susanna (Valeria Golino) tries to engage Charlie (Tom Cruise) in conversation. He remains cold and distant, emotionally closed down.

Then the Hero gets a call informing him that his father has died.

The announcement of his father's death launches the general conflict between the Hero and his dad. But since his father is deceased it's ultimately dad's trustee Dr. Bruner — the caretaker of Raymond (Dustin Hoffman), Charlie's autistic brother — who will soon stand in as Adversary.

Charlie tells Susanna a bit about his sad family history; his mom died when he was two and he's had issues with his father. They never got along. Charlie's casual about it, even seems uncaring, but this hints strongly at long repressed emotion inside of him.

(Charlie's actual TRAUMA — the moment that his loving relationship with his special brother the "Rain Man" was torn away from him when Charlie was only a toddler — won't be revealed until the Midpoint.)

The Hero cancels the weekend pleasure trip with Susanna and turns the car around.

**Fresh News for HGS #2:** *Charlie suddenly finds himself heading off for his father's funeral.*

So in HGS #2 of *Rain Man*:

*a.) The Inciting Incident takes place — Charlie Babbitt gets a call telling him his father has died;*

*b.) The general conflict begins — Charlie and his antagonistic relationship with his father will be explored;*

*c.)  The Hero's inner emotional suffering is revealed through his inability to share feelings with Susanna, and through his too casual comments about a difficult history with his father.*

EXAMPLE: HGS #2 of *Erin Brockovich*.

Catching up: Hero Erin hustles her personal injury attorney Ed Masry (Albert Finney) into giving her a job, which is the Fresh News for an unusually long Hero Goal Sequence₍®₎ #1.

And then…

**Hero Goal #2:** *Having finally found employment, Erin wants to be a good file clerk and mother and just collect her paycheck.*

Erin begins her new gig. On the homefront she meets a new neighbor, biker George, who enters the story as a potential Love Interest character.

We also first witness Erin being rejected and disrespected by her female coworkers. They don't help her or include her in lunch plans. The pain of Erin's inner emotional suffering surfaces; when slights are inflicted on Erin she turns confrontational and it causes people to dislike her. This reveals her inner turmoil over self-worth.

(Her actual TRAUMA, when she set out to save the world by serving as Miss Wichita only to find out she was completely powerless to change anything, is revealed later.)

Erin receives a box of *pro bono* case papers, about some small-time real estate deal in Hinkley, California, involving health records. Her curiosity grows and she asks her boss Ed Masry if she can look into it.

**Fresh News for HGS #2:** *Erin gets off-handed permission from her boss to investigate a puzzling new case.*

So in HGS #2 of *Erin Brockovich*:

*a.)  The general conflict between Erin and Pacific Gas & Electric first shows up when Erin's curiosity is piqued by the Hinkley pro bono case;*

*b.)  The Inciting Incident takes place when Ed Masry thoughtlessly gives Erin permission to look into it;*

*c.) The Hero's emotional suffering over low self-worth is revealed as girls at the office snub her... and ex-beauty queen Erin becomes testy when she doesn't get any respect.*

Placing the Inciting Incident in Hero Goal Sequence® #2 can be considered tried and true, but not a rule. In *Spider-Man* the Inciting Incident shows up in HGS #1. *Hitch* springs the Inciting Incident in HGS #3, and *Up* in HGS #4. Remember: the Inciting Incident can arrive anywhere in Act One.

Most commonly though, it will be found right here in Hero Goal Sequence® #2.

## HERO GOAL SEQUENCE® THREE

These are the story elements that often occur in HGS #3:

*a.) A Call to Adventure arrives for the Hero;*
The Call to Adventure comes straight from the mythological story structure pointed out by Joseph Campbell and interpreted by Chris Vogler. It finds a primary home in Hero Goal Sequence® #3. Here's when an opportunity for real change arrives for the Hero.

*b.) New plot-enhancing characters are introduced;*

*c.) The pace of the story picks up;*

*d.) The Love Interest character first appears, or the romance function of an existing character becomes established to challenge the Hero emotionally;*

*e.) A trap is set for the Hero.*

I believe it was UCLA Professor Lew Hunter who said that in Act One, three things happen: a trap gets set, the Hero steps into the trap, then the trap springs shut. Consider Hero Goal Sequence® #3 an excellent place to lay a bear trap that will clamp shut on the Hero just before the end of Act One.

EXAMPLE: HGS #3 of *Spider-Man*.

Catching up: In HGS #1, we meet Peter Parker in his ordinary world of teen angst and inability to connect with the beautiful girl next door. Then — Fresh News and Inciting Incident — on a museum field trip he is bitten by a genetically designed super-spider.

In HGS #2 Peter falls ill and begins experiencing some unpleasant changes in his body. But ultimately the changes aren't so bad since they result in better vision and greater strength. Pretty good for a nerd.

So next:

**Hero Goal #3:** *The Hero wants to find out how far these wonderful new body changes will go and if they might make Mary Jane Watson take notice.*

Peter finally does get her attention in the school cafeteria when "M. J." mentions his nice eyes. Here, Mary Jane first enters Peter's life as a realistic romantic goal.

During a fight with the school bully Peter discovers that his new powers allow him to beat the bully easily. So cool. But Mary Jane isn't impressed by the way Peter humiliates Flash.

The effortless victory over Flash brings a powerful ego boost to Peter.

In **Subplot Cutaways** during this sequence the Adversary character, rich scientist Norman Osborn (Willem Dafoe) — soon to become the Green Goblin — discovers he also has superpowers. But Osborn's powers are driving him crazy. Osborn's life-or-death clash with Peter becomes inevitable here.

**Fresh News for HGS #3:** *Now Peter finds he can shoot a stream of web silk from his palms all the way across the street, allowing him to swing from building to building for the first time.*

So in HGS #3 of *Spider-Man*:

a.) *A Call to Adventure arrives in the form of Peter's ego-inflating superpowers;*

b.) *New characters are introduced;*

*c.) The story pace picks up;*

*d.) The Hero first discovers that his Love Interest character has become a realistic goal and she first speaks to him as his challenging conscience;*

*e.) A trap gets set for Peter with the creation of an insane Adversary, the Green Goblin.*

EXAMPLE: HGS #3 of *Rain Man.*

**Hero Goal #3: Charlie Babbitt wants to find out how much he will inherit from his father.**

At his father's funeral, then at dad's house, memories of his troubled childhood flood back for Charlie. Girlfriend Susanna offers him understanding and she comes into focus here as serving the functions of a true Love Interest character. But Charlie doesn't see the value of such challenging intimacy yet.

He's blinded by anger at dad, and his fear of losing his imported sports car business. Charlie just wants the cash he feels his father rightfully owes him as the man's only son.

Charlie Babbitt hears from an attorney that he's been cut out of the estate altogether, except for an old car and some rose bushes. All the money will go to an "anonymous beneficiary" and be overseen by one Dr. Bruner.

The Hero is furious that dad's three million dollars remains just out of reach. So typical of his father to pull this.

**Fresh News for HGS #3: Charlie won't accept getting cut out and he launches a crusade to discover who this "anonymous beneficiary" is.**

So in HGS #3 of *Rain Man:*

*a.) A Call to Adventure arrives when the Hero gets disinherited by his father;*

*b.) New characters turn up in the Hero's world — an estate lawyer, Dr. Bruner, and an anonymous beneficiary;*

*c.) The pace quickens;*

*d.) Charlie's girlfriend first officially serves the function of a Love Interest character by challenging the Hero's inner emotional life;*

*e.) A trap gets set for the Hero with the appearance of so much money just out of reach, driving Charlie to take action.*

## HERO GOAL SEQUENCE® FOUR

We can usually look for the following to happen in Goal Sequence #4:

a.) *New characters continue to be introduced, and relationships develop;*

b.) *Often a Mentor character appears, and, if not already present in the story, a Love Interest or Sidekick may show up, too;*

c.) *The pace increases even more as the Hero pursues his general goal;*

d.) *The Hero is forced to take a risk;*

e.) *The Hero steps into the trap set for him back in HGS #3 (moves into trap either here in HGS #4 or in #5).*

EXAMPLE: HGS #4 of *Scarface.*

Catching up: By this time in the story Tony Montana works as a dishwasher in a Miami hamburger stand. But he has been offered a chance at a small-time drug deal to prove himself to Omar (F. Murray Abraham), a low-level crime boss.

All of Tony's upwardly mobile dreams depend on carrying out this test assignment well.

So then…

**Hero Goal #4:** *Anti-Hero Tony wants to prove himself by buying a big stash of cocaine for street gangster Omar.*

Now Tony thinks through how to do it, while buddy Manny isn't really taking the job too seriously.

Tony goes up to the designated dope deal apartment with friend Fernando and leaves Manny in the car horsing around.

The deal turns out to be a setup. The cocaine seller captures Tony and Fernando and demands to know where their purchase cash is. The dealer chops Fernando into pieces with a chainsaw to make his point.

But Tony's courage buys time. Eventually Manny comes to the apartment to see what's up. Tony turns the tables and kills the chainsaw wielding thug. Tony grabs the cocaine and keeps the cash, too.

The Hero impresses not only Omar, but Omar's boss, Frank Lopez (Robert Loggia).

**Fresh News for #4**: *High on success, Tony makes his first big career move — and demands to meet Omar's boss Frank, who controls the real money.*

So in HGS #4 of *Scarface*:

a.) *New characters are introduced in Tony's world;*

b.) *His relationship with Sidekick Manny develops as they become drug criminals together;*

c.) *The pace continues to pick up as the Hero pursues his general goal of making big money fast;*

d.) *The Hero takes a huge risk as he pursues this coke-buying job;*

e.) *The Hero steps into a nasty trap of drug dealing and violence.*

EXAMPLE: HGS #4 of *Finding Nemo*.

Catching up: in HGS #2, widowed father Marlin reluctantly takes his only surviving child to the boy's first day of school. Marlin nervously sees Nemo off on a science field trip with a kindly stingray. Then Fresh News for #2 — after Nemo is gone, Marlin learns that the field trip will take his son to "the Drop Off," a frightening edge of deep open ocean.

In HGS #3 Marlin rushes to the Drop Off to order Nemo home. The boy is playing a game of "chicken" with new friends as they dare each other to swim out the farthest toward a boat in deep water. Fresh News arrives when suddenly a human diver scoops Nemo into a small net.

Marlin is blinded by a photographic flash, but when his eyes clear he sees the diver lifting Nemo aboard the boat.

Before Marlin can catch up, the speedboat engine jumps to

life and the boat rockets away across the waves. Marlin watches in horror. This is the Inciting Incident for the film.

Then...

**Hero Goal #4:** *Clownfish Marlin tears off into open ocean trying desperately to catch the speedboat.*

He swims as far and as fast as he can but loses sight of the craft.

Soon Marlin begins asking passing fish if anyone saw which way the boat went. The Hero meets ditsy surgeonfish Dory, a new character who will become his Sidekick and teach Marlin many important lessons about life.

**Fresh News for HGS #4:** *A huge shark sneaks up — and invites Marlin and Dory to attend a party with him.*

Marlin feels he must go to keep the shark friendly...

So in HGS #4 of *Finding Nemo:*

a.) *New characters are introduced — including Bruce the Shark on his way to a 12 Step meeting;*

b.) *A Sidekick enters the story in the form of ditzy Dory;*

c.) *Pace picks up tremendously;*

d.) *The Hero takes a big risk when he agrees to go with Bruce to a "party;"*

e.) *The Hero steps into a trap when he tears off swimming alone into open ocean following the speedboat.*

## HERO GOAL SEQUENCE® FIVE

Hero Goal Sequence® #5 frequently contains:

a.) *A revelation of the Hero's primary DESIRE;*

The DESIRE is not the focused physical goal of the plot. That will be defined in HGS #7. But the Hero's DESIRE provides emotional motivation for achieving the highly specific visible goal yet to be established.

The DESIRE is the Hero's equivalent of "what's in it for me?"

The Hero is not yet aware of his own need for character growth. That comes out later in Act Two. However, here in Hero Goal Sequence® #5 an audience should understand the nature of the Hero's *underlying emotional hope*. Sometimes it's conscious, sometimes not quite yet conscious. In *Spider-Man* it's here in HGS #5 that Peter Parker prepares to fight a wrestling match as "The Human Spider" so he can win money for a car to impress Mary Jane.

At this point, Peter's only motivation to become Spider-Man is his DESIRE for a hot car.

*b.) Second thoughts arise about the danger in any possible Call to Adventure and the Hero momentarily Refuses the Call;*

Mythological structure requires a Hero at first to "Refuse the Call" to adventure. If it's appropriate for your story, this is usually the place where doubts appear.

*c.) The Hero steps into a previously set trap — unless that already happened in HGS #4.*

The Hero has to step into the trap in either HGS #4 or HGS #5 because that trap must spring closed in Goal Sequence #6.

*d.) An introduction of the Hero to the Adversary, or to the power of the Adversary, takes place;*

This intro can be for the very first time or it might be the first time an Adversary who has previously been placed in the Hero's world actually crosses paths with the Hero. Sometimes the Adversary doesn't show up in the flesh but all the same it's here that a Hero first encounters the social stature or power of his Adversary.

However, the Hero does NOT yet know that this is the person he will personally fight for all the marbles. That contest won't begin in earnest until Act Two.

In *Chinatown*, Jake Gittes (Jack Nicholson) doesn't physically meet his Shapeshifter Adversary, the obscenely wealthy Noah Cross, until the Midpoint. But in Act One, in HGS #5, while searching for the missing Hollis Mulwray, Jake first enters the top offices of the L.A. Department of Water and Power and personally sees the enormous influence over the city held by the man who will be revealed later as his Adversary. Here Jake is surrounded by framed photos of Noah Cross (John Huston) and his daughter Evelyn (Faye Dunaway). Jake's just not paying full attention.

The Adversary *must* be established as a powerful presence within the Hero's world before Act One ends. Usually it happens here in HGS #5.

EXAMPLE: HGS #5 of *The Matrix*.

Catching up: In Sequence #4 Mentor Morpheus tells Neo on the phone that Neo is, in some way, incredibly important. "You are The One." Now Neo's curious to find out what it means to be The One.

So next...

**Hero Goal #5:** *Hero Neo wants to go with Trinity and meet Morpheus.*

On a dark, rainy street, a car stops to pick up Neo. Trinity and Switch invite him inside. Switch points a gun at Neo, demands he take off his shirt.

Neo will have none of it and opens his door to get out of the car. He suddenly has serious second thoughts about the dangers involved with finding out if he's The One.

As the Hero looks down the wet, grubby city street stretching before him, Trinity says, "You know that road. You know exactly where it ends."

Neo's dissatisfaction with his life wins out. He remains in the car.

Trinity points a weapon-like machine at him that tracks a mechanical "bug" inside Neo's stomach cavity. He's horrified.

Neo experiences the true, enormous reach of Agent Smith for the first time.

**Fresh News for HGS #5:** *Trinity rips the "bug" from Neo's stomach cavity and he now knows his recent interrogation by Agent Smith wasn't just a dream after all — "That thing's real!"*

So in HGS #5 of *The Matrix*:

*a.) The Hero's primary personal DESIRE becomes — find out what it means to be The One;*

*b.) When doubts surface about the dangers of this Call to Adventure, Neo momentarily Refuses the Call;*

*c.) The Hero steps into a trap when he chooses to stay in the car — now he will be led into a terrifying new world from which there is no turning back;*

*d.) Neo discovers the true power of his Adversary in the form of a grotesque mechanical bug implanted in his stomach.*

EXAMPLE: HGS #5 of *Collateral*.

Catching up: in HGS #4, when cabbie Max drops Assistant District Attorney Annie at her destination he sees how stressed she is, so Max gives her his visor photo of the South Seas island. "You need it more than I do." Grateful, Annie hands him her card and invites Max to get in touch (Fresh News for #4).

He's delighted that she's interested... but cautious too, since class-wise, Annie is a world above him.

**Hero Goal #5:** *Cabdriver Max wants to get back to work while feeling on top of the world because Annie just expressed interest.*

Sharp dresser Vincent climbs into the cab, and Max meets his Adversary. But Max has no idea yet that this is a hitman. A smart and soulless student of human nature, Vincent quickly sizes Max up as a talker, not a doer.

Probing with personal questions, Vincent pushes Max to reveal his DESIRE — Max longs for the courage to launch his own limo company, Island Limos. But Max has been driving this cab for twelve years and he just can't find the guts to go for his own business.

For the first time we really see Max's great need for the courage to live his life fully.

Vincent wants to hire Max as his driver for the whole night, waves money at him. Max declines. It's against company policy.

Vincent keeps after him. Finally, cautious Max takes the cash. **Fresh News for HGS #5:** *Max makes a deal to drive one fare, Vincent, for the rest of the night.*

So in HGS #5 of *Collateral*:

a.) *Max's DESIRE becomes clear — find the personal courage to start a business and pursue Annie;*

b.) *Max Refuses the Call to Adventure at first by turning down Vincent's offer of an all-night hire;*

c.) *The Hero steps into a trap by finally accepting Vincent's deal;*

d.) *The Hero meets his Adversary for the first time, not yet knowing that Vincent is a killer.*

## HERO GOAL SEQUENCE® SIX

We know that at the end of Act One a critically important story structure event occurs called Stunning Surprise #1 (S.S. #1). It comes out of the blue, and the Hero's life will never be the same. The Fresh News for Hero Goal Sequence® #6 is *always* Stunning Surprise #1.

Here in HGS #6 the trap springs shut. Then as Act One ends, the Hero gets thrown into a much scarier special world of big challenge and great danger. Whatever story event happens here, it must surprise the Hero and grab the audience.

The Hero's general goal of Act One at this point becomes highly specific and now the Hero's obsessive struggle to achieve that focused goal begins in earnest. This S.S. #1 event defines the Hero's action line for the rest of Act Two.

So in HGS #6:

a.) *The trap springs shut on the Hero;*

b.) *Stunning Surprise #1 takes place;*

*c.) The specific physical goal that the Hero will now pursue throughout the rest of Act Two becomes clear.*

EXAMPLE: HGS #6 of *Chinatown*.

Catching up: Jake Gittes' latest "private" investigation of Hollis Mulwray's infidelity has ended up splashed across the front page. Not good for business. So Jake wants to find the still missing Mulwray and help the man fight this public embarrassment.

Then...

**Hero Goal #6:** *Jake heads out to a Water Department reservoir where Evelyn Mulwray just told him he will find Hollis Mulwray exercising on his lunch break.*

Jake cons his way into the restricted reservoir area.

The P.I. runs into Lieutenant Escobar, an old cop acquaintance. They chat and catch up. These men are mutually respectful, but not quite friends. Jake belittles as corrupt another cop he runs into there — old antagonisms surface.

Then Jake declares he wants to talk to Mulwray. Escobar points to a reservoir spillway. That's where Jake can find him. Jake saunters over to the spillway and sees... Mulwray's body being dragged up out of the reservoir.

**Fresh News for #6/STUNNING SURPRISE #1:** *Wealthy Hollis Mulwray has drowned during a drought and now Jake suddenly finds himself in the middle of a life or death murder case.*

So in HGS #6 of *Chinatown*:

*a.) The trap springs shut when Jake finds cops all over the reservoir — he'll soon be up to his sliced nose in a dangerous mystery;*

*b.) When Jake sees Hollis Mulwray's body dragged up the spillway, the Hero experiences Stunning Surprise #1;*

*c.) What this movie is about — Jake's obsessive pursuit of a murder case involving the enigmatic Mrs. Mulwray — becomes clear.*

EXAMPLE: HGS #6 of *Spider-Man*.

**Hero Goal #6:** *Peter wants to win wrestling prize money so he can buy a hot car and impress Mary Jane.*

Uncle Ben (Cliff Robertson) drops Peter off at the downtown library. He offers the boy a life lesson, "With great power comes great responsibility." Peter snaps back, "You're not my father!" Ben is clearly hurt by the comment.

Instead of going to the library, Peter sneaks away and enters a sleazy wrestling match. Wearing his baggy homemade costume, to the surprise of the blood-lusting crowd Peter wins.

In a crummy office the fight promoter refuses to pay Peter the advertised amount, just tosses a few meager bucks on the desk and tells him to beat it. The boy storms off, furious at the injustice.

Just then the promoter gets robbed, and Peter is so angry he lets the thief run right past him and escape. When the promoter complains, "You could have stopped him from getting away with my money!" Peter echoes the promoter's own words and says, "I missed the part where that's my problem."

Tasting sweet revenge, Peter struts outside to meet his uncle for a ride home.

On the corner he sees a crowd gathered.

**Fresh News for #6/STUNNING SURPRISE #1:** *Peter pushes his way through the spectators to discover Uncle Ben has been shot by the very crook Peter let get away — and Peter's beloved Mentor dies on the sidewalk.*

Devastated, Peter tears off after the killer. The real Spider-Man is born.

So in HGS #6 of *Spider-Man*:

*a.) The trap springs shut on Peter Parker when he lets the thief escape with the promoter's money for a petty personal reason, to get revenge.*

*b.) Stunning Surprise #1 arrives when Peter shoves his way through the crowd to discover Uncle Ben dying on the sidewalk — proving in a most painful way that "with great power comes great responsibility."*

*c.) The specific physical goal of the story, Peter trying to protect the city from evildoers and soon the Green Goblin in particular, is revealed.*

# FINAL THOUGHTS ON THE SIX HERO GOAL SEQUENCES₍ₑ₎ OF ACT ONE

Looking at these Act One Goal Sequences from a number of successful films, an important point becomes clear: it takes one heck of a lot of story to draw an audience into your movie.

Professional screenwriters must develop a strong command of plot dynamics. A movie story needs to leap forward repeatedly to the next level of interest not just a couple times per hour, but every few minutes. Lengthy dialogue sequences simply won't do that.

Every Hero needs to undertake six distinct, separate actions in Act One to keep an audience connected to the story. And each of these short-term physical actions must be unique. No sequence goal can exactly repeat.

*Change* remains the soul of every plot.

Including six complete Goal Sequences in each first act you write guarantees you'll have an active Hero. It will get your screenplay up to speed quickly and keep it fascinating. Moreover, it will create a context in which all essential story and character information can be communicated to an audience through action, at just the right times, for the strongest possible impact.

All it takes is a whole lot of imagination, planning, and persistence.

## SUMMING UP:

• **Human expectation in the ritual of storytelling allows us to get fairly specific about what goes on in most Hero Goal Sequences₍ₑ₎. We can generally predict what story elements can be expected to appear, and at what point they should appear in successful scripts.**

• Hero Goal Sequence₍ₑ₎ One should include:
   a.) A short glimpse of the Hero's ordinary life;

   b.) Reasons to like the Hero immediately, even if the character is an Anti-Hero;

c.) A first use of the Hero's personal emotional SHIELD;

d.) Some form of danger or Unfair Injury appearing as the Hero pursues an active goal;

e.) Establishing that the Hero is not happy with the ordinary world as he finds it.

- Hero Goal Sequence® Two often includes:
  a.) Beginning of the general story conflict;

  b.) Arrival of the Inciting Incident;

  c.) The first demonstration of the Hero's inner emotional pain caused by a trauma in the past.

- Hero Goal Sequence® Three often includes:
  a.) A Call to Adventure arriving for the Hero;

  b.) The introduction of new, story-enhancing characters;

  c.) Pace accelerating in the story;

  d.) The first appearance of the Love Interest character, or the romance function of an existing character being revealed to challenge the Hero emotionally;

  e.) A trap getting set for the Hero.

- Hero Goal Sequence® Four often includes:
  a.) New characters and relationships developing;

  b.) First appearance of a Mentor, Love Interest, or Sidekick;

  c.) The pace increasing even more as the Hero pursues his general goal;

  d.) The Hero being forced to take a risk;

  e.) The Hero stepping into the trap.

- Hero Goal Sequence® Five often includes:

    a.) Revelation of the Hero's DESIRE, providing personal emotional motivation for achieving the goal;

    b.) An introduction of the Hero to the power of the Adversary, or to the Adversary directly;

    c.) The Hero having second thoughts about the risks of any Call to Adventure, or flat-out Refusing the Call;

    d.) The Hero stepping into a previously set trap (if not in HGS #4).

- Hero Goal Sequence® Six ALWAYS INCLUDES:

    a.) The trap springing shut on the Hero;

    b.) The arrival of Stunning Surprise #1;

    c.) The main movie action-line and what specific goal the Hero will now pursue being made clear.


EXERCISE:

Get a copy of *Avatar*. View the first 45 minutes.

This movie runs 2 hours 34 minutes, so you can expect Hero Goal Sequences® to run longer than in a conventional length film like *The Proposal*.

This is a one-Hero story about Jake Sully (Sam Worthington). The Mentor is Dr. Grace Augustine (Sigourney Weaver), the Love Interest is Neytiri (Zoe Saldana) and the Adversary is Colonel Quaritch (Stephen Lang).

NOW:

Write notes describing the six Hero Goal Sequences® in Act One of *Avatar*. Write down the HERO'S focused single physical GOAL for each sequence, and then the sequence- ending FRESH NEWS that concludes the current goal and creates the next one.

- I'll give you the first sequence…

For HGS #1 the HERO GOAL is — *Get to Pandora and replace Jake's dead twin brother there.* FRESH NEWS comes when — *Wheelchair-bound Jake first meets his new avatar body face to face and he sees that this assignment might get interesting.* With opening credits, sequence runs 9 min. 40 sec.

- So… in HGS #2 the HERO GOAL is now — *Take his new avatar out for a wobbly first trial.* What does Jake discover as his FRESH NEWS? (Has to do with learning the truth about Dr. Augustine.) This sequence runs 9 min. 32 sec.

- Then in HGS #3, what's the Hero's new HERO GOAL? (Working hard to do what?) What FRESH NEWS changes things? (It involves Colonel Quaritch's request.) This sequence runs 4 min. 30 sec.

- What's the HGS #4 HERO GOAL? (It has to do with guard duty.) And FRESH NEWS? (It involves getting wet.) This one runs 8 min.

- In HGS #5, what's the HERO GOAL? (Something about camping skills.) And FRESH NEWS? Runs 5 min.

- Then for HGS #6, what's the HERO GOAL? And what's the FRESH NEWS, which is also STUNNING SURPRISE ONE (Some small but magical event opens a path for the Hero into a whole new world.) This runs 5 min. 15 sec. — making Act One of *Avatar* 41 min. 55 sec. long.

REMEMBER — Subplot cutaway scenes where the Hero does not appear *do not count* toward the Hero's pursuit of a current Hero Goal, or the Hero's experience of Fresh News. *But the running time of these subplot cutaways must be included in a Hero Goal Sequence total time.* Take a stab at these Hero Goal Sequences®, then you'll find the answers at the end of Chapter Eleven.

## ANSWERS FOR CH. 9,
## HGS 1-6 IN ACT ONE OF *THE PROPOSAL*:

### HGS #1:
HERO GOAL — *To pursue another day of being great at her job.*
FRESH NEWS — *Margaret's top boss wants to see her right away.*
Time: 9 min.

### HGS #2:
HERO GOAL — *To see her boss and hit him up for another raise.*
FRESH NEWS — *Canadian Margaret is getting deported... so she lies that she's engaged to her assistant, American Andrew, in order to stay in the country and keep her job.*
Time: 4 min.

### HGS #3:
HERO GOAL — *Do the INS paperwork to make engagement official.*
FRESH NEWS — *Her INS caseworker is a hard nose... and to convince him, Margaret must now go to Alaska and tell Andrew's family that they are getting married.*
Time: 6 min. 28 sec.

### HGS #4:
HERO GOAL — *Get her assistant Andrew to make their travel arrangements.*
FRESH NEWS — *Andrew extorts a promotion out of Margaret and forces her to actually be nice to him.*
Time: 2 min. 24 sec.

### HGS #5:
HERO GOAL — *Fly to Alaska and pull the wool over the eyes of Andrew's family.*
FRESH NEWS — *When the plane arrives, Andrew's Mom and Gammy turn out to be savvy people, and this ruse won't be nearly as easy as Margaret had assumed.*
Time: 3 min. 22 sec.

**HGS #6:**

HERO GOAL — *Drive to Andrew's hometown of Sitka and check into a hotel.*

FRESH NEWS (STUNNING SURPRISE ONE) — *Margaret discovers that Andrew's family lives in a mansion... and "poor" Andrew is actually very wealthy!*

Time: 3 min. 46 sec.

*chapter eleven*

# FIRST HALF OF ACT TWO: SEQUENCES® 7~12

———— ✆ ————

Every Hero comes tumbling into Act Two, toes over tea kettle, down the rabbit hole.

Now she must pick herself up, dust herself off, and try to figure out what the heck just happened. So a Hero starts off in Act Two dazed and unsure of herself as she struggles to take in the lay of a strange new Wonderland.

## HERO GOAL SEQUENCE® SEVEN

In Goal Sequence #7 often we will find:

a.) *The Hero flounders for a plan of action;*

The general conflict of Act One has now become a highly specific fight for a particular goal against strong opposition, and the Hero must quickly come up with a plan with which to charge ahead toward victory. At Stunning Surprise #1 in *Finding Nemo*, an ocean full of old World War II ship mines explodes, throwing Marlin into a dark and frightening world landscape with no way to find his son Nemo. But soon Marlin retrieves a diver's mask dropped by the kidnappers. Dory reads the address label on it, revealing where Nemo has been taken, and now the Hero has a specific plan: find a way to get to Sydney, Australia.

*b.) The Hero commits himself to this specific physical plot goal which will require some type of long-term struggle;*

It's here clownfish Marlin commits himself not just to chase the boat that kidnapped his kid, but specifically to cross the whole Pacific ocean to reach Nemo. He knows he will face many dangers — but sets off anyway.

*c.) The Hero's inner conflict — that tension between pain caused by his TRAUMA and the personal isolation created by the use of his SHIELD — rises to the surface;*

That first step of the Character Growth Arc — EXPRESS the need for change — can happen anywhere between HGS #7 and #10. But at the least, *more evidence of the need for change* within the Hero will emerge here in Goal Sequence #7 during all the emotional turmoil caused by the startling end of Act One.

This need for growth may show itself in a number of ways. Often it's an ironic or double-entendre statement from the Hero, or from someone close to the Hero in a moment of confrontation. It may not yet be fully, consciously understood by the Hero, even if clearly spoken. But the Hero at least gets it on an intuitive level.

*d.) The nature of this inner conflict reveals the theme of the movie;*

In *Scarface,* Tony Montana wants to grab big-time dope money so he can win drug boss Frank's girl, Elvie (Michelle Pfeiffer), Tony's dream woman. In HGS #7 Tony forms his plan and tells Manny, "First get the money. With money comes power. *Then* you get the woman."

So Tony picks Elvie up to give her a ride somewhere. Flush with his first drug cash, the Hero has bought a used gold Cadillac convertible with zebra stripe upholstery. Elvie says of Tony's taste in cars, "It looks like somebody's nightmare," and thereby EXPRESSES Tony's inner flaw. He's blind to the fact that his plan to get rich through drug money is really a horror.

Thus theme comes to the surface: pursuing material success without caring how many people you destroy to do it is no dream, it's a nightmare.

*e.) New characters enter the Hero's life and he must begin sorting out allies from enemies;*

Commonly Heroes meet a number of new people in Hero Goal Sequence® #7, and the need to sort out helpers from troublemakers adds extra tension while choosing up sides for the clash to come.

In *Avatar*, deep in Pandora's jungle, after Sully gets saved from the wolf-like creatures by Neytiri, he scampers along behind her trying to make friends as Neytiri scornfully orders Sully to get lost. But the floating, magical Seeds of the Sacred Tree gather around the Hero, drawn to his brave heart (S.S. #1).

Neytiri suddenly sees proof that Sully is someone very special. She now tells him to follow her.

Then in HGS #7, Sully meets a Na'vi hunting party that nearly kills him. The warriors take him as a captive to the Sacred Tree, where Sully meets scores more Na'vi characters including Neytiri's powerful father and mother, who also debate whether or not to kill him.

Sully begins sorting them all out — possible friends from possible foes.

EXAMPLE: HGS #7 of *The Matrix*.

Catching up: in HGS #6, Neo emerges naked and gasping from a birthing pod to discover a world of mechanized horror that he never imagined existed beyond the ordinary world. (Stunning Surprise #1).

**Hero Goal #7:** *Neo wants to get reborn into the world of the rebellion and be physically prepared to handle life there.*

Morpheus immediately starts rebuilding Neo's body musculature so the Hero can adapt to this special new world.

Neo is disoriented, awed, frightened.

Discovering he's aboard the rebel hovercraft Nebuchadnezzar, Neo is introduced to the crew. Among this group are both future loyal friends and one traitor.

Morpheus grows ever more convinced that Neo is "The One." Whatever that means, Neo doesn't want the responsibility and thinks it can't possibly be true. But there's no going home again; he's stuck with the rebels, and he *is* curious. Neo finds himself haunted by inner conflict. He struggles to form a plan.

Morpheus loads a history program into Neo's mind.

**Fresh News for HGS #7:** *Neo finally sees the true surface reality of Earth, a post-apocalyptic landscape destroyed by war between humans and machines.*

"Welcome to the desert of the real," Morpheus says. So in Hero Goal Sequence₍ᵣ₎ #7 of *The Matrix*:

a.) *Confused and dazed, the Hero flounders for a plan;*

b.) *The Hero commits to a new, highly specific goal — preparing for life in this real world to help the rebels fight a war of liberation against the machines;*

c.) *The Hero's inner conflict between longing to be a commoner in his ordinary world again and the frightening prospect he might be The One in this new world, rises to the surface...*

d.) *...which brings out the film's theme: to discover your destiny you must first know who you really are;*

e.) *The Hero meets new characters and begins sorting out allies from enemies.*

EXAMPLE: HGS #7 of *Rain Man*.

**Hero Goal #7:** *Charlie Babbitt wants his girlfriend Susanna to take care of Ray at a hotel while Charlie figures out what to do next.*

After impulsively kidnapping his autistic brother from Wallbrooke Sanatorium (S.S. #1), Charlie registers at a hotel for the night with Raymond and Susanna. She demands to know why Charlie brought Raymond to a hotel. He answers, "Because they want him and I've got him!"

Charlie is angry at Dr. Bruner for carrying out dad's wishes and not giving the Hero any of dad's money. Soon the Hero forms a plan involving Raymond: "I'm going to keep him until I get my half."

Charlie works the hotel telephone, trying desperately to save his imported car business back in L.A.

Susanna grows more upset over Charlie's callous attitude toward Raymond. She accuses Charlie of using everyone.

Then Susanna walks out on him.

**Fresh News for HGS #7:** *Suddenly Charlie finds himself sole caregiver for a very needy autistic brother who he doesn't understand and doesn't care about.*

So in HGS #7 of *Rain Man*:

*a.) Charlie flounders for a plan;*

*b.) Charlie decides on a goal that will shape the rest of Act Two — hold onto Raymond until Dr. Bruner pays Charlie half of his father's estate;*

*c.) Susanna tells Charlie, "You don't need anybody. You use everybody!" Thus she EXPRESSES the Hero's inner problem, that he hides behind a SHIELD of emotional detachment from where he manipulates people...*

*d.) ...and so theme emerges: to lead a fulfilling life you must put loving relationships before selfish desires;*

*e.) In sorting allies from enemies, Charlie cannot yet see this nuisance of a brother or Susanna as the emotional allies they truly are.*

## HERO GOAL SEQUENCE® EIGHT

Now that the Hero has committed himself to pursuing the main goal of Act Two, it's time to drive up the stakes and demonstrate just how incredibly difficult victory will be. Here in Hero Goal Sequence® #8, often the Adversary comes into focus as a key player and displays his enormous strength ever more convincingly.

Also, Heroes need to be trained. They must master special skills as they prepare for the battle ahead. Schooling for the Hero often begins in HGS #8, as it does in *Gladiator* when Maximus is forced to start training to be a gladiator, in *Avatar* when Jake Sully starts training to master life as a true Na'vi, and in *Men In Black* when Agent J begins training to track down space alien scum as a freshly minted member of the Men In Black.

Allies and enemies continue to show up in #8, testing the Hero's ability to tell the difference.

And it can often be here that the first step in character growth appears: the Hero EXPRESSES, or hears expressed, the nature of her own inner conflict and her need for change.

The acknowledgement of inner conflict must be clear but natural. Even subtle. Avoid creating neon billboards emblazoned "author's message!"

This moment is most commonly expressed in dialogue and can even be stated ironically.

Most frequently an EXPRESS moment shows up in HGS #8 or #9, occasionally in HGS #7, and once in a rare while in HGS #10. In *Shrek*, the moment appears quite early in Hero Goal Sequence® #7 when Shrek tells Donkey, "Ogres are like onions, they have layers!" and so EXPRESSES his inner personal conflict over being misunderstood and rejected.

But in *Legally Blonde* it's here in HGS #8 that Elle Woods, tricked into wearing a bunny costume to a non-costume Harvard party, tries yet again to get her ex-boyfriend's attention. When Warner dismisses her as not smart enough to make it at Harvard, Elle's EXPRESS moment dawns on her: "I'm never going to be good enough for you, am I?" Now Elle's character growth can begin. She must stop trying to be what other people want and start becoming the very best Elle Woods possible.

So in HGS #8 you can often expect to see:

a.) *The great strength of the Adversary being visibly demonstrated;*

b.) *Stakes increasing;*

c.) *The Hero undergoing some sort of training or instruction to master needed skills;*

d.) *The further sorting of allies and enemies;*

*e.) The first step in character growth appearing — to EXPRESS the Hero's inner emotional need for growth.*

EXAMPLE: HGS #8 of *As Good As It Gets.*

Catching up: in HGS #6 Obsessive-Compulsive romance writer Melvin pursues waitress Carol, and artist neighbor Simon gets beaten by burglars. Melvin is forced to look after Simon's dog Verdell while Simon recovers in the hospital.

A major reversal appears when Melvin falls hard for the little dog, and it's the first time he has genuinely loved anything. A new world opens to the Hero (S.S. #1).

In HGS #7 Simon comes home from the hospital and Melvin must give the dog back. The Hero suffers an anxiety attack over losing Verdell. Fresh News for HGS #7: playing the piano, Melvin weeps. Loving even a dog means letting pain into his life.

Then:

**Hero Goal #8:** *Melvin Udall wants to find emotional support in a time of personal crisis.*

Desperate, Melvin barges into his psychiatrist's office and hollers "Help!" Dr. Green insists... no appointment, no session. The doctor councils Melvin to develop emotional self-control.

Exiting through the waiting room, Melvin stops to ask the other patients, "What if this is as good as it gets?" His fellow patients gasp in horror at the thought.

Here Melvin EXPRESSES his inner conflict — what's the point of living if he must forever remain a miserable captive of Obsessive-Compulsive Disorder, doomed to hide behind his shield of bitter vitriol?

He must either fight his OCD or live his whole life alone.

He now understands the stakes are life or death.

Melvin rushes to the comfort of his routine meal at Café 24, but Carol isn't there.

His new waitress does everything wrong and the Hero loses it, yells at her. The café manager orders Melvin out. The other customers burst into applause.

Exiting, Melvin bribes the busboy to give him Carol's last name.

**Fresh News for HGS #8:** *Melvin learns Carol's full name —* *so now he can look up her address.*

In HGS #8 of *As Good As It Gets*:

a.) *The true strength of Melvin's Love Interest-Adversary Carol and the emotional power she holds over the Hero becomes established;*

b.) *Stakes are pumped up to metaphorical life or death;*

c.) *The Hero gets schooled by his Mentor psychiatrist to develop more emotional self-control;*

d.) *Allies and enemies must be dealt with in the form of a doctor, other patients, a hostile café manager, ill-wishing café customers, and one helpful busboy;*

e.) *The first step in Melvin's character growth journey appears when he EXPRESSES his inner problem, "What if this is as good as it gets?"*

EXAMPLE: HGS #8 of *Erin Brockovich*

Catching up: in HGS #7 Erin works long hours on Donna Jensen's *pro bono* real estate case. Erin receives the first signs of growing respect from the other women in Ed's office.

Fresh News for HGS #7 — another husband and wife from Hinkley show up to see Erin, so her pollution case expands from one suffering family to two.

And then:

**Hero Goal #8:** *Erin wants to find even more clients for the growing case against PG&E.*

Erin works hard to expand the case while strains appear between the Hero and her family. She is seldom available for them. When Erin arrives home late again, her young son refuses to speak to her.

The Hero EXPRESSES, figuratively and subtly, her inner struggle when she says to the boy, "Don't you want mommy to be good at her job?" In other words, don't you want mommy to be worthy of both self-respect and the respect of others? Her son, of course, just wants her home. So as the Hero begins winning stature in Ed's office, she starts losing it in her personal life. It seems Erin's inner need for accomplishment can only be won at the cost of her family's love.

Erin visits more homes in Hinkley and sees the destruction of the town's health brought about by a Goliath-like Adversary. She now understands that all the people of Hinkley have been abused by PG&E and they need her help.

Stakes and urgency rise.

**Fresh News for HGS #8:** *Erin is introduced to a little girl in Hinkley who is dying of cancer, and the true life and death human dimension of the suffering in this case hits her hard.*

Therefore, in HGS #8 of *Erin Brockovich*:

*a.) The strength of the Adversary, revealed by the damage PG&E has done to Hinkley, is demonstrated;*

*b.) The stakes of human suffering keep rising;*

*c.) The Hero undergoes on-the-job training as a legal investigator while she comes to understand the true dimensions of this case;*

*d.) More allies are established among the families in Hinkley while the Hero's own family turns against her to function as a kind of emotional enemy;*

*e.) The Hero EXPRESSES her inner emotional conflict to her son —  her unfulfilled longing for self-worth and worldly respect — and so begins character growth.*

## HERO GOAL SEQUENCE® NINE

Sequences #9 and #10 take us through the middle section of the first half of Act Two, and here new energy needs to burst loose.

It's now been a while since the audience felt the jolt of Stunning Surprise #1. It's time for another interesting plot kicker to push things up a notch as the story pace accelerates.

A good story isn't just inner angst and rumination. The Hero must show what she's physically capable of doing. So an Action Burst frequently appears here.

Also, the Hero often takes a big risk at this point... but it backfires.

The Hero may even consider giving up on the crucial main objective of the story. However, by this time other people are depending on him and he can't disappoint them.

So in Hero Goal Sequence® #9 you can usually expect to see:

*a.) An Action Burst or moment of high emotion that drives up tension and picks up the pace or scope of the story;*

*b.) The Hero shows what she's capable of doing physically;*

*c.) The Hero takes a risk that backfires;*

*d.) The Hero considers giving up.*

EXAMPLE: HGS #9 of *The Matrix*.

Catching up: In sequence #8 Neo learns that the Matrix is a fictional construct created by the machines so they can farm humans as an energy source.

Waking up back in his bunk aboard the Nebuchadnezzar, Neo listens to Morpheus explain how he has searched years for a prophesied savior among the last humans alive: "I believe that search is over." Morpheus relates the mythology of The One. Fresh News for #8 — Morpheus thinks Neo is destined to save all humanity.

Then in #9...

**Hero Goal #9:** *Neo works to develop special skills for the battle ahead.*

Next morning Tank enters Neo's room and reveals his excitement over Neo being The One. This is an EXPRESS moment where Tank directly confronts the Hero with the responsibility he faces as a messiah. Some very oversized shoes to fill.

Other people are depending on Neo now. But how can it be true?

Neo's real inner journey begins. To pursue his destiny he must find out who he is. For a minute Neo wants to give up and wishes he could just go home.

Tank downloads skills programs into Neo's brain. An Action Burst begins as Neo and Morpheus spar with each other in a dojo.

Suddenly Neo finds himself standing high on a skyscraper rooftop with Morpheus one hundred stories up. Morpheus runs and leaps across a cavernous divide to the next rooftop. There he waits for Neo to join him.

Neo screws up his courage, runs and leaps into the unknown. But he looks down and panics. Neo falls screaming all the way to the street so far below.

Aboard the Nebuchadnezzar once more, Neo discovers that his mouth is bleeding. He asks, "If you die in the Matrix, you die here, too?"

**Fresh News for HGS #9:** *Yes. If you die in the Matrix you're dead for real.*

So in HGS #9 of *The Matrix*:

*a.) An Action Burst ensues as Neo works to master extreme martial arts;*

*b.) The Hero shows what he can do physically;*

*c.) The Hero takes a risk, tries to leap to another rooftop — but the risk backfires and he falls;*

*d.) For a moment the Hero wants to give up, but now other people are counting on him;*

*e.) The EXPRESS inner conflict moment takes place here when a common man, Tank, shares his joy over finding the messiah and what it means to everyone — but how can Neo accept he is to be the savior of all humanity?*

EXAMPLE: HGS #9 of *Erin Brockovich.*

**Hero Goal #9:** *Erin wants to gather enough evidence to bump up this small pro bono real estate case to a full class action negligence suit.*

Still shaken from meeting a dying child, Erin demands that her lawyer boss Ed Masry raise their case against Pacific Gas & Electric from a simple real estate dispute to a huge toxic tort class action case involving scores of families.

Ed yells that they'd be taking on a multibillion-dollar corporation, it would take forever and cost a fortune. Erin won't let up. People are suffering and need their help.

Finally Ed relents and tells Erin if she can gather enough evidence to prove the case, he'll do it.

So begins a sweeping, active sequence of short scenes as Erin bags evidence from around the plant in Hinkley. She scoops up dead mutant frogs and yucky pollution, showing how far she'll go physically to get the goods on PG&E.

She climbs down a toxic well to risk taking water samples. Tough guys run out to stop her. Erin jumps in her car and roars away.

At home, as boyfriend George plays games with her kids, Erin gets a phone call.

**Fresh News for HGS #9:** *A gruff anonymous voice threatens Erin — and the case suddenly gets dangerous.*

Erin realizes she may have put her kids in harm's way. Troubled, for a moment Erin wonders if she should dump the whole thing.

So in HGS #9 of *Erin Brockovich:*

a.) *An Action Burst unfolds as Erin gathers evidence;*

b.) *Erin shows how far she'll go physically to get the goods on PG&E;*

c.) *The Hero takes a risk by going to war with a corporate giant and the risk backfires when she receives a threatening phone call;*

d.) *For a moment Erin wrestles with her fear — maybe she should just give up.*

## HERO GOAL SEQUENCE® TEN

Once in a while the Action Burst will not turn up until Goal Sequence #10.

It's during HGS #10 of *Gladiator* that Hero Maximus, the top Roman general fallen into slavery as a gladiator, first rises to local stardom as The Spaniard during an Action Burst. And it's also in HGS #10 of the striking drama *A Beautiful Mind* where a car chase and shootout between spies cuts loose as the largest Action Burst in the whole movie.

But you'll more often find here in HGS #10:

*a.) The Hero gets hit with a setback;*

*b.) A new Mentor is consulted;*

*c.) An unexpected physical obstacle pops up;*

*d.) A subplot cutaway unfolds in which the Hero does not physically appear.*

EXAMPLE: HGS #10 of *As Good As It Gets*.

Catching up: when waitress Carol's severely allergic son gets a very high temperature, she demands that Melvin rush them the hospital in a cab — providing a burst of action and emotion for HGS #9.

Carol orders Melvin to leave her alone and stay out of her life for good.

Then:

**Hero Goal #10:** *Melvin wants to help Carol's son Spence in some way so that Carol will allow Melvin back into Café 24 and serve him breakfast as usual.*

Melvin stews and struggles to come up with a way to surmount this setback of Carol's insistence that he get lost.

In a subplot cutaway scene where the Hero does not appear Melvin's neighbor Simon, just home from the hospital, hears from friend Jackie that he's flat broke and cannot afford to keep his apartment. Jackie says Simon needs to call his parents for money, something Simon feels he cannot do.

Melvin consults a previously unknown Mentor at her office, his publisher, to ask a favor. He's figured out a way the publisher can help him get Carol back in his life. The publisher reluctantly agrees.

On his way out, Melvin's exit is blocked by his publisher's receptionist. Turns out she's a big fan and she moves in on him gushing with sappy romanticism over his books. It's Melvin's worst "fan" nightmare.

In another subplot cutaway scene, waitress Carol returns home to her apartment and finds a doctor there attending to her chronically ill son. This doctor is the publisher's husband and this was Melvin's requested favor. The doc orders tests previously denied by Carol's cheap health insurance and he promises that Spence will be feeling better soon. Carol and her mom are euphoric.

Dr. Bettes tells Carol that Melvin Udall asked to be billed.

A knock at Melvin's door. He opens up and Simon's housekeeper asks if Melvin would walk Verdell every day while Simon recuperates. What luck!

**Fresh News for HGS #10:** *Melvin gets to keep his relationship with the dog he loves, Verdell.*

So in HGS #10 of *As Good As It Gets:*

*a.) Melvin must deal with a setback when Carol demands he stay away from her;*

*b.) The Hero consults a Mentor, his publisher, for a favor;*

*c.) Melvin faces an unexpected physical obstacle when a dimwitted gushing fan blocks his way;*

*d.) Subplot cutaway scenes take place with Simon and Carol where the Hero does not appear.*

EXAMPLE: HGS #10 of *Finding Nemo.*

As Marlin's desperate journey continues…

**Hero Goal #10:** *Marlin must reach the East Australian Current which lies on the other side of a spooky undersea trench.*

The Hero consults a passing Mentor-like school of tuna, and they inform the Hero that to reach Sydney, Marlin must leap aboard the East Australia Current. And to reach the EAC, Marlin and Dory need to pass through a scary undersea trench.

Marlin darts off in that direction.

But the tuna specifically warn Sidekick Dory not to go over the trench. She and Marlin must swim through it. Dory suffers from short-term memory loss and forgets to tell Marlin that part. Reaching the creepy trench, Marlin insists they swim over the dangerous looking passage and he heads upward.

Swimming above the trench, Marlin and Dory find themselves trapped in the middle of a dangerous unforeseen physical obstacle…

**Fresh News for HGS #10:** *Marlin and Dory are surrounded by thousands of deadly jellyfish.*

In a subplot cutaway scene to the dentist's aquarium, son Nemo despairs that his father will never come to save him because dad is afraid of the open ocean. All seems lost for the young lad.

So in HGS #10 of *Finding Nemo:*

a.) *The Hero encounters a setback when he and Sidekick Dory face a scary undersea trench they're supposed to swim through;*

b.) *The Hero consults a new Mentor — the helpful cheerleading school of tuna;*

c.) *The Hero hits an unforeseen physical obstacle when he's trapped in the middle of a vast gathering of deadly jellyfish;*

d.) *A subplot cutaway involving Marlin's son Nemo takes place where the Hero does not appear.*

## HERO GOAL SEQUENCE® ELEVEN

Goal Sequence #11 can often contain what Joseph Campbell called the Approach to the Inmost Cave, where a Hero nears the most dangerous heart of the Adversary's power.

In sequence #11 of *Star Wars*, it's where Luke, Han and Chewbacca approach and sneak aboard the Death Star, the very center of Darth Vader's conquering army, as the Hero undertakes searching for Princess Leia there.

In *Gladiator*, sequence #11 unfolds when Hero Maximus, now a slave gladiator, gets transported to the catacombs beneath the Roman Coliseum, which is the center of all power belonging to evil Emperor Comodus. Maximus approaches the Inmost Cave of his Adversary's empire.

And here in HGS #11 conflict grows more intense, reaching the point of open warfare. Fighting for principles becomes person-to-person combat — usually with an agent or proxy of the Adversary and not yet with the Adversary directly.

A sense of urgency continues to mount. This is the Hero's last chance to consult a Mentor, train, and gather tools… and his last opportunity to bail out.

In HGS #11 you will frequently find:

a.) *The Hero approaches the seat of power or the Inmost Cave belonging to the Adversary;*

b.) *Conflict becomes more intense;*

c.) *A battle breaks out between the Hero and a proxy of the Adversary;*

d.) *Urgency and stakes rise sharply;*

e.) *It's the last chance for Mentor consultation, training, and gathering tools or weapons;*

f.) *The last chance to abandon pursuit of the Hero's goal.*

EXAMPLE: HGS #11 of *A Beautiful Mind.*

Summarizing the story so far: in Act One, genius John Nash struggles to find a worthy student project to undertake at Princeton. He almost misses his chance at world recognition in this competitive stampede to come up with one truly original idea. But the great idea finally does strike John, so he's rewarded with a plum scientific work placement and teaching position.

In HGS #6, in the first class he teaches, emotionally isolated John meets Alicia (S.S. #1), the woman who changes his world and who'll ultimately save his life.

Then in the first half of Act Two, John Nash begins a secret code-breaking assignment for the government. Soon John finds himself followed by shady-looking characters who might be Russian spies.

In HGS #10 he is swept into a car chase shoot-out as his boss Agent Parcher (Ed Harris) fights to save John from the Russians.

The Hero tries to quit, but Agent Parcher won't let him. The Russians are closing in and spies follow John everywhere.

Nash insists that his wife Alicia go stay with her sister for her own protection. Alicia refuses to leave him.

Both stakes and urgency rise sharply.

Now...

**Hero Goal #11:** *Math whiz John Nash, delivering a lecture, must escape when he sees Russian spies closing in to kill him.*

Speaking at a Harvard conference, John rambles incoherently, too nervous to think, seeing men in fedoras show up at the back of the hall. Certain that Russians have come to kill him, John runs from the building. He's soon cornered.

John punches the head Russian in the jaw as henchmen grab the Hero, hold him down and jab a needle into his arm.

They drag John to an ominous black car and push him in, screech away.

John wakes up to find he's chained to a wheelchair in an opulent, Edwardian-style office. The head Russian, now claiming to be one Doctor Rosen, tells John he's being held in a psychiatric hospital.

The Hero insists he was never involved in military spying. Then, half hidden in a corner of the office, John spots his college roommate, Charles, who is looking troubled.

John suddenly realizes that "dear friend" Charles is in on this with the bad guys. Charles is a traitor.

Rough men drag John down a hall in Dr. Rosen's lair as the Hero yells out that he's being held against his will.

Here John Nash approaches the Inmost Cave of complete madness. He still believes that all his delusions about Russian spies are real.

**Fresh News for HGS #11:** *John is locked in a cell inside a Russian "insane asylum."*

So in HGS #11 of *A Beautiful Mind*:

a.) *John Nash Approaches the Inmost Cave of madness — the realm of his true Adversary, Agent Parcher — as he is locked in an insane asylum;*

b.) *Conflict becomes far more intense between the Hero and his delusions;*

c.) *The Hero enjoins battle with Adversary proxies — the head "Russian spy" Dr. Rosen and John's fantasy of a traitorous roommate, Charles;*

d.) *Urgency and stakes rise sharply;*

e.) *John meets an as yet unrecognized new Mentor, Dr. Rosen;*

f.) *Dr. Rosen offers John a last chance back to sanity.*

EXAMPLE: HGS #11 of *Scarface*.

**Hero Goal #11:** *At the Babylon Club, center of the Miami drug dealing world, Tony Montana works to establish himself as a new Mr. Big.*

Tony strolls into the club and presents himself as a new tough guy boss to reckon with.

The Babylon Club stands as the center of Tony's decadent ambitions. Coke dealers far more powerful than Tony gather here, so this is the key political location for his attempt to become a boss.

But Tony spots his twenty-year-old sister Gina dancing wildly with some small-time Lothario. The Hero is troubled to see her here in his own sex-and-drugs world.

Chief Narcotics Detective Bernstein braces Tony and squeezes the Hero for payoff money. Dirty cop Bernstein explains to this newcomer how a drug dealing relationship with the police works.

Tony's boss Frank and Frank's girl Elvie arrive at the club and as soon as Elvie is left alone, Tony moves in. Tony plays to the whole room, openly puts the make on Frank's girlfriend.

Frank hustles over and tells Tony to get lost. Tension rises. Tony's true Adversary in this story is Alejandro Sosa, a top Bolivian cocaine producer. But one test set for Tony by Sosa was to deal with Frank Lopez.

Urgency and stakes rise sharply.

Tony spots his little sister Gina staggering off toward the restrooms while her sleazy date gropes her. Enraged, Tony storms after them, kicks open a men's restroom stall door to find Gina snorting coke and having sex. Tony goes nuts, throws loverboy out, then hits his sister.

The Hero claims total physical domination over Gina. Not because he loves his sister, but because he feels he owns her. This Anti-Hero's tragic flaw — the fact that he cannot genuinely love anyone — distorts his every action.

**Fresh News for HGS #11:** *Tony discovers that his own sister is being corrupted by the very drugs he sells.*

So in HGS #11 of *Scarface*:

*a.) The Hero Approaches the Inmost Cave of drug power in the Babylon Club;*

*b.) Conflict grows more intense as Tony's sister gets involved in his sex-and-drugs world;*

*c.) Open battle erupts with the Hero's boss Frank Lopez, a proxy offered up by Tony's true Adversary, Sosa;*

*d.) Urgency and stakes rise when Tony catches Gina doing drugs and having sex in the men's room;*

*e.) The Hero consults a new negative Mentor, Detective Bernstein;*

*f.) This is Tony's last chance to bail out before he becomes a major drug boss with a target on his back.*

## HERO GOAL SEQUENCE® TWELVE
## THE MIDPOINT SEQUENCE

Whether a film feels long or short has a lot to do with how well the Midpoint Sequence works. If the necessary dramatic events don't occur in Goal Sequence #12 it will seem like the first half of the story isn't taking us anywhere and audience interest will quickly wane.

Reiterating from Chapter Seven: in the Midpoint Sequence — Hero Goal Sequence® #12 — you will find many of the following actions occurring:

*a.) The Hero reaches a Point of No Return beyond which there's no turning back;*

*b.) The second step in character growth appears where the Hero BATTLES his inner need for emotional growth;*

*c.) Lovers kiss or go to bed for the first time either literally or metaphorically — or with buddies a partnership becomes official — which greatly deepens mutual commitment;*

*d.) Mood and storytelling style differ from anything else in the picture;*

*e.) Conflict with the Adversary becomes personal;*

*f.) A "ticking clock" time limit gets set in motion;*

*g.) An unmasking takes place, literally or metaphorically;*

*h.) A real or symbolic death and rebirth takes place. representing the end of adolescence and the beginning of adulthood for the Hero.*

EXAMPLE: HGS #12 of *Erin Brockovich.*

**Hero Goal #12:** *Erin wants to take an all-or-nothing legal shot as Ed Masry asks a lone judge whether their class action suit against Pacific Gas & Electric will go to trial or be dismissed.*

Outside the Hinkley PG&E plant a man in emotional agony throws rocks at the plant buildings and wanders through the scrub brush weeping. Bathed in moody, unnatural blue light, this scene unfolds as an abstract jump-cut montage unlike anything else in the film.

The weeping man turns out to be the husband of Erin's good friend Donna Jensen. Donna's just found out she now faces her third battle with cancer. She's dying.

Hero Erin sits by Donna's bed and does what she can to comfort her friend. The fight gets very personal for the Hero. Stakes couldn't be higher. A clock starts ticking on Donna's survival to witness the outcome and see justice done. For the Hero, walking away isn't an option anymore.

In a courtroom Erin sits nervously beside Ed Masry, looking just like she's a lawyer, too, waiting to hear the ruling. The judge finds merit in the case and rules that it will go to trial. Erin and Ed are delighted.

Ed offers Erin respectful congratulations and he treats her like his true partner for the first time.

Back at Ed's law office, three classy PG&E attorneys show up to offer a twenty-million-dollar settlement, but Erin attacks it as grossly inadequate to pay for all the human suffering PG&E has caused in Hinkley. The Hero intimidates the intimidators with a fiery display of self-confidence and purpose.

Rising to the second stage of character growth, Erin wages masterful BATTLE with her inner lack of self-worth and for a few moments she shines as brightly as any experienced attorney. Ed is proud of her.

But arriving home, Erin finds her live-in boyfriend George with a packed suitcase. He's tired of Erin's endless criticism. Erin hasn't said a kind word to him in six months.

So as Erin gains more respect at work, her home life falls apart. She still has a lesson to learn: before Erin can receive respect she must give respect to others.

**Fresh News for HGS #12:** *At the moment of a big legal victory Erin's live-in boyfriend George walks out on her.*

In HGS #12 of *Erin Brockovich*, the Midpoint Sequence, we see:

a.) *A Point of No Return crossed when Erin refuses the 20 million dollar settlement offer by PG&E;*

b.) *Erin undertaking the next stage of character growth as she BATTLES interior conflict by taking on PG&E's top lawyers;*

c.) *Erin and Ed join together in court for the first time as true partners;*

d.) *The style and focus of the montage is unlike anything else in the movie;*

e.) *Conflict with the Adversary becomes personal when Erin learns friend Donna is dying of the cancer caused by PG&E;*

f.) *A ticking clock begins — the case must be resolved soon or the outcome will arrive too late for Donna.*

g.) *An unmasking takes place when George reveals the depth of his unhappiness to Erin;*

h.) *A symbolic death takes place when George ends their relationship — Erin must now seek her new emotional "adulthood" alone.*

EXAMPLE: HGS #12 of *A Beautiful Mind.*

**Hero Goal #12:** *John Nash wants to get out of the insane asylum where Russian spies are trying to convince him he's crazy.*

Here in the Midpoint Sequence, for the first time in this story, focus switches completely away from Hero John Nash and over to the Love Interest character, John's wife Alicia.

This allows the screenwriter to bring both Alicia and the audience up to speed on what is real in the Hero's world and what isn't.

Dr. Rosen informs Alicia that people she has previously believed to be important in her husband's life — Charles, the child Marcee, and Agent Parcher — actually don't exist. They are delusions.

Stunned, Alicia rushes to see Sol and Bender, John's work colleagues. She demands that they allow her into John's office. She finds there scattered across the walls a tangled web of strings and nonsensical magazine clippings.

Alicia investigates John's work and sees for the first time behind her husband's disguise of sanity and into his madness.

Alicia goes to John's secret drop-off spot, an abandoned building. She discovers dozens of sealed envelopes left by John containing his "decoding" of secret messages in magazines. None of his envelopes have ever been collected.

At the hospital, Alicia wells with compassion. She truly knows John for the first time and their relationship changes fundamentally; from husband and wife to patient and caregiver.

The Hero begs her to get him out of the madhouse. Alicia shows John all the secret envelopes that no one collected, surely proof Agent Parcher doesn't exist.

Refusing to believe it, John storms from the visiting hall.

But later that day in his room...

**Fresh News for HGS #12:** *The Hero rips open the flesh of his own arm looking for the "secret implant" decoding device left by Parcher, but it isn't there — and John must accept he has lost his mind.*

So we see in HGS #12, the Midpoint Sequence of *A Beautiful Mind*:

*a.) A Point of No Return crossed since now the Hero must confront the fact of his insanity;*

*b.) The Hero BATTLES inner conflict about whether his delusions are real or not;*

*c.) Alicia truly sees her husband for the first time, a metaphorical first kiss which deepens mutual commitment;*

*d.) Style differs from anything else in the film when the story shifts completely to Alicia's point of view;*

*e.) Conflict with the Adversary becomes personal as John realizes the true enemy is Agent Parcher who exists only in John's own mind;*

*f.) A kind of ticking clock appears... if John cannot conquer his insanity soon he will lose forever his goal of world recognition;*

*g.) An unmasking takes place;*

*h.) There's a symbolic death and rebirth as cocky genius John Nash dies and a humbled, frightened man struggling to recapture his sanity gets born.*

## SUMMING UP

- In Hero Goal Sequence₍ₐ₎ SEVEN you frequently find that:
    a.) The Hero flounders for a plan of action, either on her own or in concert with others;

    b.) The Hero commits herself to the specific plot goal of the movie which requires some type of struggle;

    c.) The Hero's inner conflict surfaces...

    d.) ...and reveals the theme of the movie;

    e.) New characters enter the Hero's struggle and she must begin distinguishing allies from enemies.

- In Hero Goal Sequence₍ₐ₎ EIGHT you frequently find that:
    a.) The strength of the Adversary is demonstrated;

    b.) The stakes are increased;

    c.) The Hero undergoes training or instruction to master special skills needed for the battle ahead;

    d.) Allies and enemies are further established;

    e.) Often the first step in character growth appears, when the Hero or someone close to the Hero EXPRESSES in dialogue the Hero's inner emotional problem. (This first step in character growth can appear anywhere between HGS #7 and HGS #10, but HGS #8 is the most common placement.)

- In Hero Goal Sequence₍ᵣ₎ NINE you frequently find that:
  a.) An Action Burst or highly emotional moment occurs that drives up the tension and picks up the pace or scope of the story;

  b.) The Hero shows what he can do physically;

  c.) The Hero takes a risk, and that risk backfires;

  d.) The Hero considers giving up.

- In Hero Goal Sequence₍ᵣ₎ TEN you frequently find that:
  a.) The Hero gets hit with a setback;

  b.) A new Mentor is consulted;

  c.) An unexpected physical obstacle pops up;

  d.) A subplot cutaway unfolds in which the Hero does not physically appear.

- In Hero Goal Sequence₍ᵣ₎ ELEVEN you frequently find that:
  a.) The Hero Approaches the Inmost Cave or seat of power belonging to the Adversary;

  b.) Conflict becomes more intense;

  c.) A battle breaks out with a proxy of the Adversary;

  d.) Urgency and stakes rise sharply;

  e.) A last chance for training, instruction, or consultation with a Mentor is offered.

- In Hero Goal Sequence₍ᵣ₎ TWELVE, THE MIDPOINT SEQUENCE you frequently find that:
  a.) The Hero reaches a Point of No Return beyond which turning back is no longer an option;

b.) The second major step toward character growth appears where the Hero directly BATTLES whatever inner conflict is keeping him from achieving his goal;

c.) Lovers kiss or go to bed for the first time either literally or metaphorically — or with buddies a partnership becomes official — which deepens mutual commitment;

d.) Mood and storytelling style differ from anything else in the movie;

e.) Conflict with the Adversary becomes deeply personal;

f.) A "ticking clock" time limit gets set in motion;

g.) An unmasking takes place, literally or figuratively, and an inner truth gets revealed;

h.) A literal or symbolic death and rebirth takes place representing the end of childhood and the beginning of adulthood for the Hero.

**EXERCISE:**

Get a DVD of *The Bourne Identity*. View the first 70 minutes.

Jason Bourne (Matt Damon) is the lone Hero. His Adversary is CIA Treadstone Director Conklin (Chris Cooper), and his Love Interest is Marie (Franka Potente).

NOW: Describe the Hero Goal Sequences® in the first half of Act Two of *The Bourne Identity*, HGS 7-12. Note the HERO'S physical GOAL and FRESH NEWS for each sequence.

Some hints are provided below. This film contains a strong Adversary subplot and shows that many cutaways from the Hero do not alter the Goal Sequence structure.

• TO CATCH UP — HERE'S THE END OF ACT ONE in *The Bourne Identity*:

HGS #6… HERO GOAL: *Bourne wants to buy a car ride to Paris from Marie*. Climbing in, he finally takes a close look at Marie —

FRESH NEWS (STUNNING SURPRISE #1) — Bourne is immediately captivated by this woman who will change the whole nature of his isolated world.

(NOTE: The life changing S.S. #1 in stories with strong romance threads is often the first meeting of the Hero and Love Interest.)

Then there are cutaway scenes where *Conklin activates three deadly hit men. "I want Bourne in a body bag by sundown!"* Stakes are clear — life or death.

Act One total running time: 29 min. 13 sec.

• I'll give you sequence seven… In HGS #7 the HERO GOAL is — *Finally trust someone and confide in Marie.* (In the middle of HGS #7 there's an Adversary cutaway, then back to Hero.) FRESH NEWS — *In Paris, Marie expresses romantic interest in the Hero.* Sequence time with cutaway: 7 min. 20 sec.

• In HGS #8 the HERO GOAL becomes — *Check out Bourne's Paris apartment for clues as to his identity.* What does Bourne next discover as his FRESH NEWS? (He figures out something while on a phone call.) 5 min. 56 sec.

• Then in HGS #9, what's the Hero's new HERO GOAL? (It has to do with expecting something and dealing with it when it arrives.) What FRESH NEWS changes things? (Has to do with photos and flying.) 4 min. 3 sec.

• In HGS #10, what's the HERO GOAL (it has to do with Marie), and what's FRESH NEWS? (about Marie sending a message through auto safety.) 5 min. 59 sec.

• For HGS #11, what's the HERO GOAL? (Quite straight forward.) And FRESH NEWS? 6 min. 29 sec. with end cutaways.

• In HGS #12 what's the HERO GOAL? (He needs to get something.) This is the MIDPOINT SEQUENCE and it includes: Hero scenes; Cutaway scenes; The Hero and Love Interest first make love; Bourne and Marie first work as a team; A Point of No Return when someone gets murdered; A 24-hour Ticking Clock established.

Then... what's the Hero's FRESH NEWS? (It's about Marie, and happens before the Adversary cutaway that actually ends HGS #12.)

Answers can be found at the end of Chapter Twelve.

## ANSWERS FOR CH. 10, HGS 1-6 IN ACT ONE OF *AVATAR*:

### HGS #1:
HERO GOAL — *Get to Pandora and replace his dead twin brother.*
FRESH NEWS — *Wheelchair-bound Jake first meets his new avatar face to face... sees this assignment could get interesting.*
Time: 9 min. 40 sec.

### HGS #2:
HERO GOAL — *Take his new avatar body out for a wobbly first trial.*
FRESH NEWS — *Jake runs into Dr. Grace Augustine in her avatar form, she throws him fruit, and Jake sees she is not the enemy but a Mentor.*
Time: 9 min. 32 sec.

### HGS #3:
HERO GOAL — *Learn how to "drive" his avatar.*
FRESH NEWS — *Jake gets an assignment from Colonel Quaritch... to spy for Quaritch while working for Dr. Augustine.*
Time: 4 min. 30 sec.

### HGS #4:
HERO GOAL — *Guard his first research mission into the jungle.*
FRESH NEWS — *Hero escapes an attacking beast, but now he's lost with no weapons.*
Time: 8 min.

**HGS #5:**

HERO GOAL — *Survive the night in the jungle alone with just a knife.*
FRESH NEWS — *A female Na'vi warrior, Neytiri, saves him from being eaten by wolf-like creatures, but she thinks Jake is stupid.*
Time: 5 min.

**HGS #6:**

HERO GOAL — *Follow Neytiri as she tries to get ride of him.*
FRESH NEWS (STUNNING SURPRISE #1) — *Seeds from the Sacred Tree suddenly surround Jake, choosing him. Seeing this as an important sign, Neytiri now tells Jake to come with her. A door into the heart of the Na'vi has suddenly opened for the Hero.*
Time: 5 min. 15 sec.

Total Act One running time — 41 min. 55 sec.

*chapter twelve*

# SECOND HALF OF ACT TWO: SEQUENCES 13~18

—— ꙮ ——

## RACING TOWARD THE CLIMAX

Heroes charge forward from the Midpoint Sequence with a do-or-die look burning in their eyes. No turning back now. The pace continues to quicken as Heroes race onward toward their fate.

All plot setups should be complete by now. All battle lines clearly drawn.

This last half of Act Two should be about confrontation and payoff. Very seldom will you find any important new characters introduced here who are not Agents of an already well-established Adversary. If your story needs un-foreshadowed, out-of-the-blue plot machinery suddenly popping up here in order to keep it afloat, your script is telling you something. Go back and rethink your Goal Sequences from the beginning.

## HERO GOAL SEQUENCE₍ₐ₎ THIRTEEN

The Hero presses onward from HGS #12 with renewed commitment to the physical task at hand.

But frequently in HGS #13 a Hero's inner emotional defensiveness returns. He retreats once more behind his battered shield of isolating self-protection. In the Midpoint Sequence the Hero tried to BATTLE and overcome that inner conflict which forces him to use his emotional SHIELD. He stepped out from behind his protection for a time. But geez, that was scary. Here in HGS #13 the inner need for self-isolation returns.

One step forward, two steps back.

During the HGS #12 Midpoint Sequence of *As Good As It Gets*, Melvin Udall hears a late night knock on his door. It's waitress Carol in her rain-soaked, clinging T-shirt. She's come to tell Melvin how grateful she is for the doctor he sent to help her son... but Carol will never, ever sleep with Melvin. Her wet T-shirt and awkwardness, however, carry a subtext that hints otherwise.

Then after she leaves, Melvin does an amazing thing. Stirred up by Carol's impassioned declaration, he buys hot Chinese soup and takes it over to neighbor Simon as a "get well" gesture. Melvin opens his heart to Simon like a true friend and talks about his feelings. It's a huge growth step for Melvin — sharing himself emotionally. Melvin BATTLES inner conflict and, for a moment at least, becomes Mr. Open.

But the very next day in Café 24, now in HGS #13, Carol approaches Melvin's table to read a long thank you letter and Melvin refuses to hear it. His SHIELD comes back up.

Melvin's feelings for Carol are still too powerful to allow them out in the light of day. Self-protection returns.

Struggling to change the emotional patterns of a lifetime can never be easy. Falling back into old habits in HGS #13 means that the Hero has lost his first battle in pursuit of personal connection. But at least he fought the good fight.

Also in HGS #13, as new complications emerge, further proof will be found that conflict between the Hero and Adversary has turned deeply personal. An important source of the renewed commitment felt by the Hero in HGS #13 comes from seeing that this clash is now so singular. So it's him-or-me.

In Hero Goal Sequence₍ᵣ₎ #13 we often see that:

*a.) The Hero presses onward with renewed determination to complete the physical task;*

*b.) A new complication crops up;*

*c.) The Hero lifts again her battered inner SHIELD of self-defense and isolation;*

*d.) Additional proof is found that the conflict between Hero and Adversary has become very personal.*

EXAMPLE: HGS #13 of *Erin Brockovich.*

**Hero Goal #13:** *Erin must pursue the Hinkley PG&E case, now burdened by the need to take her kids with her everywhere.*

Erin storms forward from HGS #12 with determination to sign up as many plaintiff families as possible. But she carries an extra weight.

In the Midpoint Sequence boyfriend George left her. Caught without the built-in babysitting George provided, Erin must now travel everywhere with three children in tow. Stress increases. A new layer of complication has been added.

In Hinkley the Hero tries again to win over her most resistant prospect, housewife Pamela Duncan. Like everyone else, Pamela and her family have experienced serious health trauma from the PG&E pollution. But she tells Erin, "I don't want to feel it all over again and then not have it come out right."

Pamela explains how she once rushed her children to the emergency room with severe nosebleeds, and the staff immediately assumed Pamela was abusing her kids.

Erin's feeling of outrage toward PG&E grows.

Full of renewed purpose, Erin convinces Pamela Duncan to fight alongside the other Hinkley families.

With Erin's kids still forced to come along, she rushes back to Ed Masry's law office while arguing with her son over transportation to roller-hockey.

From the reception area Erin spots Ed deep in private consultation with a man in a power suit. Erin's ticked off that she wasn't invited to the meeting.

Ed comes to her and announces, "This is our new partner, Kurt Potter. He'll be handling Hinkley now." Erin's jaw drops. The case she created has just been handed over to a stranger and she wasn't even consulted.

Erin's anger rises and her self-worth plummets. She retreats into her old self-protective confrontational mode.

**Fresh News for HGS #13:** *A big-time lawyer steps in to grab all the glory away from Erin.*

So in HGS #13 of *Erin Brockovich*:

*a.) The Hero presses on with renewed courage as she signs up even the most resistant families to the case;*

*b.) A complication appears when Erin suddenly needs to take her kids with her everywhere;*

*c.) Further proof arrives that the conflict has grown more personal when Erin hears Pamela Duncan's story, and when a hotshot lawyer wounds Erin's ego by grabbing the Hinkley case away from her;*

*d.) Excluded and disrespected, the Hero retreats from character growth to hide again behind her SHIELD of anger and emotional isolation.*

EXAMPLE: HGS #13 of *A Beautiful Mind*.

**Hero Goal #13:** *John Nash must undertake treatment for schizophrenia.*

Recognizing at last that he suffers from serious mental illness, John musters courage and submits to a severe course of treatment — insulin shock therapy five times a week for ten weeks.

Under the burden of long-term treatment, the Hero's mind becomes foggy. Friends avoid him.

John faces new complications: shock therapy, medications that muddle thought, loss of job and status in the world, and a permanently altered relationship with his wife... while on the medications he can't make love with Alicia.

John's genius, the very thing that made him so unique, slips away.

Alicia invites John's colleague Sol over to the house. Sol appears nervous about seeing John. The Hero tries lamely to lighten the conversation.

Then John tells Sol he's working on an important mathematical hypothesis and he offers a draft to Sol for his opinion.

In the notebook Sol finds only childish scribbles. He mutters, "There are other things besides work…" Despairing, John asks, "What are they?"

The Hero retreats into severe self-doubt and shame.

**Fresh News for HGS #13:** *John cannot return to his work in advanced mathematics while he's on the meds… his latest hypothesis is drivel.*

So in HGS #13 of *A Beautiful Mind:*

a.) *With renewed courage the Hero moves forward to undergo harsh shock treatment for schizophrenia;*

b.) *Complications crop up when medication dulls John's mind and destroys his ability to work;*

c.) *The Hero finds in the loss of his love life with Alicia further proof that his battle against his unreal Adversary grows ever more deeply personal;*

d.) *The Hero retreats once more behind his battered SHIELD of emotional isolation and insecurity.*

## HERO GOAL SEQUENCE₍ₐ₎ FOURTEEN

Not every sequence needs to be more frantic than the last. Tempos should vary.

After the spike of new energy set loose in HGS #13 it's only natural that things should calm down a bit in sequence #14. The Hero needs a moment to think it all through and perhaps talk things over with someone.

Then there suddenly appears on the scene a Big New Idea to challenge the Hero.

Goal Sequence #14 is never dull.

Since the next sequence, HGS #15, will most often contain the second Action Burst of Act Two, #14 serves as a small lull before the upcoming storm. And the Big New Idea that drives the second Action Burst first appears here in #14 as a particularly large and important Fresh News announcement.

Also in Hero Goal Sequence® #14 we usually find another demonstration of just how much his inner conflict still mucks things up for the Hero. In this quieter moment a Love Interest character or Sidekick or Mentor might confront the Hero's inner wound to keep him focused on the character development work yet to be accomplished.

The third step in character growth, confronting and OVER-COMING inner conflict, will soon appear in HGS #16 or #17. So this is one of the last chances available to address the emotional suffering still crippling the Hero before the final showdown with the Adversary.

In Hero Goal Sequence® #14 we often find that:

*a.) Pace slows down a bit and offers the Hero a contemplative moment;*

*b.) A Love Interest or Sidekick or even the Hero himself brings up inner conflict issues the Hero would rather not deal with right now;*

*c.) A Big New Idea arrives to challenge the Hero...*

*d.) ...and this Big New Idea paves the way for story development in the Action Burst coming up during HGS #15.*

EXAMPLE: HGS #14 in *Shrek*.

Catching up: In HGS #13, having escaped from the dragon's keep, Shrek, Donkey, and the Princess plod back toward Duloc to turn Fiona over to Lord Farquaad. This demanding princess is getting on Shrek's nerves. Then suddenly she realizes that the sun is going down. Princess Fiona insists they stop. She orders Shrek to find her shelter before sunset!

So...

**Hero Goal #14:** *Shrek must make camp for the night with Side-kick Donkey and a feisty princess.*

Shrek locates a cave. Fiona hurriedly rips off a slab of tree bark to make a door and shuts herself in mere seconds before the sun goes down.

Shrek and Donkey bed down beside an open campfire.

The Hero contemplates a starry sky and tells stories to Donkey about great ogre heroes from days of yore.

In this quiet moment Shrek lets down his guard and for the first time starts treating Donkey like a true friend.

But Donkey keeps asking annoying questions, cutting to the core of Shrek's inner pain. Donkey also wants to know what "we" will do when "we" get "our" swamp back.

Shrek snaps, "There is no *we!* There is no *our!*"

The Hero growls that he will return to live in his swamp all alone. And for good measure he intends to build a ten-foot wall around his whole property!

Donkey keeps after him. Shrek shouts that he'll keep out all the people who judge him before they even know him. Secretly, Princess Fiona overhears. Donkey reminds Shrek that he never judged the ogre when they first met. "I know," Shrek says, calming.

Next morning, much to their shock, Princess Fiona cooks up a breakfast of fresh eggs for the boys — because they all got off on the wrong foot, she says, and wants to make it up to them.

Shrek gapes at her. She's not what he expected at all. A Big New Idea arrives for Shrek... the possibility of falling hard for this princess.

**Fresh News for HGS #14:** *Princess Fiona shows her sweet, down-to-earth side... and throws Shrek for a loop.*

So in HGS #14 of *Shrek:*

*a.) The pace slows and offers the Hero a contemplative moment by a campfire;*

*b.) The Hero once more wrestles with inner conflict as Sidekick Donkey points out unfinished character growth that the Hero would rather not deal with;*

*c.) A Big New Idea arrives to challenge the Hero as the possibility of romance appears...*

*d.) ...paving the way for the Hero to fall in love with the Princess during an Action Burst coming in HGS #15.*

EXAMPLE: HGS #14 in *Rain Man.*

Catching up: Charlie Babbitt hears in HGS #13 that his European sports car inventory has been repossessed by the bank. His business is finished. So...

**Hero Goal #14: *Charlie Babbitt needs money fast to pay back his customers' deposits so he won't go to jail.***

On the road with Raymond, still heading toward L.A., Charlie turns thoughtfully inward. He's now got legal troubles, and no source of income.

The tempo of the journey slows as Charlie's 1949 Buick rolls into, then straight out of, Las Vegas with barely a glance from Charlie as his problems press down on him.

Next morning the Hero stops at a desert store to buy sun block for Raymond.

Charlie is looking after his brother's needs in a more thoughtful, affectionate way — in direct conflict with Charlie's life-long shield of avoiding all emotional connections.

Eating breakfast in a diner booth, Charlie snaps at Ray to stop flipping through the song index pages of the tabletop jukebox. Raymond stops. But then Ray starts reciting the call letters for every song he hears played.

Charlie looks up. He recognizes that his brother just memorized all the jukebox index listings in a matter of seconds.

The Hero sparks with sudden excitement. He jumps up, rushes Raymond outside to the convertible.

On the trunk hood of the old Buick Charlie spreads out most of a deck of playing cards face up. Still keeping a few cards secret in his hand, Charlie asks Raymond to name the undis-closed cards. Raymond calls them out. Perfectly. A Big New Idea hits Charlie. He quickly stuffs Ray back in the Buick.

Charlie jumps in and lays rubber turning around, stomps on the gas, roars back toward the Blackjack tables of Las Vegas.

**Fresh News for HGS #14:** *Charlie discovers that Raymond is a natural card counter, which means he can possibly beat the casino Blackjack tables.*

So in HGS #14 of *Rain Man*:

*a.) The pace slows and offers the Hero a contemplative moment;*

*b.) Charlie once more wrestles with his self-protective emotional defenses as he smears sunblock on Ray and discovers he feels affection for someone;*

*c.) A Big New Idea strikes when Charlie figures out that Raymond can count cards and they roar off for the Vegas Blackjack tables...*

*d.) ...paving the way for an Action Burst in HGS #15 where Ray and Charlie will gamble and win big.*

Take note that Charlie Babbitt's Big New Idea does not come to him out of the blue as a sudden "realization." Physical, visible actions demonstrate what the Big New Idea is, how Charlie arrived at it, and why the idea comes to him now and not earlier or later.

Screen story development is strongest when communicated through behavior. And it must be motivated.

## HERO GOAL SEQUENCE® FIFTEEN

Now comes a second major Action Burst right in the middle of the second half of Act Two. An eruption of new excitement and visual energy.

Deciding what form of action, of course, will always depend on the genre of your story.

But however you dramatize the second Action Burst for HGS #15, an energized plotline should allow the Hero to think she's winning this round against the Adversary. Temporarily. Because soon the bottom will drop out.

When the Hero first feels victorious, or at least like she's fighting the powerful Adversary to a draw, her hope swells. She thinks that maybe she can pull off the impossible after all.

This moment of mood uplift is called the *False Victory*. It brings a fleeting, counterfeit sense of security to the Hero.

For example, in *Sideways* the False Victory arrives for Hero Miles in HGS #15 when, after finally making love the night before, he and Maya go out to share a picnic together. On a blanket under a beautiful oak tree they relax, read, speak warmly. Maya asks Miles if he can stay over for the whole weekend. It's everything Miles has longed for — a relationship with a wonderful woman who shares his passions. The woman who could help him grow beyond obsession with his ex-wife Victoria. Victory! But… Miles accidentally lets slip that his friend Jack is getting married in a few days. Maya is stunned. Then furious. Jack has just told Maya's best friend Stephanie that he loves her! How could Miles have been part of such a thing!

Miles' False Victory comes to a sudden, crashing end. Hope raised, then quickly dashed. So begins an Action Burst as Maya rages and demands that Miles take her home.

In Hero Goal Sequence® #15 we often find that:

*a.) An Action Burst arrives where physical action or dramatic confrontation kicks upward;*

*b.) The Hero experiences a False Victory or believes she has fought the Adversary to a draw, so her ultimate goal does not seem impossible anymore;*

*c.) A fleeting sense of security arrives for the Hero, soon to be dashed;*

*d.) The Hero's involvement in Action Burst Two can be motivated by conflict with a Love Interest character.*

Often this Burst of action originates from quarreling between the Hero and a Love Interest character, as in *Sideways*.

And in HGS #15 of *Mr. & Mrs. Smith*, John and Jane Smith steal a minivan to escape assassins while revealing to each other in dialogue their true romantic histories. Under armed attack by three SUVs, the Smith's personal truth vetting turns into an argument. The whole tempo of this blazing action sequence plays off of the comedic husband-wife romantic fracas taking place in the foreground, inside a minivan under heavy fire.

So the Action Burst fireworks can frequently be provided by a romantic relationship.

EXAMPLE: HGS #15 of *A Beautiful Mind*.

**Hero Goal #15:** *John Nash wants to get back to work.*

Since John Nash can no longer think clearly and no longer physically respond to his wife, he surreptitiously stops taking his anti-hallucinatory medications.

Soon John begins hearing things, sees darting shadows of sinister men. He's drawn into the woods behind his house and finds himself surrounded by armed agents.

Parcher steps forward. "Time to return to work, soldier."

Confusion about what's real overwhelms John once more. Agent Parcher leads the Hero to an abandoned garage where a spy command center has been set up just for him.

The Hero swells with renewed pride. He triumphantly returns to the center of his own self-aggrandizing psychotic universe, feeling back in control of his genius.

Days later as a storm approaches, John's wife Alicia runs outside to pull in laundry from the line while John draws the baby's bath upstairs.

As bathwater deepens around the helpless infant, John wanders off, talking to his non-existent friends.

Outside, Alicia hears a garage door banging in the wind.

Storm blowing, she pursues the sound and discovers the shed. Inside — scores of magazine pages pinned to the walls, incoherent scribbles, string criss-crossing it all. Madness.

Alicia spins and tears off through the driving rain back toward the house and the baby. Tension shoots up.

Mere seconds before the baby would have drowned, Alicia grabs him from the bathwater and runs in horror down the stairs to the telephone. She calls Dr. Rosen. John chases after her, yelling insanely.

John claims Agent Parcher has just ordered him to stop Alicia from calling the doctor. Alicia screams that there's no one else in the room. But John sees Parcher, Charles, and the child Marcee clearly — as they insist that John stop his wife.

Parcher pulls out his .45 and takes aim at Alicia. John leaps in front of Parcher to deflect the shot but John accidentally bangs into Alicia, knocks her and the baby to the floor.

Alicia grabs the baby and runs from the house.

John's head swirls with a crescendo montage of images — Parcher, Charles, little Marcee — most especially Marcee. He's frantic to understand what's happening to him.

At the curb Alicia fumbles to start the car and get away from her raving husband. But John leaps in front of the car, leans on the hood stopping her.

Revelation in his eyes. Understanding. "Marcee can't be real," he says...

**Fresh News for HGS #15:** *John Nash notices that one of his delusions, the child Marcee, "...never gets old." Ultimate proof to John that she isn't real.*

So in HGS #15 of *A Beautiful Mind*:

*a.) Action Burst Two offers suspense and a rise in energy, physical action, and confrontation;*

*b.) For a short while the Hero enjoys a False Victory as his delusions return and he regains self-importance in his madness;*

*c.) The euphoria John feels working again for Agent Parcher soon crashes when he realizes he has nearly injured Alicia and the baby;*

*d.) A romantic relationship drives this Action Burst Two as John and Alicia clash.*

EXAMPLE: HGS #15 in *Hitch*.

Catching up: At the Midpoint of *Hitch*, this Date Doctor finds himself falling ever more in love with Sara, a reporter for a gossip newspaper. So he has invited Sara to his apartment where he plans to cook dinner for her.

But in a HGS #14 subplot, Sara discovers, unbeknownst to Hitch, that he is in fact the Date Doctor of urban legend. Sara wrongly believes that Hitch was to blame for getting a sleazy guy into bed with Sara's best friend and breaking her heart.

Then...

Sequence #15 begins with a **subplot cutaway** where Love Interest Sara pushes angrily ahead with her plan to publish her exposé about Hitch and his client Albert Brennaman conniving to hoodwink rich socialite Allegra Cole into a romance with Albert.

But Hitch doesn't yet have any inkling of her intentions.

**Hero Goal #15:** *Hitch wants to get to know Sara better over dinner in the Hero's apartment.*

Hitch expertly prepares dinner while waiting for Sara to arrive.

When she shows up, the Hero feels a real sense of victory that he has finally reached the end of his "short game" romances, where he's always been afraid to let a woman into his heart.

As he cooks dinner Sara plays the melodramatically exaggerated role of a love-struck female, and so mocks Hitch. Her angry bitterness seeps ever more into the open as Hitch tries to figure out what's up.

The scene builds into a full-scale shouting match with thrown vegetables and dumped food. Sara finally storms out of his apartment.

The next day Sara's gossip news story breaks wide. Albert Brennaman loses all hope of winning Allegra, and Hitch's career as the Date Doctor comes crashing to an end.

**Fresh News for HGS #15:** *Everybody in town now knows who Hitch is, but they've been misled about what he really does.*

So in HGS #15 of *Hitch*:

*a.) Action Burst Two comes in the form of a high energy fight between the Hero and his Love Interest-Adversary;*

*b.) The Hero enjoys a False Victory — he temporarily believes he and Sara are falling in love and that his "short-game" romances are behind him;*

*c.) The euphoria Hitch feels soon crashes and becomes open warfare that destroys both his own prospects for romance and those of his favorite client, Albert;*

*d.) A romantic relationship drives this Action Burst.*

Some films provide the Action Burst of fresh energy or confrontation in HGS #16, or even HGS #14. In *Collateral*, for instance, the nightclub shootout, where Max gets pulled to freedom by a detective only to see the cop gunned down by Vincent — all takes place in #16. The second Action Burst for *Chinatown*, on the other hand, shows up in Hero Goal Sequence® #14, when Jake and Evelyn snoop around a retirement home and gunsels shoot at Jake as he narrowly escapes.

But most frequently you'll find the second Action Burst right here in Sequence #15.

## HERO GOAL SEQUENCE® SIXTEEN

The energy set loose in HGS #15 sweeps onward and upward in #16. No time to take a break now. Dramatic action swells and becomes more intense.

The Hero may achieve an increased degree of confidence at this point. Battle tested, he is now wise in the ways of the wily Adversary and understands the true nature of the problem at hand. There is often some form of rededication by the Hero here to achieving his goal, come what may.

This leads the Hero to discover a new angle or previously unconsidered outlook on the problem. A strong, fresh take on things should come from the Hero here, advancing plot development.

Sometimes this can be accomplished with a simple attitude change for the Hero, or even just an arena change. Moving the conflict to a new location can allow for unexpected fresh obstacles and reactions. Not just a move from the kitchen to the living room, mind you, but from the kitchen to Monte Carlo on New Year's Eve.

Also in HGS #16 you may find the third step in character growth, where the Hero OVERCOMES her inner conflict and beats it in a demonstrable way. This requires action on the part of the Hero. We must see it happen, not merely be told about it as a "realization." This third character growth step most often takes place in HGS #16 or #17.

In HGS #16:

*a.) The dramatic energy coming out of HGS #15 continues to rise, not as more physical action but as a growing intensity of conflict;*

*b.) The Hero feels greater confidence in his abilities and rededicates himself to the ultimate goal;*

*c.) The Hero discovers some important new outlook on the central conflict;*

*d.) The third step in character growth arrives — and the Hero OVERCOMES his inner emotional turmoil (here or in HGS #17).*

EXAMPLE: HGS #16 of *Erin Brockovich.*

Catching up: The new stuffed-shirt attorney Kurt Potter and his priggish partner Theresa completely ruin relations with the earthy residents of Hinkley. Erin's PG&E case is suddenly falling apart.

Ed Masry comes scurrying back to Erin, begging for help. Now the only legal move they've got left is arbitration. Then...

**Hero Goal #16:** *After the new attorneys mess up, Erin works desperately to save the PG&E class action case.*

Erin and Ed hold a big meeting in Hinkley to try and explain binding arbitration to their clients and why it's the only chance to see real compensation anytime soon. They must get 90% of the residents to agree.

It's an angry, rowdy meeting. When Ed points out that in an arbitration process there will be no jury — that everything depends on the ruling of one judge — many people start to walk out. They demand a jury of their peers or nothing.

Ed turns them around masterfully. He asks if they remember Three Mile Island? The people who suffered from radiation poisoning there won in that trial... but almost twenty years later they still haven't gotten a penny. Legal wrangling can drag on for decades.

As Erin watches her boss she's impressed.

Ed Masry convinces the people of Hinkley that arbitration is better. Erin and Ed get signatures from practically everyone at the meeting. But they're still about 160 signatures short of the 90% needed — and Ed says they also urgently need some kind of "smoking gun" proof that PG&E knew about the pollution and lied about it. The Hero will personally go door to door to collect signatures.

On the way out, Erin stops. She turns back to Ed and says, "Hey. You did good."

It's at this simple moment Erin finally understands that to receive respect, first she must give it to others.

Erin drove her Love Interest character George away with constant criticism. She demanded respect and love from George but never gave any back. At work with Ed, with the office staff, even with Potter — although desperate for respect herself, Erin never thought to give it to anyone else.

Here, in an empty meeting hall in Hinkley, Erin finally sees the light. "Hey," she tells Ed, "you did good."

**Fresh News for HGS #16:** *Erin needs to collect 160 more signatures and find a Smoking Gun.*

So in HGS #16 of *Erin Brockovich*:

a.) *The energy coming out of HGS #15 — where Erin gets complaints from Hinkley residents and she sees the whole case falling apart with Potter in charge — carries over and intensifies the conflict in HGS #16 as Erin comes riding back to the rescue;*

*b.) The Hero feels a rising confidence and rededicates herself through action to victory in the central conflict;*

*c.) The Hero finds an important new outlook on the case — if she gets 160 more signatures and finds one smoking gun she will win;*

*d.) The third stage in character growth for Erin appears, OVERCOMING inner conflict as she steps away from her own need for respect long enough to offer it to another.*

EXAMPLE: HGS #16 of *Finding Nemo*.

Catching up: The curtain drops on sequence #15 when Marlin and Dory are scooped into the mouth of a monstrous whale.

Fade to ominous black. Then... A **subplot cutaway** begins #16 as we discover little Nemo has successfully jammed the fish tank filter and now the tank has become good and slimy inside. The fish friends overhear their owner making plans to clean the tank tomorrow.

Maybe Nemo will still get a chance to escape down the drain before fish killer Darla gets there!

**Hero Goal #16:** *Marlin must escape from the gullet of a whale.*

Back with the Hero and Dory inside a whale's huge mouth... Marlin throws himself against the inner jaw over and over, trying desperately to break out.

On the other hand, Dory frolics and plays in the sloshing water on the whale's immense tongue. Marlin gives up, sinks to the bottom of the whale's mouth in despair, feeling he will never save Nemo now. Dory tries to cheer him up and tells him it will be okay.

Marlin sighs, "No, it won't. I promised Nemo nothing would ever happen to him."

Dory says, "That's a funny thing to promise. If you never let anything happen to him then nothing would EVER happen to him."

Dory tries speaking "whale" to ask their host what's up. Marlin is irritated because he's convinced Dory cannot speak whale.

Then the water level in the whale's mouth starts dropping. It's all draining back deep into the throat of the huge creature. The massive tongue shifts position to form a cliff, dropping everything back down into the black depths below.

Marlin hangs onto the tongue for dear life. The end is near.

Dory tells him the whale says it's time to let go.

"How do you know something bad isn't going to happen?!" Marlin hollers in panic.

Dory answers, "I don't." And she let's go, falling down into the darkest reaches of the whale's gullet.

The moment of truth arrives for our Hero.

Marlin's inner conflict has been that he always expects the worst, never trusts anyone, and so never lets Nemo learn anything on his own. "You can't!" have been Marlin's favorite words, always spoken in anger and fear.

Now it's time for Marlin to OVERCOME his fear and let go.

The Hero finally releases the whale's tongue and falls into blackness.

Next, Marlin finds himself shooting up high into the air, pushed out the whale's blow hole on a huge stream of water. He splashes back down into the ocean and realizes... the whale has placed them right in the middle of Sydney harbor.

Dory did know how to speak "whale" after all.

In a gush of joy Marlin cries, "We're gonna find my son! We can do this!"

The Hero has battled and OVERCOME his inner conflict.

**Fresh News for HGS #16:** *The Hero has finally reached Sydney, Australia, and is much closer to saving his son.*

So in HGS #16 of *Finding Nemo*:

*a.) The dramatic energy coming out of HGS #15 when Marlin and Dory were swept into the mouth of a whale continues to rise in a growing intensity of conflict inside the whale's jaw;*

*b.) Arriving in Sydney, the Hero finds a greater confidence in his abilities and rededicates himself to the goal;*

*c.) The Hero discovers an important new point of view toward the central problem — let go of negativity;*

*d.) The Hero undergoes his third step in character growth, finally OVERCOMES his fear of everything and learns to trust others.*

## HERO GOAL SEQUENCE® SEVENTEEN

Now a growing sense of impending payoff must develop.

For most movie stories, if it didn't happen in #16 this will be the screenwriter's last chance to wrap up step three of the Hero's Character Growth Arc as he OVERCOMES his inner struggle and finally learns to live honestly and openly, without camouflage or emotional armor.

So in HGS #17 you can usually expect to find:

*a.) Final preparations completed for the act climax showdown with the Adversary or Adversary Agents;*

*b.) The formidable strength of the Adversary demonstrated again, but this time in the most personal terms possible for the Hero;*

*c.) The ticking clock approaching zero hour, or the high-stakes threat drawing near;*

*d.) The Hero's full strength and courage on display as she demonstrates through action just why she is exceptional — often through the character growth step of OVERCOMING interior conflict (if not in #16).*

EXAMPLE: HGS #17 of *As Good As It Gets*.

Catching up: In sequence #15 Melvin Udall was asked by Simon's art agent Frank to drive Simon to his parents' hometown so Simon could ask them for money. Melvin saw a great opportunity in this trip to pursue Carol, and he asked her to come along.

HGS #16 involves the drive to Simon's parents' seaside hometown as Carol bonds with Simon, not Melvin.

Then…

**Hero Goal #17:** *Melvin Udall wants to go on a dinner date with waitress Carol.*

In their adjoining rooms at a hotel, Carol speaks on the phone with her son Spencer, worried that he sounds like he is having another allergy attack. But in truth Spencer just kicked a big game-winning goal for his soccer team! Carol is thrilled.

She feels like celebrating and asks Simon and Melvin to take her out for dinner and dancing. (See? *Everything* must be motivated, even Carol's reason for going to dinner with Melvin.)

Simon's tired, won't go. That means Carol is stuck with Melvin. Melvin's delighted at the prospect. He'll just hop in for a quick shower.

The shower takes an hour.

Eventually, as Melvin and Carol approach a quaint pier restaurant they pass many happy people. Carol smiles, tries to look forward to the evening even though it's with Melvin. Melvin nervously asks everyone if the restaurant has hard shell crabs. He wants to be certain it's the perfect place. The perfect date.

Inside, the reservations host offers to lend the Hero a restaurant-owned sport coat and tie. There's a dress code.

Melvin stares in horror at the jacket and its billions of germs. The date with Carol looks to be falling apart before it begins.

Melvin tells Carol to wait, he'll be right back. He tears off to find an open men's store.

Spots one. Saved! Throws open the door to the shop, and stops cold. The entry linoleum presents a pattern of crisscrossing lines. Melvin just can't step on a line. So he points from the doorway — *that* jacket, *that* tie.

Melvin speeds back to the restaurant.

Soft romantic music plays as people dance. The reservation host points out that Carol is waiting for Melvin over at the bar.

Should he get her for the gentleman?

Now spotting Carol talking with some good looking guy at the bar, Melvin gives a revealing answer.

"No, that's all right," he says, "I'll just watch."

Melvin moves slowly into the room, glowing with one of the most remarkable expressions of pure love ever captured on film. He's not even jealous that Carol is chatting with another man. Nor is he any longer nervous or in a hurry to get every last detail of the evening just right.

Melvin simply stops to appreciate this extraordinary woman who has stolen his heart. "A woman," he will soon say, "who if you make her laugh, you've got a life."

In this moment Melvin Udall finally OVERCOMES his inner struggle with emotional isolation. Busts free from his lifetime jail sentence of living narcissistically.

He's a changed man.

**Fresh News for HGS #17:** *Melvin is truly, unselfishly in love with a woman for the first time... and it feels great.*

So in HGS #17 of *As Good As It Gets*:

*a.) Final preparations for the Act Two climax face off with Love Interest-Adversary Carol are made;*

*b.) The formidable strength of the Love Interest-Adversary is demonstrated in a deeply personal way — she has given him the motivation to change;*

*c.) The stakes soar as he now must find out once and for all if he can win her.*

*d.) The Hero's strength and courage are demonstrated as he pursues the third step in character growth by OVERCOMING his OCD isolation and truly falls in love.*

EXAMPLE: HGS #17 of *A Beautiful Mind*.

Catching up: With Alicia's encouragement, John Nash has again stopped taking medications in order to clear his mental fog — only this time with a better grip on what is real. He still struggles with hallucinations, but now seeks his own self-control solution.

Then...

**Hero Goal #17:** *The Hero wants to end his isolation and fit in once more at Princeton.*

John returns to the hallowed halls of Princeton.

Martin Hansen, John's bitter academic rival back when they were students, now is Chair of the Math Department. John enters Martin's office and humbles himself, says "You won."

Martin replies, "We were wrong, John. Nobody wins."

Martin Hansen serves this story as a Gate Guardian character. In the first act Martin refused the Hero entrance into the elite club of recognized Princeton geniuses. Now he becomes John's ally.

John is shocked at Martin's kindness. And his stress calls up the hallucination of roommate Charles, who demands that John declare his greatness to Martin. John shoos Charles away.

The Hero asks Martin if he could just hang around on campus. No office needed, the library will do. Martin agrees.

Walking back across the quad, John starts raging in furious argument with Agent Parcher. Students gape at him. Martin runs up and tries to calm him, but John stumbles off, burning with humiliation over his insane display.

He tells Alicia how awful it was, thinks he should return to the mental hospital.

Alicia takes his hand and says — try again tomorrow.

As time passes, John becomes the resident eccentric on campus. But he keeps going back, keeps trying.

Then one day on his way to audit a math course, John stops. His hallucinations still walk beside him everywhere he goes. So John turns to speak to Marcee, the child who never gets old.

He lovingly tells Marcee goodbye. He will not speak to her again. Nor to Charles, or Agent Parcher. From this moment forward, whatever they say, however they hound him, John will ignore them. He kisses the child farewell on the forehead.

Then John walks to a doorway and requests permission to audit the course. The professor is honored to have him.

Humbled, willing to learn from others at last, John enters the room.

**Fresh News for HGS #17:** *The Hero says goodbye to his hallucinations and starts real life over, as a student.*

So in HGS #17 of *A Beautiful Mind*:

*a.) Final preparations for John Nash's Act Two climax showdown with Agent Parcher are completed as the Hero fully reenters the real world;*

*b.) The strength of the Adversary is demonstrated in a deeply personal way as John screams at Parcher on campus and so reveals his insanity to everyone;*

*c.) A high-stakes threat draws near as the Hero reenters the world with his Adversary Parcher ever at his side, waiting to reclaim him;*

*d.) The Hero demonstrates why he is exceptional by refusing to ever acknowledge his hallucinations again, and so OVERCOMES his inner conflict between head and heart.*

## HERO GOAL SEQUENCE® EIGHTEEN

Now you've arrived at the Act Two climax, an important sequence of high conflict. And any way you build it, this sequence *MUST* contain Stunning Surprise #2.

Whether the audience realizes it consciously or not, getting hit by Stunning Surprise #2 tells them Act Two is over and that the story will now jump up to the final level of conflict resolution in Act Three.

So in HGS #18 you often find:

*a.) Usually a longer than average sequence — sometimes as much as ten minutes or more;*

*b.) An Act Two climax that hits the peak of conflict and action — but the central question is NOT fully resolved;*

*c.) The Hero demonstrates her new, evolved self;*

*d.) The Hero believes she has conquered inner conflict;*

*e.) Stunning Surprise #2 provides the biggest reversal in the story for the Hero — usually to the negative.*

In many romantic comedies it is here at Stunning Surprise #2 that the central pretense or fraud in the story gets revealed and the pain of betrayal physically separates the lovers, apparently for good.

EXAMPLE: HGS #18 of *Mr. & Mrs. Smith.*

**Hero Goal #18:** *Now hunted by an army of killers, Jane and John Smith decide to get themselves a bargaining chip — grab something more important to their pursuers than the Smiths are themselves.*

Catching up: John and Jane know the government still holds their target Benjamin Danz in captivity deep under the Federal Courthouse. Danz was the mark the Smiths were hired separately to bump off back in the first act, but Danz got away because they tripped over each other.

Getting to him now looks like mission impossible. But Jane and John love a challenge.

A climatic sense of do-or-die builds around their two-person operation as they prepare to break in and grab Danz.

Still working on their relationship issues, the Smiths drive to the courthouse with all the latest high-tech military equipment. John asks Jane the how-many-partners question. Boasts that for him it's in the high fifties — low sixties.

Jane fires back "three hundred and twelve." That shuts her husband up.

They've been trying to find common ground but lately are having doubts again. If the mission to grab Danz fails, they'll split up to escape separately.

As John enters the courthouse through a sewer, Jane feeds him information from the van. Bickering continues.

Explosions. Bullets. John nabs Danz.

Later, interrogating Danz in a motel room, John favors the psychological approach. Jane just picks up a telephone and smashes the guy in the face — and he talks.

They learn Danz was, from the beginning, bait. Both Smiths were ordered to kill Danz at the same time on purpose. It was thought they would kill each other and eliminate the security breach of two assassins married to one another.

Then Jane asks, "*Was* bait, or *are* bait?" Holy cow. John discovers an electronic locating device hidden in Danz's belt buckle.

Attack helicopters swoop in with troops coming to kill the Smiths.

**Fresh News for #18 and STUNNING SURPRISE #2:** *Danz was bait and now Jane and John have been tricked into revealing their location.*

So in HGS #18 of *Mr. & Mrs. Smith:*

*a.) We see a longer than average Goal Sequence;*

*b.) The Act Two climax hits a peak for conflict and action — but then the central question of life or death for the Smith's is NOT fully resolved;*

*c.) The co-Heroes display their character-evolved selves as they rebuild their relationship from scratch;*

*d.) The Heroes believe they have conquered their old lying relationship and both now speak truthfully to each other.*

*e.) Stunning Surprise #2 provides the biggest reversal in the story: suddenly they're surrounded and it appears that all hope is lost.*

EXAMPLE: HGS #18 of *Scarface.*

**Hero Goal #18:** *Tony Montana must help carry out a political hit ordered by Bolivian drug lord Sosa.*

HGS #18 plays for a whopping thirteen minutes in *Scarface* and the first scene in a posh restaurant runs nearly seven minutes.

Tony gets drunk at dinner. Against his wishes he has been ordered to help the Bolivian drug lord's hit man kill a reform politician who has been naming names on TV.

Tony insists he never before killed anybody who didn't have it coming. But this hit doesn't qualify.

Tony asks Elvie and Manny, "Is this what it's all about? Eating, drinking... you got a bag for a belly... with a liver... got spots on it."

He recognizes that his life remains meaningless, but he's

blind to the reason why. Elvie announces that she's leaving Tony, and walks out.

This tragic Anti-Hero will achieve no character growth, so no Love Interest will be waiting to reward him.

Outside a New York hotel Tony waits while Sosa's hitman Alberto plants a bomb under the politician's car. But when the victim gets into his vehicle, unexpectedly his wife and two little girls join him.

Tony is wheelman as he and the hitman follow the mark's car. Alberto clutches a detonator, shouts for Tony to get closer.

Tony does not like killing a family. He gets so worked up that the Hero impulsively pulls a gun and splatters Alberto's brains to stop him from triggering the bomb.

**Fresh News for HGS #18 and STUNNING SURPRISE #2:** *Tony's one impulsive act of good conscience — saving two children by killing Alberto — ironically seals his own fate with Adversary Sosa.*

So in HGS #18 of *Scarface*:

*a.) We see a particularly long Goal Sequence;*

*b.) The Act Two climax hits a peak for conflict, action, and intensity — but the central question is NOT fully resolved;*

*c.) This Anti-Hero demonstrates once more why he CANNOT evolve — he's incapable of loving anyone. . .*

*d.) . . .so the doomed Hero can't OVERCOME inner conflict because he doesn't even recognize that change is necessary (i.e., this movie is a tragedy);*

*e.) Stunning Surprise #2 takes place and provides the strongest reversal of the story — in a split second Tony goes from king of his world to hunted animal.*

These two examples are not romantic comedies and therefore do not offer the pretense disclosure element of HGS #18 present in romance genres. Movies that do have this element would include *Maid in Manhattan*, where in HGS #18 it's revealed to Senator Marshall, the Love Interest, that Hero Marisa Ventura is not the wealthy society maven he believes her to be, but just a lowly hotel maid; and in *My Best Friend's Wedding* it's in HGS #18 that Hero Julianne Potter finally confesses to best friend Michael that she hasn't come to wish him and his bride well, but to split them up so she can marry Michael herself.

So for all romance-driven stories, add a step:

*f.) A pretense is revealed that then separates the lovers and tests the relationship.*

## SUMMING UP

- In Hero Goal Sequence₍ᵣ₎ #13 we often see that:

  a.) The Hero presses onward with renewed courage;

  b.) A new complication crops up;

  c.) The Hero again raises his battered inner emotional SHIELD of self-defense and isolation;

  d.) Additional proof turns up that conflict between Hero and Adversary has become very personal.

- In Hero Goal Sequence₍ᵣ₎ #14 we often find that:

  a.) The pace slows a bit and offers the Hero a contemplative moment;

  b.) A Love Interest or Sidekick or even the Hero himself brings up inner conflict issues the Hero would rather not deal with right now;

  c.) A Big New Idea arrives to challenge the Hero;

  d.) The Big New Idea paves the way for a second Action Burst coming in HGS #15.

- In Hero Goal Sequence₍ᵣ₎ #15 we often find:

  a.) An Action Burst where action or energy or dramatic confrontation kicks things upward;

  b.) The Hero experiences a False Victory, or at least believes she has fought the Adversary to a draw, so her ultimate goal does not seem so impossible anymore;

    c.) A fleeting sense of security for the Hero arrives, soon to be dashed;

    d.) A strong romance relationship can motivate the Hero through the Action Burst.

- In Hero Goal Sequence® #16, often you find that:
  a.) The dramatic energy coming out of HGS #15 continues to rise, not as more physical action but as a growing intensity of conflict;

  b.) The Hero feels greater confidence in his abilities and understanding and rededicates himself to the ultimate physical goal;

  c.) The Hero discovers some new point of view toward the central story conflict;

  d.) The third step in character growth can take place here (or in HGS #17), OVERCOMING the Hero's inner conflict.

- In Hero Goal Sequence® #17 you can usually expect to find that:
  a.) Final preparations are completed for the act climax showdown with the Adversary or Adversary Agents;

  b.) The strength of the Adversary is demonstrated again in the most personal terms for the Hero;

  c.) The ticking clock approaches zero hour, or the high stakes threat draws near;

  d.) The Hero's strength of courage is on display as she demonstrates why she is exceptional — often through the third step in character growth, OVERCOMING her interior conflict (if not in HGS #16).

- In Hero Goal Sequence® #18 you often find:
  a.) A longer than average sequence — sometimes as much as ten minutes or more;

b.) An Act Two climax that hits the peak of conflict and action — but does NOT fully resolve the central story question;

c.) The Hero demonstrates his newly evolved self;

d.) The Hero believes he has conquered inner conflict;

e.) Stunning Surprise #2, which provides the biggest reversal for the Hero in the entire story — usually to the negative.

f.) In Romantic Comedies it's often at Stunning Surprise #2 that the central pretense or fraud in the romance gets revealed, and the pain of betrayal tears the lovers apart, apparently for good.

**EXERCISE:**

Get a DVD of *Walk the Line.* View the whole movie.

Johnny Cash (Joaquin Phoenix) is the lone Hero. In plotline #1 he pursues Adversary dad's approval. In plotline #2, his Love Interest-Adversary is June Carter (Reese Witherspoon).

NOW: Make notes on Hero Goal Sequences® in the second half of Act Two of *Walk the Line,* HGS 13-18. What's the HERO'S physical GOAL in each sequence, and then the FRESH NEWS that creates the next goal? Hints below.

• TO CATCH UP ON THE STORY OF *Walk the Line*: In HGS #11 Johnny Cash tries for a crude on-stage kiss from June — but she rejects him.

In HGS #12... Johnny's HERO GOAL becomes — *learn to live without June, while facing dad's disapproval.* He gets ever more stoned, and June leaves the tour. She marries a race car driver. John goes off the deep end, but becomes a superstar. His wife criticizes John, just like dad does. Then... John runs into June and offers her a job.

FRESH NEWS — *June accepts the job of performing again with Johnny.*

HGS #12 running time, 8 min. 35 sec.
Total time to end of Midpoint, 70 min. 17 sec.

## SO, NOW WHAT ARE HERO GOAL SEQUENCES® 13-18?

- I'll give you sequence thirteen... In HGS #13: HERO GOAL is — *Pursue June more gently this time while they perform as a team.* FRESH NEWS — *They finally make love.* Time: 6 min. 36 sec.

- In HGS #14: HERO GOAL becomes — *Enjoy their affair.* What does Johnny next discover as his FRESH NEWS? (When June breaks it off again and John gets stoned again — which is NOT new — what happens to the tour that hasn't happened before?) This runs 6 min. 51 sec.

- Then in HGS #15, what's the Hero's new HERO GOAL? (It has to do with digging a deep hole.) What FRESH NEWS changes things for the Hero? (Has to do with a chilly place.) Sequence runs 3 min. 50 sec.

- For HGS #16, what's the HERO GOAL? (It has to do with avoiding cameras.) And what's FRESH NEWS? (Something involving kids in an automobile.) This runs 5 min. 49 sec.

- What's the HGS #17, HERO GOAL? And FRESH NEWS? (Has to do with hammers and nails.) Runs 5 min. 45 sec.

- What's the HERO GOAL in HGS #18? (It has to do with a bird.) FRESH NEWS in this sequence contains STUNNING SURPRISE TWO... so what is it? (Who saves a life and who proves to be a caring friend?) Sequence #18 running time is 8 min. 28 sec.

You'll find the answers at the end of Chapter Thirteen.

## ANSWERS FOR CH. 11,
## HGS 7-12 OF *THE BOURNE IDENTITY*:

### HGS #7:

HERO GOAL — *Hero wants to trust someone and form a plan.*
FRESH NEWS — *In Paris, Marie expresses romantic interest in Bourne.*
Time: 7 min. 20 sec.

### HGS #8:

HERO GOAL — *Check out the Hero's Paris apartment for identity clues.*
FRESH NEWS — *On the phone Bourne learns someone wants him dead, and that means there's possible danger in this apartment.*
Time: 5 min. 56 sec.

### HGS #9:

HERO GOAL — *Defend against an attack.*
FRESH NEWS — *The attacking assassin is dead, but he was carrying pictures of Bourne and Marie, which means powerful people are after them both.*
Time: 4 min. 3 sec.

### HGS #10:

HERO GOAL — *Get Marie out of there before the cops turn up.*
FRESH NEWS — *Hero gives Marie one last chance to get away from him, but she buckles her seatbelt, demonstrating she's in for the whole adventure.*
Time: 5 min. 59 sec.

### HGS #11:

HERO GOAL — *Escape from the entire Paris police force.*
FRESH NEWS — *In a car chase they lose the police, but then must abandon Marie's automobile.*
(Plus two cutaways — Wombosi visits the morgue; Conklin calls in the second hit man.)
Time: 6 min. 29 sec.

**HGS #12:**
HERO GOAL — *Get the "dead" John Kane's hotel phone bill for clues.*
FRESH NEWS — *Marie bags the phone bill for Bourne all by herself, and so proves that she's a valuable partner.*
(The sequence then ends with a cutaway to CIA headquarters that establishes the Ticking Clock at 24 hours.)
Time: 8 min. 26 sec.

*chapter thirteen*

# ACT THREE RESOLUTION: SEQUENCES 19~23

———— ⟨xɔ⟩ ————

About ninety pages ago you made a promise to your audience.

Right up front you hooked them with an engaging story opening and gained their trust. You made a deal that you'd lead them to an emotionally fulfilling resolution if they would just relax, enjoy the ride, and keep the faith.

Now it's time to reward those good people for their loyalty.

Eighteen Goal Sequences have carried your movie this far. Now you must create those final two to five Hero Goal Sequences® that will mesmerize the audience right up to the final fadeout.

The key principles for screen story resolution in Act Three are these:

1. *The Hero must bring about the finale.*

When embroiled in any final confrontation with the Adversary a Hero may receive assistance from characters who have traveled the road with him. Sidekicks or other allies can deflect the occasional spear lobbed straight at the Hero's heart by a Minion or Adversary Agent. But once the ultimate face-to-face contest of wills between the Hero and Adversary begins, if this spear is thrown by the Adversary himself — whatever metaphorical form the "spear" may take — no one else should interfere any more with their direct combat.

The Hero alone must settle the central dramatic question of the story.

In *Avatar*, at the final showdown Hero Jake Sully fights against his Adversary Colonel Quaritch to the point where the Adversary is basically beaten and no longer a threat to Pandora. The invaders' aircraft are destroyed. The Na'vi have won. But Quaritch, in his last moments of life, still remains a personal mortal threat to the wounded Hero.

Suddenly the Love Interest character Neytiri appears and formally dispatches Quaritch with her arrow. This is a thematic way of saying that love has saved the Hero's life. It echoes the idea that the Love Interest is the Hero's reward for character growth. *But all other story resolution heavy lifting has already been completed by the Hero before Neytiri finishes off the already dying Adversary.* The rule remains: Only the Hero must bring about the final resolution of the central dramatic question.

This does NOT mean the Hero must always emerge from the final battle alive. Some Heroes die so that a greater good can survive.

2. *The Hero's plan for victory, which he pursued throughout the second act, has been destroyed or rendered inoperable by Stunning Surprise #2. So now in Act Three he must improvise his way to the resolution.*

During films that include character growth for the Hero, it's in Act Three he arrives at full emotional maturity. The Hero can now demonstrate his self-actualization with new *improvisational* abilities. He gives proof of his growth by confronting the Adversary with insight and inner resources the Hero did not possess back in Act One.

3. *The Obligatory Scene must occur.*

The Act Three final confrontation can take different forms: two characters struggling through an impassioned conversation to resolve a relationship, or hundreds of fighter pilots battling space aliens for the fate of planet Earth. Both can work. But whatever the showdown, the conflict between Hero and Adversary must be resolved once and for all.

4. *Every key subplot must reach a completion.*

Any story thread big enough to be called a subplot needs an ending with emotional finality to it. Don't leave any open story questions, or the fate of any significant character dangling in the air.

5. *The Denouement must follow the Obligatory Scene.*

The Denouement wrap-up must always be found as the very last Hero Goal Sequence₀ of your picture. Before the final fadeout an audience wants to see justice — or at least equilibrium — return to the Hero's ordinary world.

And keep it simple.

## HERO GOAL SEQUENCES₀ 19 – 23

In Act Three you can use between two and five Goal Sequences, so the specific dramatic content of each becomes a bit more moveable.

For example, it's true that every final act must contain a Denouement and it has to appear as the last Goal Sequence of your movie. But that wrap-up segment can unfold in Goal Sequence 20, 21, 22, or 23 depending on which one turns out to be the end of your story.

So for this chapter, rather than explaining the content of each Goal Sequence and then giving examples as we have done so far, we will *start* with some examples of movies that contain only two Goal Sequences in their third acts, *then* we will take a look at what these film stories share in common.

We'll do the same for groups of movies with three, four, and five Goal Sequences in Act Three.

## ACT THREE USING
## TWO HERO GOAL SEQUENCES₀

Action extravaganzas like *The Matrix*, *Spider-Man*, and *The Taking of Pelham 123* frequently wrap up their third acts with only two Goal Sequences.

EXAMPLE: In *The Matrix*, the Act Two climax springs upon the Hero the greatest possible dramatic reversal: he dies.

Backing up a bit to recap:

**Hero Goal #17:** *Neo must rescue his Mentor, Morpheus, from the clutches of Agent Smith.*

In accomplishing this impossible task Neo proves he is The One. Only someone so special could pull off this miracle feat.

**Fresh News for HGS #17:** *The Hero succeeds and Morpheus is rescued.*

Then Neo's goal immediately becomes:

**Hero Goal #18:** *Get Morpheus, Trinity, and himself safely back aboard the rebel ship Nebuchadnezzar.*

Through the portal of a telephone booth in a grubby subway station Neo sends Morpheus and Trinity back to the ship — but then Neo is trapped down in the subway by Agent Smith and must fight his unbeatable Adversary alone.

Although Neo and Agent Smith go at each other ferociously, this is NOT the Obligatory Scene of the story. This subway battle ends in a draw, without any final resolution between them, and Neo makes a run for it.

With Hero Goal Sequence® #18 still in motion (since the goal of #18 — get back to the Nebuchadnezzar — has not yet ended or been fully resolved for Neo) a chase scene plays out as Neo scrambles to reach another Matrix telephone exit portal inside a rundown tenement building. He hears a phone ringing behind one apartment door and thinks it's Tank calling him home. Neo opens the door... and finds Agent Smith standing there aiming a nasty looking gun at him.

**Fresh News for HGS #18 and STUNNING SURPRISE #2:** *The Adversary blasts ten shots into Neo's chest and the Hero slides down a bloodied wall, dead.*

Being deceased can certainly be considered a Hero's darkest hour.

And the Hero Goal for HGS #18 is now resolved — the Hero can't get safely back to the Nebuchadnezzar if he's dead.

We've been thrilled by more or less non-stop action in this movie for about half an hour. The Nebuchadnezzar is now under attack by evil spider-like robots ripping off its hull, the ticking clock has reached zero hour, and the Hero has kicked the bucket.

It's time to resolve everything quickly and get out.

SO BEGINS ACT THREE.

- **Hero Goal Sequence**₍ₐ₎ **#19 of** *The Matrix*

**Hero Goal #19, the Obligatory Scene:** *Neo must rise from the dead and finish off his evil Adversary, Agent Smith.*

Back in the rebel hovercraft Trinity whispers to Neo's flat-lining corpse, "You can't be dead. Because I love you..." She kisses him. "Now get up!"

Trinity isn't battling the Adversary directly herself. She's simply standing ringside, urging the Hero to get up off the mat and keep slugging.

Back in the tenement hall Neo revives and rises from the blood-covered floor as a transformed, all powerful supernatural being, a death and resurrection moment with clear Biblical overtones.

Neo now faces down the Adversary in an Obligatory Scene that settles the central issue of the plot: the Hero stops bullets in mid-air simply by lifting his hand, then his glowing spirit jumps inside Agent Smith, who explodes in a burst of symbolic white light. The Hero overcomes the Adversary.

Once Neo gets safely back aboard the ship, Morpheus throws the power-shield switch to rescue the Nebuchadnezzar.

**Fresh News for HGS #19:** *Agent Smith has been defeated and the rebels aboard the hovercraft are now safe.*

- **Hero Goal Sequence**₍ₐ₎ **#20 of** *The Matrix*

**Hero Goal #20, Denouement:** *Neo, proven to be The One, passes on to all mankind a message of hope and rebirth.*

On a telephone call that echoes throughout the Matrix, the Hero sends his message: "I didn't come here to tell you how this is going to end. I came to tell you how it's going to begin." Neo offers the promise of a world where anything is possible. "Where we go from there is a choice I leave up to you."

The end.

*The Matrix*, with a very short third act, uses a fairly typical two Goal Sequence wrap-up for action movies: Obligatory Scene, Denouement and FADEOUT.

In general, a rising frantic pace in action movies does not allow for calm, extended resolutions. The writer builds to an action peak by the end of Act Two, moves on to dazzle with inventive final showdown fisticuffs in Act Three, then wraps it up and gets out. So only two Goal Sequences are needed.

But what about other genres that don't have any frantic action and also end the third act in a mere two Goal Sequences? *Rain Man* and *Erin Brockovich* — stories far outside the action genre — also complete Act Three using only two HGS. Why?

Let's investigate what these and some other small films that end with only two final act Goal Sequences might have structurally in common.

Take a close look at this list of movies. Consider what dramatic action they might all share at Stunning Surprise #2:

*A Beautiful Mind*

*E.T.: The Extra-Terrestrial*

*Rain Man*

*Erin Brockovich*

*The Truman Show*

Spot it?

Don't worry, you'll be able to see such patterns in time, as your screenwriter story structure sensibility becomes second nature.

In every one of these pictures Stunning Surprise #2 provides the Hero with a reversal to the POSITIVE, not to the negative.

None of these movies presents the Hero with his darkest hour as the great majority of films do at the end of the second act. They all give the Hero a huge boost toward victory at the arrival of Stunning Surprise #2.

If the Hero is already winning by the end of Act Two, Act Three better be short.

Once the Hero finds herself in a stronger position than the Adversary, major conflict dissipates quickly. It's time to resolve it all, claim victory, and fadeout. Anything else will feel protracted and anticlimactic.

EXAMPLE: In **HGS #18** of *A Beautiful Mind*, schizophrenic John Nash struggles mightily to master his delusions and reconnect with the real world of students at Princeton. He tutors study groups, then advances to teach his own classroom courses.

The Hero's tormenting Adversary, the imaginary Agent Parcher, has not left him. John simply exerts constant willpower to ignore Parcher's presence, as the Adversary lurks in the background taunting the Hero endlessly.

One day after class a man approaches John in the college hallway and introduces himself as Mr. King.

**Fresh News for HGS #18 and STUNNING SURPRISE #2**: *Mr. King informs John Nash that he is being considered for the Nobel Prize.*

Act Two of *A Beautiful Mind* ends with this major positive surprise.

SO BEGINS ACT THREE.
- **Hero Goal Sequence® #19** for *A Beautiful Mind*

**Hero Goal #19, the Obligatory Scene:** *John wants to find out why he's only being considered and not simply awarded this Nobel Prize, which is the normal procedure.*

Walking with Mr. King across campus, John figures out that King has come to discover if John Nash will be sane enough and stable enough to receive this great honor without publicly embarrassing the Nobel committee. John explains honestly that he still has hallucinations but simply chooses to ignore them.

And yes, sometimes his hallucinations get worse in stressful situations.

Mr. King offers to take John into the Princeton faculty dining room for tea.

John nervously resists and says he doesn't go in there, he just eats his sandwich alone outside on a bench. But Mr. King practically pulls John into the dining room.

We understand, as does John, that tea here in this august faculty sanctuary offers the Hero his final test.

This is his climactic showdown with madness.

Who will exert ultimate control over the life of John Nash — John himself, or Agent Parcher? Will the stress of this unexpected challenge call forth the Adversary from John's mind to destroy his one chance at world recognition? The very recognition that has been this Hero's goal from the beginning of the movie?

In the faculty dining room, as John speaks softly with Mr. King about his public limitations, other faculty members rise one at a time, step over to John's table and lay before him their fountain pens — an age-old Princeton ritual honoring a professor who attains the greatest achievement of his career.

Shocked, honored, humbled, John expresses gratitude... and remains in full control of himself.

**Fresh News for HGS #19:** *By keeping Agent Parcher at bay throughout this most unusual and touching Obligatory Scene, the Hero defeats his Adversary once and for all.*

- **Hero Goal Sequence**® **#20**

**Denouement:** *John collects his Nobel Prize and receives world recognition.*

At the Nobel ceremony this story offers a relationship wrap-up scene with John's Love Interest character.

In his acceptance speech John Nash uses his moment before the world to tell his wife Alicia, "You are all my reasons," thereby expressing his love and gratitude to her and also summarizing the theme of the film: The heart is always more important than the head.

After the ceremony John helps Alicia on with her wrap but he glances up to see Agent Parcher, Charles, and Marcee, still lurking, still waiting for John to slip back into madness and return to them.

It's a Denouement moment with Adversary Parcher.

John dismisses his fleeting delusion as nothing, and with an affectionate smile leads Alicia outside for a cab ride back to their hotel.

Victory. End of conflict.

Regardless of genre, when Stunning Surprise #2 turns out to be overwhelmingly good news, the story must wrap up quickly with only two more Goal Sequences.

It has been said by some authors on screenwriting that Act Three needs to be 25% of your movie, the same length as Act One. I, for one, disagree. Third acts can and should be a whole lot shorter than that.

## ACT THREE USING
## THREE HERO GOAL SEQUENCES®

When a movie contains three Goal Sequences in the third act it's usually because Stunning Surprise #2 proves so harshly negative that Goal Sequence #19 then requires the Hero to clear her head and rise again in preparation for the Obligatory Scene in HGS #20.

And when Stunning Surprise #2 turns out to be a strong negative, the Hero makes a last attempt to regress back behind her self-protective emotional shield once more. She tries to abandon character growth. But the Hero soon discovers she's truly a changed person and character growth, once achieved, remains permanent. It's impossible for the Hero to regress for long. The old defensive ways don't feel necessary anymore.

Goal Sequence #19 can also be used to wrap up smaller relationships or subplots and thereby remove some story baggage to lighten the load on the Denouement sequence at the conclusion.

EXAMPLE: At Stunning Surprise #2 of **HGS #18 in Mr. & Mrs. Smith**, the Smiths have been tricked into revealing their location. Scores of assassins outside their motel swoop in to blow them away.

SO BEGINS ACT THREE.

• **Hero Goal Sequence® #19 for** *Mr. & Mrs. Smith*

**The co-Heroes' mutual Goal for HGS #19:** *Jane and John want to escape from the motel with their lives.*

This sequence requires the Smiths to recover from the bad news of Stunning Surprise #2 — that they've been tricked into kidnapping Benjamin Danz in order to locate them.

John and Jane run for it, then hide under a street drain grating as an army of assassins scours the neighborhood. This gives the Smiths one last chance to discuss what they've really been fighting for — to save their marriage.

Jane backs away from character growth here. She's ready to pack it in and suggests they go their separate ways for the best chance at survival. Return to their solitary lives.

John responds, "All right, so it's a crappy marriage. I'm a mess, you're a disaster. We're both liars. But... I say we stay and fight."

**Fresh News for HGS #19:** *Jane discovers her shield of isolation doesn't work any more — so she agrees they should stand and fight the bad guys together to the end.*

• **Hero Goal Sequence® #20**

**Heroes' Goal #20, the Obligatory Scene:** *The Smiths want to make their last stand as a team and take on a horde of hit people.*

This movie is similar in structure to other films in the romantic-adventure genre like *Romancing the Stone* and *Bird On a Wire* that have two parallel storylines, the romance and the action story. Each thread contains its own Adversary character to be faced down.

In the main action storyline of *Mr. & Mrs. Smith* the "bait" character whom they capture, Benjamin Danz, serves as Adversary to both Heroes, representing the unseen forces behind Danz who want Jane and John dead.

Then a romance storyline running parallel to the action plot requires that John and Jane Smith each serve as the other's Love Interest-Adversary.

If there's only one Obligatory Scene in the story, as happens here, it means that both plotlines must be resolved within that one scene.

Benjamin Danz isn't physically present for the action plotline payoff and doesn't need to be. Danz is the personification of forces that have been unleashed on John and Jane and these forces must be fought to the death with or without the rather humorously pathetic Mr. Danz present.

The same thing happens in *The Rock, Air Force One, Déjà Vu,* and other action movies where the Adversary gets dispatched earlier in the story but the evil destruction unleashed by that Adversary must still be confronted in an Obligatory Scene.

In the extended climax of *Mr. & Mrs. Smith,* Jane and John kill every last paramilitary assassin. The scene becomes a ballet of bullets, with John and Jane moving together as an exquisite team, fluid, two bodies as one, each instinctively knowing where the other will move next.

This Obligatory Scene demonstrates visually that the Smith's marriage now works perfectly. The two have become one.

Expecting the worst at one point, Jane says, "There's nowhere I'd rather be than right here. With you."

Thus the Obligatory Scene for the romance plotline resolves itself. Jane and John have triumphed romantically: no more lies, very much in love, and married until death do them part.

As silence falls over the decimated department store, with no bad guys left to kill, the physical action-line part of the Obligatory Scene comes to an end, too.

**Fresh News for HGS #20:** *All the bad guys are dead and Jane and John have resolved their marital problems.*

Victory.

• **Hero Goal Sequence**® **#21**
**Denouement:** *In a marriage counselor's office John and Jane beam with contentment.*

They're affectionate, playful. "Ask us the sex question again," John says, grinning.

No more problems with intimacy here.

And this Act Three fadeout has been reached in three Hero Goal Sequences®.

## ACT THREE USING
## FOUR HERO GOAL SEQUENCES®

When movies use four Goal Sequences in Act Three it's usually because there are several strong subplots to be wrapped up before focusing on a grand finale Obligatory Scene, or because a new plot arena must be established late in the game to resolve the story successfully.

EXAMPLE: At the end of Act Two in **Hero Goal Sequence**® **#18 of** *Finding Nemo*, chaos breaks loose in a dentist's office.

Young Nemo pretends to be dead on a dentist's tray, trying to escape the clutches of the fish killer Adversary, little Darla. Hero clownfish Marlin and Sidekick Dory ride to the rescue inside the bill of pelican Nigel, who flies in through an open window for a desperate attempt to save Nemo.

**Fresh News for HGS #18 and STUNNING SURPRISE #2:** *Hero Marlin spots Nemo lying "dead" on the dentist's instrument tray.*

Dad suddenly believes he's arrived too late.

The dentist grabs pelican Nigel and pushes him out the window. "And stay out!"

The Hero's darkest hour, and then some.

Now the dentist drops the "dead" fish Nemo down the sink drain and Nemo falls through many pipes until he's swept into a water treatment plant. Looks like curtains for the brave little clownfish.

SO BEGINS ACT THREE.
- **Hero Goal Sequence**® **#19 of** *Finding Nemo*

**Hero Goal #19:** *Marlin wants to thank Dory, say goodbye and end his rescue mission.*

Pelican Nigel lets Marlin and Dory out of his bill and into the ocean near a lonely buoy. Nigel expresses sympathy. A real tough break, arriving too late. Nigel flies off.

Marlin expresses gratitude for all Dory's help, then tells her he's going home alone.

Dory pleads with him to stay. "When I look at you, I'm home," she says. "I don't want to lose that. I don't want to forget."

Marlin replies, "I'm sorry, Dory. I do."

The Hero turns and swims aimlessly off into a huge, cold, murky gray sea.

**Fresh News for HGS #19:** *The Hero swims away into hopelessness and defeat, inconsolable, lost.*

- **Hero Goal Sequence**® **#20**

A **subplot cutaway** starts this sequence: Nemo survives the water treatment plant and finds his way out into the open ocean. He meets Dory and asks her for help in finding his dad.

Dory has already forgotten about Marlin. "We can search together!" she offers cheerfully.

Then Dory spots the word "Sydney" stamped on a plate attached to the undersea water reclamation pipe. Seeing it, she remembers who Nemo is! (*Everything* must be motivated, even just remembering.)

With a burst of new hope, Dory finds out from a surly crab where Marlin went — to the fishing grounds.

Cut to the Hero.

**Hero Goal #20:** *Marlin wants to swim home alone and forget.*

Down-in-the-dumps Marlin gets overtaken by a school of tuna who jostle him, growl at him to move out of the way. Marlin really doesn't care anymore. About anything.

Nemo swims up joyfully. Marlin can't believe his eyes. A thrilling reunion.

But a fishing trawler's huge net scoops through the fishing grounds, catching up hundreds of tuna — and Dory. The net tightens, pulls its captives toward the fishermen's knives on the trawler deck above.

**Fresh News for HGS #20:** *Dory is trapped in a net and headed for certain death.*

- **Hero Goal Sequence® #21**

**Hero Goal #21, the Obligatory Scene:** *Marlin wants to protect Nemo, but also save Dory and the tuna.*

Nemo tells Marlin he knows what to do! The youngster's plan requires him to slip in through the net holes and join Dory inside the fishermen's trap.

The Hero yells NO! Marlin won't let his son endanger his life again, even though Nemo insists he can pull it off.

Suddenly Marlin recalls all the personal lessons he received on his long journey:

*You've got to let go.*

*Just keep swimming.*

*The little dudes can't learn unless they're set free.*

So Marlin demonstrates his character growth by expressing faith in Nemo and setting the youngster free to try his plan.

This undersea Obligatory Scene provides Marlin with the final arena in which to prove himself a changed fish.

Nemo wiggles inside the net and tells all the trapped fish to swim down together. Marlin hollers the same instructions from outside the net.

As the net is hauled ominously toward the trawler, at the last second the tuna all swim downward together. The trawler's jib arm snaps, dropping the net — and all the fish are freed.

The Hero's Adversary, cruel little Darla, was last seen back in the dentist's office at the end of Act Two with water gushing from the spit sink all over her face as she wailed. A symbolic comeuppance.

And since Darla isn't a fish, she can't participate in this Obligatory Scene underwater. But she caused Hero Marlin and his son Nemo to end up in this fine pickle, so, as in *Mr. & Mrs. Smith* and other action films, the Hero must now deal with a final challenge set in motion by the Adversary without the actual Adversary being present.

**Fresh News for HGS #21:** *Dory and the tuna are saved and Nemo declares his love for the Hero.*

• **Hero Goal Sequence® #22**
**Denouement: Marlin and Nemo, now back home, pursue a full and rewarding life together.**

The Hero's Ordinary World of the reef community has grown even more nurturing for its young. Balance has returned. Our clownfish Hero now tells knee-slapper jokes to his friends, another symbol of his character growth.

Dory returns from a Fish Eaters Anonymous meeting with shark friend Bruce and all is well for her, too. Everyone now lives together in harmony.

*Finding Nemo* reaches an Act Three fadeout with all subplot and character threads wrapped up in four Hero Goal Sequences®.

The added Goal Sequence is necessary here because a logical path must be engineered to reunite father and son. And a brand new climatic event in the fishing grounds must be set up to provide an arena for the Obligatory Scene.

## ACT THREE USING
## FIVE HERO GOAL SEQUENCES®

Some wonderful films have been written using five Goal Sequences in Act Three: *As Good As It Gets, Scarface, Shrek.*

Just remember that when a screenwriter uses five Hero Goal Sequences® in the culminating act he's pushing the outer limits of audience patience. Any such elongated resolution must crackle with inventive conflict and unexpected payoffs — and usually a SHORT Denouement.

EXAMPLE: Act Two of *Scarface* ends with **Fresh News for HGS #18 and STUNNING SURPRISE #2:** *Tony Montana impulsively kills Sosa's right hand hitman to save two kids.*

Tony's only moral impulse sets in motion his own downfall.

SO BEGINS ACT THREE.

• **Hero Goal Sequence**® **#19**

**Hero Goal #19:** *Tony must square things with Sosa and kick his own sloppy crime organization back into shape.*

Tony calls home and he finds out Manny has gone missing, Tony's sister Gina has vanished, and drug lord Sosa is demanding to speak with Tony right away.

The Hero returns to his mansion, snorts cocaine until he's covered in the stuff. A Hero submerged in self-destruction.

Sosa's on the phone and Tony tries to make light of what happened in N.Y., saying he'll take care of it soon.

**Fresh News for HGS #19:** *Sosa's furious and tells Tony there will be no next time. The Adversary declares war.*

Now we know there's horrific violence to come. But first, Tony has more immediate problems.

• **Hero Goal Sequence**® **#20**

**Hero Goal #20:** *Tony wants to find his sister, Gina.*

Tony visits his mother, who's beside herself with worry about Gina. She rails at Tony. "Why do you have to destroy everything that comes your way?"

Tony drives to a mansion address mom gave him. Manny answers the door. Inside, at the top of the stairs Gina appears, smiling, wearing only a short boudoir silk robe.

Fury floods Tony's eyes. That same jealous possessive rage he showed at the Babylon Club.

Tony pulls his gun and kills Manny. Gina, hysterical, tells Tony she and Manny just got married the day before. They wanted to surprise Tony.

**Fresh News for HGS #20:** *Tony learns too late that Manny and Gina just got married.*

- Hero Goal Sequence® #21
Hero Goal #21: *The Hero must prepare for war.*

Confusion and remorse overwhelm Tony. His henchmen convince the dazed gangster to get out of there. They stuff Gina in the car and roar off.

Tony takes his sister back to his mansion like she was one more possession to keep on a shelf. Unknown to the Hero, we see Sosa's men already sneaking into Tony's compound.

House guards go on high alert and dramatic tension builds. Slaughter in the wind.

Tony drowns his remorse in cocaine. "Why did I do that to Manny?" He has attained no self-knowledge, no growth.

Gina comes to Tony's office, silk robe open, offering herself to him. "You won't let any other man touch me. Isn't this what you want?" Then Gina reveals she carries a gun. She starts shooting at Tony, laughing at his fear.

One of Sosa's assassins jumps into the open balcony door and sprays Gina with bullets. Tony kills the goon but his sister is dead. Tony falls to his knees beside her body, sinking into a bottomless remorse.

He tells Gina's corpse, "I love you. I love Manny and I love you, too." No, he never did.

This tragic Hero was offered a chance for real love by only two people — Manny and Gina. He has now killed them both.

**Fresh News for HGS #21:** *Tony's sister is dead and the Adversary's final assault on the Hero's mansion has begun.*

- Hero Goal Sequence® #22
**Hero Goal #22, and the Obligatory Scene:** *Fight to the death with Sosa's assassins.*

Blood-letting and butchery commence. Scores of men are blasted apart.

In classic tragic Hero style, Tony Montana goes down bravely, defiantly, and pointlessly.

**Fresh News for HGS #22:** *the Hero dies.*

- Hero Goal Sequence® #23

A short Denouement: *In one long panning shot the carnage of Tony Montana's wasted life is surveyed and his ironic neon foyer sculpture echoes Tony's mistaken concept as it reads "The World Is Yours."*

The wages of sin — and lovelessness — are death.

Fadeout.

Act Three of *Scarface* concludes in five Hero Goal Sequences®.

## SUMMING UP

- The dramatic requirements for Act Three are:
  1. The Hero must bring about the finale herself;
  2. The Hero's plan for victory which she pursued throughout the second act has been destroyed or rendered inoperable by Stunning Surprise #2, so in Act Three she must IMPROVISE her way to the resolution;
  3. The Obligatory Scene must occur;
  4. Every key subplot must be resolved;
  5. A Denouement wrap-up must conclude the screenplay.

- Act Three contains from two to five Hero Goal Sequences®, the most common number being three.

- In a third act the specific dramatic content of each numbered Goal Sequence becomes portable — so a required element like the Denouement can appear in whichever sequence is last, be it #20, #21, #22, or #23.

- When Act Three consists of only TWO GOAL SEQUENCES:
  1. HGS #19 must include the Obligatory Scene, and HGS #20 must include the Denouement;
  2. The story is most likely an action movie, or one where Stunning Surprise #2 is a reversal to the positive for the Hero.

- When Act Three consists of THREE GOAL SEQUENCES it is usually because:
    1. Stunning Surprise #2 is so harshly negative that Goal Sequence #19 is needed for the Hero to clear his head and rise again before beginning the Obligatory Scene in HGS #20;
    2. The Hero tries in HGS #19 to regress back behind his self-protective emotional SHIELD once more, only to find it is no longer effective and that he is, in fact, now fully prepared for the final showdown to begin in HGS #20;
    3. The extra sequence in HGS #19 is needed to wrap up some subplots and/or relationships before moving on to the Obligatory Scene in HGS #20.

- When Act Three contains FOUR GOAL SEQUENCES it most likely means:
    1. Several strong subplots must be wrapped up before the Obligatory Scene;
    2. Entirely new location elements or circumstances must be established to resolve the story.

- Using FIVE HERO GOAL SEQUENCES® in Act Three is rare because it pushes the limits of audience patience — so any such elongated resolution must crackle with inventive conflict and unexpected payoffs.

**EXERCISE:**

Get a copy of *The Devil Wears Prada*. View the movie.

The lone Hero is Andrea Sachs (Anne Hathaway). The Adversary is Miranda Priestly (Meryl Streep). Nate (Adrian Grenier) is the Love Interest, and Nigel (Stanley Tucci), the Mentor.

NOW:

Make notes describing Hero Goal Sequences® in Act Three of *The Devil Wears Prada*, HGS 19-21. Write down the HERO'S physical GOAL and then the sequence-ending FRESH NEWS that creates the next goal.

Act Three begins 90 min. 35 sec. into the movie, and is 14 min. 49 sec. long.

- TO CATCH UP — HERE'S SEQUENCE® #18 in *The Devil Wears Prada*: HERO GOAL #18 — *Go on the ultimate Paris date with big time fashion writer Christian Thompson.* FRESH NEWS (STUNNING SURPRISE TWO) — *In Christian's apartment, Andy discovers that her powerful boss, Miranda Priestly, is about to be fired as Editor in Chief of Runway Magazine.*

SO THEN, WHAT ARE HERO GOAL SEQUENCES® 19-21?

- For HGS #19, coming off of the big discovery in S.S. #2, what's the next HERO GOAL? And what's the FRESH NEWS that upsets Andy so much? (It's discovered at a luncheon.) Runs 4 min. 42 sec.

- In this film, HGS #20 is the showdown Obligatory Scene between Hero and Adversary. What's the HERO GOAL here? What FRESH NEWS action does Andy take to resolve her central conflict with the Adversary? Runs 4 min. 3 sec.

- Then in the HGS #21 DENOUEMENT, what's the HERO GOAL? And there's even one last pleasant surprise waiting for the Hero as a FRESH NEWS tag in HGS #21... what is it?

The answers can be found at the end of Chapter Fourteen.

## ANSWERS FOR CH. 12, HGS 13-18 OF *WALK THE LINE*:

### HGS #13:
HERO GOAL — *Pursue June on stage more gently this time while they work together as a performing team.*
FRESH NEWS — *They finally make love.*
Time: 6 min. 36 sec.

### HGS #14:
HERO GOAL — *Enjoy their affair.*
FRESH NEWS — *June ends the affair, so Johnny gets higher, passes out onstage. . . and the tour is cancelled.*
Time: 6 min. 51 sec.

### HGS #15:
HERO GOAL — *Feed his ever worsening drug habit as John's star just keeps rising.*
FRESH NEWS — *Johnny gets arrested for drug possession and locked up.*
Time: 3 min. 50 sec.

### HGS #16:
HERO GOAL — *Go home and hide out from the press.*
FRESH NEWS — *His wife drives away with his kids, she wants a divorce.*
Time: 5 min. 49 sec.

### HGS #17:
HERO GOAL — *Seek the lowest depths of total oblivion while obsessing about June.*
FRESH NEWS — *Johnny passes out in a forest and wakes up to see a big beautiful house being built there, so he buys it to lure June back.*
Time: 5 min. 45 sec.

### HGS #18:
HERO GOAL — *Show dad and June how well he's doing by having both families over for Thanksgiving.*
FRESH NEWS (STUNNING SURPRISE TWO) — *John gets stoned and nearly drowns, but June saves his life and proves she does love him after all.*
Time: 8 min. 28 sec.

# chapter fourteen

# COMPLETE HERO
# GOAL SEQUENCES.
# FOR *UP*

---------- ✑✑ ----------

Screenplay *by Bob Peterson and Pete Docter*
Story *by Pete Docter*
*and Bob Peterson & Thomas McCarthy*

Now we're going to take a movie and break it down from beginning to end using Goal Sequences. You can do this with any successful American feature film that has one or two heroes.

I occasionally teach a course through the UCLA Extension Writers' Program using Hero Goal Sequences₨ to analyze current hit movies on screen. The UCLA Extension catalogue must be printed some six months before my class takes place, so the Writers' Program needs to know what films currently playing in theaters I'll be using six months down the road.

I just pick any three hit movies currently in release.

Thus the films selected for my class are announced in print usually before I see them. Before I even begin to break them down with Goal Sequences. Because I already know without any doubt that if the movies are box office hits, every Goal Sequence will be there. And each sequence will contain the exact right actions in the exact right order.

So far, I've never been wrong. *Up* has been chosen as the summarizing example here for a number of reasons, but the main three are these:

1. *Up* made a huge amount of money, which means it worked emotionally for lots of people;
2. It was Oscar-nominated for Best Picture as well as Best Original Screenplay, and won Best Animated Feature Film;
3. When I handed my students and friends a list of movie titles for possible use in this book, *Up* was hands down the favorite.

So grab your balloons — off we go!

The first step in analyzing or outlining any film is to ascertain how many heroes are in it, and to figure out the exact story function of every other key character in the plot.

This is how the cast of *Up* fits into character categories:

**Hero — Carl Fredricksen, grumpy senior citizen**

"The Hero is the person whose goal, originating from urgent high stakes, drives the story forward. All other characters function as either helpers or enemies to the Hero." *Up* is a one Hero movie.

**Mentor — Ellie, Carl's wife**

Carl's considerations of what Ellie would have wanted him to do consistently challenge this Hero. "A Mentor can be any person of any age, provided they pass on key skills or information to the Hero; the Mentor often dies; the Mentor often gives the Hero an important or lifesaving gift of vital information." Here Ellie gives Carl her Adventure Book. AND — Ellie is NOT a Love Interest character because romantic conquest is never an issue in this story.

**Shape-Shifter Adversary — Charles Muntz, the Adventurer**

"The Adversary more powerfully opposes the Hero than any other character; the Adversary appears to be unbeatable; the Adversary sees himself as the Hero of his own story; an Adversary can be the psychological flip side of the

Hero; the Adversary often has helpers who carry out his will against the Hero; the Adversary can wear the mask of friendship and not be revealed as the true opposing force until closer to the end."

## Sidekick — Russell, Wilderness Explorer in Tribe 54

"Sidekicks fight shoulder to shoulder with the Hero, challenge the Hero's motivations, keep him honest, force the Hero's inner conflict to the surface where it can be examined, and often provide comic relief; the Sidekick commits to the goal but isn't the prime mover of the story; the Sidekick isn't as skilled as the Hero and often holds a lesser social status; the Sidekick is completely loyal and trustworthy; Sidekicks cannot die; Sidekicks do not experience character growth; Sidekicks offer personal counsel and conflict."

## Helper-Follower Ally #1 — Kevin the Bird

"The Helper-Follower Ally offers special talents, skills, or assistance the Hero cannot provide himself."

## Helper-Follower Ally #2 — Dug the Dog

## Adversary Agent — Alpha the Dog

"The Adversary Agent is a significant opposition character who works for, and takes orders from, the Adversary."

## Lesser Adversary Agents — dogs Beta, Gamma, and Omega

## Independent Troublemakers — Construction Foreman Tom, Police Officer Edith, Construction Worker Steve, Nurse George, Nurse AJ, the Judge

"Independent Troublemakers oppose the Hero but are not associated with the Adversary, they provide another arena in which the Hero can prove himself; Independent Troublemakers can be major subplot characters, or minor ones."

# HERO GOAL SEQUENCES® FOR *UP*

## ACT ONE

### Action Hook — Introduction of the Shape-shifter Adversary

*Up* starts with the "Movietown News" newsreel shown in a 1930s theater, with Hero Carl as a small boy watching enraptured. Adventurer Charles Muntz, dashing and courageous, is everything the little Hero longs to become.

Muntz presents his discovery to the world — a skeleton of the "Monster of Paradise Falls." But disbelieving scientists charge him with fraud. Humiliated, Muntz boards his dirigible, The Spirit of Adventure, vowing never to return until he brings back living proof that the monster exists.

Carl in his childhood is utterly captivated.

Then:

**Hero Goal #1:** *Little Carl wants to dream of adventure while playing with Ellie.*

Playing in an abandoned house, little Carl meets little Ellie. Ellie proves to be bold, fun, and seeking adventure just like Carl. But Carl falls and breaks his arm. Adventure can be dangerous.

While recuperating in his room, Little Ellie shows Carl her Adventure Book, explaining it's her dream to go to South America and live atop Paradise Falls where Adventurer Muntz went to explore. She insists that Carl promise to take her there.

**Fresh News for HGS #1:** *Little Carl crosses his heart and swears a powerful oath he will take Ellie to Paradise Falls without fail.*

(7 min. 20 sec. including Action Hook)

So this Hero Goal Sequence® #1 includes:

a.) A short glimpse of the Hero's ordinary life;

b.) Many reasons to like the Hero immediately;

c.) A first use of the Hero's personal emotional SHIELD (here, it's dreaming of great adventure that takes Carl out of the dull, protected world he lives in);

d.) Some form of danger or Unfair Injury appearing as the Hero pursues an active goal (while seeking real adventure Carl breaks his arm — an Unfair Injury proving real adventure can be dangerous);

e.) Establishing that the Hero is not happy with the ordinary world as he finds it (here, the Hero can only play at adventure as real adventure is far out of reach).

Fade forward many years to Carl and Ellie's wedding.

**Hero Goal #2:** *Build a life with the woman he loves.*

A series of short scenes demonstrate how Carl and Ellie create a loving life right in their old home town. But Ellie finds she cannot have children. She's crushed, and Carl does all he can to support her.

The Hero never forgets his promise about taking Ellie to Paradise Falls. They save money for a trip to South America, but the money must be spent on practical things.

They grow old together. Ellie becomes ill. On her hospital bed Ellie gives Carl the gift of her Adventure Book.

**Fresh News for HGS #2:** *Ellie dies... and without her the world looks very dark to Carl.*

(4 min. 17 sec.)

So this HGS #2 includes:

a.) Beginning of the general story conflict (Ellie gives Carl her Adventure Book so he now thinks himself responsible for Ellie's unfulfilled dream);

b.) The first demonstration of the Hero's inner emotional pain caused by a trauma (Ellie's death);

c.) In this film, the Inciting Incident will not arrive until HGS #4.

**Hero Goal #3:** *Defend his house against greedy developers.*

Carl's small town has grown into a city and major construction is underway all around his little house. The Hero becomes a cranky old guy.

Building contractors want to buy Carl out but he refuses.

A young Wilderness Explorer knocks on Carl's door, hoping to earn a merit badge by helping an old person. Carl meets sweet, irksome Russell.

In an altercation over Ellie's mailbox, Carl hits a construction worker with his cane. Now Carl has unwittingly handed the developers a way to get him out.

**Fresh News for HGS #3:** *A judge declares Carl a "public menace," and he will be taken away to an old age home the very next morning.*

(7 min. 41 sec.)

This HGS #3 includes:

a.) A Call to Adventure arriving for the Hero (he's being forced out of his home and away from the lifetime of love it represents);

b.) The introduction of new, story-enhancing characters (Russell, land developers, a judge, nurses);

c.) Pace accelerating in the story (as the developers close in);

d.) First appearance of a Love Interest Character (here, there is no Love Interest in the story so a future Sidekick appears who will provide the same emotional confrontations that a Love Interest would);

e.) A trap getting set for the Hero (Carl is forced to consider actions that are about to throw him into harm's way).

This sequence runs long because it includes an extended comic confrontation with the boy Russell to establish another key character.

Notice that Carl becomes a grumpy old man, sure, but we care deeply about him because we see his Unfair Injuries of losing Ellie and then losing his home.

**Hero Goal #4:** *Prepare to leave the home he shared with Ellie.*

From the closet Carl pulls down his suitcase and Ellie's Adventure Book. Carl crosses his heart once again, acknowledges the oath he never kept.

The next morning men show up to take Carl to the retirement home. Carl asks for a few moments to say goodbye to the old place.

**Fresh News for HGS #4 and INCITING INCIDENT:** *Carl releases thousands of helium balloons on strings attached to his home and soon the house is airborne.*

*"So long, boys! I'll send you a postcard from Paradise Falls!"*

(2 min. 42 sec.)

This HGS #4 includes:

a.) New characters being introduced, relationships developing (here, Carl's central relationship with Ellie is furthered by a physical commitment to her dream);

b.) The first appearance of a Mentor (Ellie is established as Mentor now, and the driving force behind everything Carl will do);

c.) In *Up*, the Inciting Incident appearing (the Inciting Incident can arrive any time in Act One);

d.) The pace increasing even more as the Hero pursues his general goal (Carl's general goal is to keep his promise to Ellie);

e.) The Hero being forced to take a risk (as he launches his house into the sky to escape developers);

f.) The Hero stepping into a trap (taking action to fulfill his promise now puts Carl in direct danger).

**Hero Goal #5:** *Get the feel of his "craft" and set sail for South America.*

Carl has even created makeshift sails as a way to navigate. He flies over the city working out the kinks in his homemade dirigible.

There's a knock at the front door. Huh?

Carl discovers the boy Russell trapped on his front porch. The Wilderness Explorer asks politely if he can come inside.

**Fresh News for HGS #5:** *Carl now has an unwanted passenger complicating his voyage.*

(3 min. 20 sec.)

This HGS #5 includes:

a.) A revelation of the Hero's DESIRE, providing personal emotional motivation for achieving the goal (to find purpose in life again from Carl's promise to his wife — "We're on our way, Ellie!");

b.) An introduction of the Hero to the power of the Adversary (here, it's feeling the power of Charles Muntz' courage to fly away into the unknown for real);

c.) The Hero has second thoughts about the risks of any Call to Adventure (when Russell happens aboard, Carl must ponder the danger to the boy);

d.) The Hero steps into a previously set trap, if he hasn't already done so in HGS #4 (Carl already did this in #4).

**Hero Goal #6:** *Navigate to Paradise Falls while trying to get rid of the boy.*

Carl considers ways to drop Russell off, but nothing feels safe. Turns out the boy has a flair for navigation.

A huge, dark storm overtakes them. In the buffeted house Carl desperately tries to save his SHIELD — the mementos he has of Ellie. Carl gets knocked unconscious. He awakens to sunny skies. Russell claims that he has navigated the floating house to South America. Carl remains skeptical... but he cuts a few balloons loose to lower his blimp down through cloud cover and see where they are.

In thick mist Carl discovers his house now floats just a few feet above a rocky mountain plateau.

Heavy wind sweeps the house toward a cliff. From the ground Carl grabs the attached gardening hose and pulls hard to stop the structure from slipping over the edge, barely saving Ellie's house.

**Fresh News for HGS #6, and STUNNING SURPRISE #1:** *The fog lifts and Carl suddenly sees only a few miles off -Paradise Falls! He's almost made it!*

Carl has arrived in the strange new world of ACT TWO. (6 min. 51 sec.)

So in HGS #6:

a.) The trap springs shut on the Hero (a nasty storm blows him thousands of miles to a mysterious new land);

b.) Stunning Surprise #1 takes place (suddenly he can see Paradise Falls just a few miles off and the possibility of keeping his promise to Ellie becomes a reality);

c.) The specific physical goal the Hero will now pursue becomes clear (to get Ellie's house right next to the falls where she wanted it).

Act One = 32 min. 11 sec.

## ACT TWO

**Hero Goal #7:** *Get his house over to the falls.*

Carl is upset that he got Ellie's house so near to Paradise Falls and yet still so far away.

The Hero struggles to come up with a plan. Russell suggests they pull the floating house by the garden hose and walk it around to the falls.

Sounds good to Carl. They set off.

A ticking clock is established — Carl says they have only three days until all the helium leaks from the balloons.

**Subplot cutaway:** a pack of vicious dogs chase an as yet unseen creature through a jungle.

**Returning to the Hero:** the killer dogs chase their prey near Carl and Russell, unseen by Carl. The Hero's hearing aid squeals and drives the dogs away.

Russell wants a bathroom break.

**Subplot cutaway:** In the bushes Russell spots huge tracks left by the unknown creature.

Using candy as a lure Russell meets a very large, strange bird. This colorful creature is clearly the "Monster of Paradise Falls" that Charles Muntz set out to capture back when Carl was a kid.

**Returning to the Hero:** The boy leads his new friend "Kevin" up to Carl. The creature proves to be a playful troublemaker. Carl insists Russell cannot keep the bird. Russell pleads. Carl growls "No!" Cut to:

**Fresh News for HGS #7:** *Pulling the house onward Carl has picked up another unwanted passenger, Kevin the Snipe, complicating his task even more.*

(7 min. 43 sec.)

So in HGS #7:

a.) The Hero flounders for a plan of action, either on his own or in concert with others (Carl must figure out how to get the house across the plateau to the falls);

b.) The Hero commits himself to the specific plot goal of the movie, which requires some type of struggle (get Ellie's house moved to the falls — across a hostile mountaintop);

c.) The Hero's inner conflict surfaces (his grumpiness reveals a desire to live in the past with Ellie rather than put up with Russell and Kevin in the here and now)...

d.) ...and that reveals the theme of the movie ("To live a fulfilling life one must let go of the past");

e.) New characters enter the Hero's life, and he must begin distinguishing allies from enemies (At first Carl thinks Kevin just an obstacle and he does not yet see the bird as the Ally she really is).

**Hero Goal #8:** *Carl wants to get rid of the giant bird as he treks onward.*

Russell lures Kevin along behind them with his chocolate bar as Carl grumbles.

A friendly dog trots up wearing a collar device that allows him to talk. Chatty dog Dug says he's been sent on a mission to find a colorful bird, so Dug asks permission to take Kevin home with him as his prisoner.

Russell pleads to keep the dog as a pet, too. Carl yells "No!"

**Fresh News for HGS #8:** *A talking dog joins Carl's little troop and yet another irksome complication has been added to his journey.*

(2 min. 43 sec.)

**Subplot cutaway:** Alpha the Dog is introduced as a dangerous Adversary Agent who lords it over the other dogs.

Through a collar monitor screen Alpha sees Dug has actually found the bird. The collar maps Dug's location. Alpha leads the dogs off to capture Kevin.

So in HGS #8 we find:

a.) The strength of the Adversary is demonstrated (we meet a vicious pack of Adversary Agent dogs hunting down Kevin with the big advantage of technology created by the as yet unknown Adversary);

b.) The stakes are increased (we see genuine danger closing in on Carl);

c.) The Hero undergoes training or instruction (Carl learns more about this strange world from Dug and Kevin);

d.) Allies and enemies are further established (Ally Dug the Dog enters the story, and also enemy Alpha);

e.) In this film, the first EXPRESS moment of character growth won't take place until HGS #10 (it can happen anywhere between #7 and #10).

**Hero Goal #9:** *Escape from the extra burden of Kevin and Dug.*

Dug announces that he loves Carl as his new master. Carl yells, "I am not your master!" The Hero wants no new relationships crowding his attempt to live in the past with Ellie.

Carl tries to drive off Kevin and Dug, but it doesn't work. So he pulls a tennis ball from the bottom of his cane walker and throws it — Dug tears off after the ball. Then Carl grabs a hunk of chocolate, tosses that, and Kevin races away chasing it.

Carl hurries onward with Russell, lugging the house as fast as he can, bumping into things, but at last escaping to a distant hilltop where Carl is sure he's rid of the two animals for good.

"I think that did the trick!"

**Fresh News for HGS #9:** *Loyal Dug and Kevin turn up right beside the Hero, and Carl sees that he is stuck permanently with Russell's two "pets."*

(4 min. 43 sec.)

So in HGS #9 we find:

a.) An Action Burst occurs that picks up the pace or scope of the story (Carl suddenly runs and pulls the house quickly up a mountain to escape Kevin and Doug);

b.) The Hero shows what he can do physically (this old codger demonstrates his physical skills);

c.) The Hero takes a risk, and that risk backfires (Carl throws the ball and candy and makes a run for it through wild country, but Kevin and Doug zoom up beside Carl even more bonded to the Hero).

d.) The Hero considers giving up (Carl sees it's futile trying to get rid of Russell's pets).

**Hero Goal #10:** *Get through a nighttime rainstorm.*

Camped under his floating house as thunder cracks, Carl sees that Russell doesn't even know how to put up a tent. Why doesn't the boy's dad teach him?

Russell explains that his parents are divorced and he rarely sees his father any more. Russell hoped his dad would be present to pin on his final merit badge at the big Wilderness Explorer ceremony coming up, but Russell's not sure dad will show.

Carl's heart begins to open to the boy. Russell pleads again to keep Kevin and Dug. Carl softens, says yes.

Russell makes the Hero cross his heart — just like Ellie did — then the boy falls asleep. Carl says, "What have I gotten myself into, Ellie?"

This is STEP ONE in the Hero's Character Growth Arc. Here Carl EXPRESSES his longing to keep living in the past with his loving memories of Ellie — he even carries his late wife's house around tied to his back, quite a SHIELD — but life keeps pulling him toward new relationships that Carl wants to block out. This is Carl's inner conflict.

The next morning Kevin reveals that she's a girl bird by collecting Carl's food and darting off to feed her babies. Russell wants to follow and be sure Kevin's babies are safe.

Carl insists it's more important to get Ellie's house to Paradise Falls because time is running out.

The vicious pack of dogs led by Alpha suddenly encircles Carl and Russell.

**Fresh News for HGS #10:** *Carl and Russell are hijacked by nasty dogs and forced to follow Alpha, while still pulling Ellie's house along above them.*

(6 min. 3 sec.)

In HGS #10 we find:

a.) The Hero gets hit with a setback (Carl and Russell are captured by Adversary Agents);

b.) A new Mentor is consulted (Russell offers Carl a positive opportunity to live in the present if he will become the boy's father figure — thus providing another Sidekick function as teacher to the Hero);

c.) An unexpected physical obstacle pops up (an overnight storm forces Carl to stop);

d.) A subplot cutaway unfolds in which the Hero does not physically appear (that doesn't happen here because the Adversary Agent dogs show up to face Carl directly — and the presence of Charles Muntz is held back as a surprise to launch the Midpoint Sequence, *which leaves no other key characters available to provide a cutaway in HGS #10).*

**Hero Goal #11:** *Carl must go and meet the nasty dogs' Master —
or else.*

Carl and Russell are led by the dogs through stark canyons.
Menace hangs in the air. They arrive at a large cave opening
where even more vicious-looking dogs creep forward toward the
Hero....

Then stepping out from the deep cave shadows comes the
original Adventurer himself, Charles Muntz. The Adventurer
questions Carl to find out why the Hero has come.

When Muntz learns that Carl's purpose is not to capture
the Monster of Paradise Falls (Kevin) his tone lightens.

**Fresh News for HGS #11:** *Muntz suddenly turns into a
charming and pleasant host, invites Carl and Russell into his cave home
for supper.*

(2 min. 15 sec.)

In HGS #11 we see:

a.) The Hero Approaches the Inmost Cave or seat of power
belonging to the Adversary (here, Carl literally approaches the cave home of the Shape-Shifter Adversary);

b.) Conflict becomes more intense (suddenly the Hero is
terrorized by a nasty pack of dogs);

c.) A battle breaks out with a proxy of the Adversary (the
Hero gets captured by the dog Alpha);

d.) Urgency and stakes rise sharply (now it's life or death);

e.) A last chance for training or instruction, or consultation
with a Mentor (it appears that Charles Muntz will teach
Carl the wonderful ways of adventuring — but Muntz
is a false Mentor, really an Adversary in Shape-Shifter
disguise).

**Hero Goal #12 — MIDPOINT SEQUENCE:** *Carl
wants to make a friend of this world-famous explorer and learn about his
exploits.*

Carl moors Ellie's balloon house inside the Adventurer's

huge cave, and Muntz invites Carl and Russell into his blimp home. Carl is thrilled.

Passing through Muntz's private skeleton collection, the Adventurer reveals in subtext that he is a selfish man who kills animals just to display their bones. A man who lies and cheats and harbors grudges. Muntz is the dark reflection of Carl, without Carl's loving heart, because both men live in the past.

Over a meal catered by dog servants, Carl hears that Muntz has one great prize left to capture. The Adventurer shows off the skeleton of a huge bird.

Carl recognizes it as an ancestor of Kevin. He's suddenly worried about Muntz's intentions.

The boy innocently blurts out that the skeleton looks like Russell's pet bird who follows them everywhere!

Muntz turns menacing. He makes a murderous threat, demands that Carl reveal where the bird is.

Carl spots Kevin right outside Muntz' window, on Ellie's house roof! The Hero demurs and backs Russell toward the exit. But the bird caws loudly outside.

The Adventurer spots the bird. Carl grabs Russell and runs. Muntz orders his dogs to get them.

**Fresh News for HGS #12:** *The Adventurer is revealed as a dangerous villain who will stop at nothing to capture Kevin.*

(5 min. 55 sec.)

So in HGS #12, the Midpoint Sequence:

a.) The Hero reaches a Point of No Return (now it's escape from Muntz or die);

b.) The second major step toward character growth appears, where the Hero directly BATTLES inner conflict (he must stop living in the past long enough to save his new friends Russell and Kevin in the present);

c.) Lovers kiss for the first time, or the partnership of buddies deepens into mutual commitment (for the first time Carl, Russell, and Kevin begin acting like a true team of buddies when they set out to escape);

d.) Mood and storytelling style differ from anything else in the movie (here, it's Muntz playing the charming host with his private bone museum and Carl playing the tourist in a blimp with dog servants that's wildly different);

e.) Conflict with the Adversary becomes personal (Muntz informs the Hero that he is willing to kill Carl to get Kevin — and that's pretty personal);

f.) A "ticking clock" time limit gets set in motion (now Carl faces immediate danger, which leaves even less time to get Ellie's house to Paradise Falls than before);

g.) An unmasking takes place (the charming Adversary's mask of friendship comes off);

h.) A literal or symbolic death and rebirth takes place (Carl the codger-living-in-the-past dies, and Carl the-true-Hero gets born, determined to save his team).

**Hero Goal #13:** *Escape the attacking dogs and get Ellie's house out of the cave to safety.*

With dogs closing in on two sides, Carl and Russell unmoor the house. But the cave entrance is blocked. So Dug leads them deeper into the cavern to show Carl another exit.

Carl's team escapes and the Hero pulls Ellie's house outside. Many balloons pop. The house is barely airborne now.

Kevin helps the crew fly across a deep gorge and away from the dogs — but Alpha chomps into Kevin's leg during the escape and the giant bird is wounded.

They escape Muntz' dogs, but Carl sees that his house won't stay afloat much longer. He must get it to the falls immediately.

Russell wants to drop everything and take wounded Kevin safely home to her children.

In a further demonstration of STEP TWO character growth...

**Fresh News for HGS #13:** *Carl agrees to help get Kevin home to her babies before anything else.*

(3 min. 31 sec.)

So in HGS #13:

a.) The Hero presses onward with renewed courage (here Carl fights hard against a much stronger enemy to save his team);

b.) A new complication crops up (Carl reaches a huge canyon cliff with no way across as Muntz's dogs attack from behind);

c.) The Hero again resorts to his inner emotional self-defense and isolation (Carl worries the house won't float much longer and he still wants desperately to fulfill his promise to Ellie — but his SHIELD isn't officially lifted back up again until HGS #15);

d.) Additional proof turns up that conflict between Hero and Adversary has become very personal (Adversary Agent Alpha seriously wounds Kevin and Carl sees real blood shed by his team for the first time).

**Hero Goal #14:** *Get wounded Kevin safely to her home.*

Under cover of night, Carl and Russell pull Ellie's house behind them as they take Kevin home.

The boy recounts a simple memory, when his father and Russell sat on a curb together playing a car counting game and eating ice cream. He says, "I think it's the boring stuff I remember the most."

Carl makes the connection to his own memories of Ellie. The Hero listens like a caring friend. Suddenly flood lights blast on and Muntz' blimp shows up overhead. A net shoots out over Kevin. Villainous Muntz descends the blimp ramp to face Carl.

**Fresh News for HGS #14:** *Muntz throws a lantern under Ellie's house and sets it ablaze.*

So in HGS #14:

a.) The pace slows a bit and offers the Hero a contemplative moment (as Carl listens to Russell's touching memory);

b.) A Love Interest or Sidekick or even the Hero himself brings up inner conflict issues (Russell's story about his disinterested father forces Carl to weigh his own wish to live in the past against caring for a boy who needs his support in the present);

c.) A Big New Idea arrives to challenge the Hero (when Muntz sets Ellie's house on fire);

d.) The Big New Idea paves the way for a second Action Burst coming in HGS #15 (as Carl fights the fire).

**Hero Goal #15:** *Carl must put out the fire.*

Carl runs to fight the flames — while bad guy Muntz drags Kevin aboard The Spirit of Adventure. The blimp departs. Carl finally puts out the last of the flames.

Russell is shattered that Carl chose to save Ellie's house instead of saving Kevin. "You just… gave her away." When cornered, Carl still chooses the past.

The Hero says, "This is none of my concern! I didn't ask for any of this!" Living in the past remains less painful than living for the present, and the Hero lifts his SHIELD once more.

**Fresh News for HGS #15:** *Carl proclaims that he is going to get Ellie's house to Paradise Falls without help, even if it kills him.*

(I min. 54 sec.)

So in HGS #15:

a.) An Action Burst appears, where dramatic confrontation kicks things upward (Carl fights to save Ellie's house rather than stop Muntz from grabbing Kevin, causing Russell to confront Carl);

b.) The Hero experiences a False Victory, or at least believes that he has fought the Adversary to a draw (at least Muntz no longer has reason to stop Carl from achieving his goal since the Adversary already has Kevin);

c.) A fleeting sense of security for the Hero arrives, soon to be dashed (no dogs are hunting him at the moment);

d.) A strong romance relationship can motivate the Hero through the Action Burst (Carl's deep love for Ellie causes him to revert to saving her house before anything else).

**Hero Goal #16:** *Carl must haul his battered house to the waterfall by himself.*

Carl drags his barely floating burden toward Paradise Falls. A glum Russell trails behind, not helping.

The Hero finally arrives at his goal.

Russell throws down his Merit Badge sash. Says he doesn't want it any more.

Carl enters his home, now mostly a broken relic. He pulls up his easy chair right next to Ellie's and sits.

Victory... sort of.

**Fresh News for HGS #16:** *Carl keeps his promise to Ellie — but it doesn't feel nearly as good as he expected.*

(2 min. 4 sec.)

In HGS #16 we see:

a.) The dramatic energy coming out of HGS #15 continues to rise, not as more physical action but as a growing intensity of conflict (the emotional conflict between Carl and Russell coming out of #15 grows more intense);

b.) The Hero feels greater confidence and rededicates himself to the ultimate goal (Carl feels the confidence of victory. He did it. But what would Ellie really want him to do next...?).

c.) The Hero discovers some new point of view toward the central story conflict (even after achieving his specific Act Two goal, Carl discovers that Ellie's house still feels empty);

d.) The third step in character growth can take place here or in HGS #17 (for Carl it will happen in #17).

**Hero Goal #17:** *Live in his house and fulfill Ellie's dream.*

Inside, Carl looks around at the old shattered keepsakes.

But Ellie still isn't sitting in her chair next to him. So Carl places Russell's unfinished merit badge sash in Ellie's empty chair... a symbol of the future and a boy's life yet to be lived.

Carl picks up Ellie's Adventure Book, sadly turns to the last page titled "STUFF I'M GOING TO DO!"

But instead of empty pages beyond that Carl is surprised to find snapshots, Ellie's cherished record of two people deeply in love who were lucky enough to grow old together.

On the last page Carl finds a note left by Ellie: "Thanks for the adventure — now go have a new one! Love, Ellie."

At last Carl gets it. Ellie herself wants him to live in the present, not the past.

The Hero steps outside to check on Russell.

He sees the boy floating away, tied to a few balloons and using a leaf blower for power. Russell calls out, "I'm going to help Kevin even if you won't!"

Carl knows he must keep Russell safe. But Ellie's house won't fly anymore.

So Carl starts tossing things out to lighten it. Furniture, the old mementos, he heaves it all out the front door.

Here Carl OVERCOMES his interior conflict once and for all. He throws away his SHIELD, the burdensome stuff that kept him weighed down in the past.

Now it's Russell who needs him.

**Fresh News for HGS #17:** *Freed at last from his past, Carl's house rises again into the air ready for new adventure.*

(3 min. 40 sec.)

In HGS #17 we see:

a.) Final preparations are completed for the act climax showdown (Carl throws out all his furniture to create a fighting-weight attack blimp);

b.) The strength of the Adversary is demonstrated again, in the most personal terms for the Hero (here, it's seeing Russell fly off to save Kevin when Carl knows the boy alone doesn't stand a chance against Muntz);

c.) The ticking clock approaches zero hour, or the high stakes threat draws near (Carl races off toward his final showdown with Muntz);

d.) The Hero's courage is on display as he demonstrates why he is exceptional — often through the third step in character growth, OVERCOMING interior conflict (which is exactly what Carl does).

**Hero Goal #18:** *Carl must catch up with Russell and help the boy save Kevin.*

Now airborne again, the Hero heads off to the rescue.

A knock at the front door. Huh?

This time it's Dug the Dog, trapped out on the porch, asking if he can come in because he loves Carl. Displaying his character growth, Carl says, "You're my dog, aren't you?! And I am your master!" Dug is delighted, licks him like crazy. "Good boy, Dug!"

**Subplot cutaway:** Russell maneuvers himself up alongside Muntz's dirigible in the clouds, climbs in through an open window. The Adventurer's dogs quickly capture Russell and tie him in a chair.

Muntz sees Carl's house approaching, too.

The cruel Adversary pulls a lever... and the boarding ramp of the blimp begins lowering, with Russell tied in a chair that starts sliding down the ramp toward open sky.

**Fresh News for HGS #18 and STUNNING SURPRISE TWO:** *Maneuvering his house up closer to the Spirit of Adventure, Carl is horrified to spot Russell sliding down the ramp toward certain death.*

(2 min. 40 sec.)

(Act Two total running time, 42 min. 7 sec.)

In Hero Goal Sequence #18 we see:

a.) A longer than average sequence (not in *Up*);

b.) An Act Two climax that hits the peak of conflict and action — but does NOT fully resolve the central story question (Carl flies in to begin the showdown at peek conflict, but the central question is not yet settled);

c.) The Hero demonstrating his newly evolved self (now Carl is pure action Hero);

d.) The Hero believing he has conquered inner conflict (now Ellie's house is only a tool to be used in Carl's new higher calling — save Russell);

e.) The arrival of Stunning Surprise #2 which provides the biggest reversal for the Hero in the whole story, usually to the negative. (Carl sees helpless Russell slipping toward certain death.)

**Hero Goal # 19: *Save Russell and Kevin!***

Carl swoops in, throws his garden hose grappling hook over the dirigible ramp railing. Slides down the hose to the ramp just in time... he catches Russell's chair and saves the boy.

Carl heaves the chair back inside Ellie's house, but he won't untie the boy. Carl says he wants Russell safe.

The Hero rushes back aboard The Spirit of Adventure with Dug, distracts all the guard dogs and sneaks past them to reach Kevin.

**Subplot cutaway:** Russell shakes free of the chair ropes but falls off the porch and into open sky. Grabs the dangling hose. Hangs on for dear life.

As Muntz steers his dirigible he watches Russell get dragged across the blimp window while clutching the garden hose. The Adversary orders his dogs to attack Carl's house.

Russell climbs back up to the floating house. Attacking in toy biplanes, the dogs shoot darts at him.

**Back to the Hero** — Carl tries to sneak across Muntz's museum room and escape with Kevin and Dug.

**Fresh News for HGS #19:** *Carl spins around to discover Muntz right behind him, attacking with a huge broadsword!*

(3 min. 11 sec.)

So in HGS #19:

a.) The Hero Carl *improvises* his way toward his ultimate goal... to keep Russell, Kevin, and Dug safe;

b.) By chasing after Russell to protect him, it's Carl and no one else who *brings about his own showdown with the Adversary;*

c.) Fresh News here *causes the Obligatory Scene to commence,* when Carl turns to see Muntz attacking.

**Hero Goal #20 and the OBLIGATORY SCENE:** *The Hero fights to overcome his Adversary once and for all.*

The final showdown battle begins — two old guys with arthritis going for the gold.

Carl almost gets run through, but Muntz trips. Escaping, Carl and Kevin climb out a window and head up the outside ladder on The Spirit of Adventure.

**Subplot cutaways:** In the pilot room Alpha moves in to destroy Dug, but Dug thinks fast and slaps the Cone of Shame dog collar around Alpha's neck.

That leads Dug to become the new alpha dog of the pack!

Still flying Ellie's house, Russell sees Carl in trouble on top of the blimp. The boy navigates the house in closer to help.

**Back to the Hero:** Carl collects Kevin and Dug as Russell swoops in, and they all jump into Ellie's house. But Muntz appears with a shotgun. Blasts the balloons. Carl falls off the house and back onto the blimp. Russell, Dug and Kevin are still inside... as the now less buoyant house slides toward the edge of the blimp tail fin.

Carl grabs the hose and stops the house from slipping over.

Muntz shoots his way into Ellie's house. Russell and Dug

cling to Kevin as Carl lures the giant bird back to the dirigible with chocolate, thus saving them all.

Trapped in balloon strings, Adversary Muntz falls to his just deserts far below.

Then Ellie's house breaks loose from the garden hose and drifts away downward, disappearing into lower clouds. Carl watches his little house vanish forever. Russell says he's sorry.

Carl answers, "It's just a house."

**Fresh News for HGS #20:** *Carl has beaten his powerful Adversary Muntz and saved Russell, Dug, and Kevin.*

(5 min. 38 sec.)

In HGS #20 we see:

a.) The Obligatory Scene play out as Carl and Muntz fight hand to hand in several locations for ultimate story resolution;

b.) The Hero personally brings about conflict finality when Carl cleverly lures Kevin, with Russell and Dug clinging to the bird, back to safety on the blimp — thereby defeating the Adversary Muntz;

c.) The Hero proves the completion of his Character Growth Arc when Ellie's home is lost forever and Carl can say, "It's just a house."

**Hero Goal #21 and DENOUEMENT:** *Live a new, full life.*

Carl gets Kevin home to her babies and symbolically gives his cane away to the big bird. Doesn't need it any more.

With Russell, Dug, and all of Muntz's dogs aboard, Carl flies The Spirit of Adventure dirigible home. At Russell's Wilderness Explorer Merit Badge ceremony Carl stands in for the boy's missing dad and pins on Russell Ellie's bottle cap: "The highest honor I can bestow, the Ellie Badge."

Then Carl, Russell, and Dug sit on a curb eating ice cream and playing Russell's car counting game like he used to do with his dad. Overhead floats the symbolic Spirit of Adventure, as Carl's rewarding new life begins.

(3 min. 1 sec.)

In HGS #21 we see:

a.) The wrap up of all key relationships: Kevin is returned safely home and her babies are shown to be thriving, Dug and the other dogs are taken back to civilization to be cared for with no animal characters harmed;

b.) Carl officially expanding his love for Ellie to include Russell when he gives the boy the symbolic "Ellie Badge" bottle cap,

c.) The beginning of Carl's new bonded relationship with Russell made visible when they eat ice cream together on the curb;

d.) One last scene even reveals that Ellie's house did float down safely and end up right where it should be, at the top of Paradise Falls;

e.) This story leaves no lose ends. Running time for Act Three: 11 min 40 sec. Total running time: 1:25:58 without credits.

*Up* contains 21 Hero Goal Sequences®, the most common number. All story elements are positioned exactly where the Hero Goal Sequences® paradigm predicts they will show up. And audiences the world over loved this movie.

## EXERCISE:

Pick your own movie for analysis. It must be a financially successful, single hero, mainstream Hollywood film.

Now break the story down into Hero Goal Sequences® and discover why the movie works so well for audiences.

Are you beginning to see the enormous advantages of outlining your next screenplay using Hero Goal Sequences®?

## ANSWERS FOR CH. 13,
## ACT THREE HGS 19-21 OF *THE DEVIL WEARS PRADA*:

### HGS #19:

HERO GOAL — *Warn Miranda Priestly that she is to be fired and try to help Miranda save her powerful job at Runway Magazine.*

FRESH NEWS — *Miranda already knows, and has schemed to save herself by stabbing Mentor Nigel in the back and destroying his career.*

Time: 4 min. 42 sec.

### HGS #20:

HERO GOAL (OBLIGATORY SCENE) — *Confront Miranda to find out how the Adversary pulled off this cruel, selfish maneuver.*

FRESH NEWS — *The Hero walks away from Miranda and tosses her own cell phone in a fountain. . . thus Andy quits her job to live a less selfish life.*

Time: 4 min. 3 sec.

### HGS #21:

HERO GOAL (DENOUEMENT) — *Rebuild her old life. Wrap-ups: Andy gets back together with old boyfriend Nate; Andy makes peace with work rival Emily; and. . .*

FRESH NEWS — *When applying for a new job, Andy discovers she's gotten a splendid reference from Miranda. Her Adversary appreciates her after all.*

Time: 6 min. 4 sec.

# EPILOGUE

———— ୧୨ ————

We writers spend our days stuffing life in as fast as we can. It's a two-fisted job. We're gluttons at the feast.

And each time we open a book on screenwriting or walk in the door of a screenwriting class eager to expand our storytelling skills, it's always because somewhere deep inside there's another movie about to burst forth. A new tale demanding to be told.

It's a splendid feeling, this passion for storytelling.

But since writers are also condemned at birth to be honest with themselves, we know that the most important lessons about this passion will never be found in any book or class.

The most critical truths about movie writing art can only be discovered on our personal journey to the center of the universe. That lonely journey to the center of self.

Because only there will we ask the really tough questions.

Who am I?

Why do I want to write screenplays?

What is it *exactly* that I burn so deeply to share with an audience?

Am I willing to alter my daily life and that of my family in order to support the many challenging years required to pursue this dream?

Am I tough enough to stand naked before the world asking to be judged?

Writers swim in a sea of questions. Most of them can never be fully answered, of course, but asking them does keep us sharp.

We watch. We observe. We notice details about people and about everyday life that many others miss.

Often a bit guarded, most of us take comfort in solitude and tend toward quiet obsessions. But writers, like all artists, are also those souls most in touch with their own humanity.

We puzzle over the good and bad in our species — why we are here on Earth at all and, each in our own small way, what we might help humanity to become. Writers are sage explorers of complex inner worlds.

And we are time travelers, every one.

I always recommend to new screenwriters that they do some acting. Doesn't matter if you're good at it or not, although you'll never know until you try. Many writers are terrific actors. In a workshop or community playhouse go learn what it takes to deliver a line of dialogue in a believable way, find out how hard it is to lift words from a page and make them come alive. Discover what it feels like to lose yourself inside a character while an audience watches your every move. Experience first hand the ultimate end use of your own dramatic writing.

Then as you write, cherish the memory of Franz and Vincent.

Both labored long and hard, completely unrecognized throughout their lives. Both died broke and undiscovered. Yet Franz Kafka and Vincent Van Gogh were two of the greatest creative minds ever to walk the planet.

Did the lack of income from writing make Franz any less a writer? Vincent any less a painter?

Always remember that being a screenwriter isn't just about selling. Selling is great, and an important goal. Selling brings its own kind of validation and allows you to continue your journey. But you earn the right to call yourself a screenwriter the very first day you sit down to do the work.

Then, too, we writers must steel ourselves against the naysayers of the world. Even the well-meaning ones who love us.

I've never known a successful screenwriter who wrote just for the money. Some scribes in a cynical mood might say so, but keep after them and they'll eventually confess it isn't true. If it's really only the money you find attractive there are other ways to make more bucks more quickly.

You still want to write? Then write about what matters to you, what moves you, what gets your blood up. If you really care about what you're writing you can't help but make your audience care, too.

So here are three final summary recommendations for the committed screenwriter:

1. **Read produced screenplays.** Incessantly. By the score. You cannot expect to write well in a literary form that you do not read.

2. **Love, collect, and play with words.** Your degree of skill at using language to create a movie in the mind of your reader remains crucial to communicating any vision you may have for your screenplay. As you write — to paraphrase Norman Mailer — never settle for the almost-right word. Screenwriters use language. Bathe in words every day.

3. **And finally, this challenge.** If you are serious about mastering screenwriting, get copies of the three produced scripts you most admire. Three movies you really love. Then sit down at your keyboard... and retype them. Word for word. Line for line. FADE IN to FADE OUT.

In retyping the work of master screenwriters you will submerge yourself in the smallest textures and nuances of great screenwriting. You'll experience the conceptualization and construction of effective descriptive passages, and live the rhythms in the sentences. You'll discover how professionals drive one scene forward into the next. You'll learn what it feels like to have rich, masterful dialogue pouring through your fingers. And your screenplay vocabulary will be forever strengthened.

There is no way to come out the other side of such an experience unchanged as a writer. Consider the gauntlet thrown down.

Herein presented are the tools of your trade. May they serve you well.

I truly believe that over time, as you study more movies more carefully and submit more scripts to be judged by professional eyes, the truth will emerge. Hero Goal Sequences® can set you free.

In a book on the craft and art of screenwriting such as this one, only a certain sort of person reads to the very end. The obsessive writer sort.

So if you're still reading — welcome to the club.

Now go love strong, laugh lots, and write with fire.

# FILMOGRAPHY

———— ⊘⊙ ————

Movies on this list are referred to in *The Story Solution*. A couple dozen of them are great films. Many are terrific entertainment. A few are real dogs. But for screenwriters, the close study of all kinds of movies remains essential. Pick some of these films and watch them a number of times to uncover their secrets: story structure, character arcs, dramatic weaknesses and strengths. How do they achieve character sympathy? If they don't, why not? Which create strong emotion in you, and which do not? Why? Practice mapping Hero Goal Sequences® with them. And don't avoid the dogs. Pinpoint the reasons a movie is bad — so you will not make the same mistakes yourself.

*A Beautiful Mind* (2001) Written by Akiva Goldsman, book by Sylvia Nassar

*A History of Violence* (2005) Screenplay by Josh Olson, graphic novel by John Wagner and Vince Locke

*A League of Their Own* (1992) Screenplay by Lowell Ganz & Babaloo Mandel, story by Kim Wilson & Kelly Candaele

*Air Force One* (1997) Written by Andrew W. Marlowe

*Along Came a Spider* (2001) Screenplay by Marc Moss, novel by James Patterson

*An Officer and a Gentleman* (1982) Written by Douglas Day Stewart

*Animal House* (1978) Written by Harold Ramis & Douglas Kenney & Chris Miller

*Apocalypse Now* (1979) Screenplay by John Milius and Francis Ford Coppola, novel by Joseph Conrad

*Apollo 13* (1995) Screenplay by William Broyles Jr. & Al Reinert, book by Jim Lovell & Jeffrey Kluger

*As Good As It Gets* (1997) Screenplay by Mark Andrus and James L. Brooks, story by Mark Andrus

*Avatar* (2009) Written by James Cameron

*The Aviator* (2004) Written by John Logan

*Babel* (2006) Written by Guillermo Arriaga

*Bagdad Café* (1987) Screenplay by Eleonore Adlon and Percy Adlon and Christopher Doherty

*Batman Begins* (2005) Screenplay by Christopher Nolan and David S. Goyer, story by David S. Goyer, characters by Bob Kane

*Bird on a Wire* (1990) Screenplay by David Seltzer and Louis Venosta & Eric Lerner, story by Louis Venosta & Eric Lerner

*The Blair Witch Project* (1999) Written by Daniel Myrick & Eduardo Sanchez

*Body Heat* (1981) Written by Lawrence Kasdan

*The Bourne Identity* (2002) Screenplay by Tony Gilroy and W. Blake Herron, novel by Robert Ludlum

*The Brave One* (2007) Screenplay by Roderick Taylor & Bruce A. Taylor and Cynthia Mort, story by Roderick Taylor & Bruce A. Taylor

*Braveheart* (1995) Written by Randall Wallace

*Breach* (2007) Screenplay by Adam Mazer & William Rotko and Billy Ray, story by Adam Mazer & William Rotko

*The Break-Up* (2006) Screenplay by Jeremy Garelick & Jay Lavender, story by Vince Vaughn & Jeremy Garelick & Jay Lavender

*Bridget Jones' Diary* (2001) Screenplay by Helen Fielding and Andrew Davies and Richard Curtis, novel by Helen Fielding

*Bringing Down the House* (2003) Written by Jason Filardi

*Chaplin* (1992) Screenplay by William Boyd and Bryan Forbes and William Goldman, story by Diana Hawkins

*Chinatown* (1974) Written by Robert Towne

*Citizen Kane* (1941) Screenplay by Herman J. Mankiewicz and Orson Welles

*Collateral* (2004) Written by Stuart Beattie

*Con Air* (1997) Written by Scott Rosenberg

*Contact* (1997) Screenplay by James V. Hart and Michael Goldenberg, story by Carl Sagan and Ann Druyan, novel by Carl Sagan

*Dancing at the Blue Iguana* (2000) Screenplay by Michael Radford and David Linter

*The Dark Knight* (2008) Screenplay by Jonathan Nolan and Christopher Nolan, story by Christopher Nolan & David S. Goyer, characters by Bob Kane

*Dead Man Walking* (1995) Screenplay by Tim Robbins, book by Helen Prejean

*Déjà Vu* (2006) Written by Bill Marsilii & Terry Rossio

*The Departed* (2006) Screenplay by William Monahan from the film "Mou gaan dou" screenplay by Alan Mak and Felix Chong

*The Devil Wears Prada* (2006) Screenplay by Aline Brosh McKenna, novel by Lauren Weisberger

*Dexter* (TV Series, 2006- ) from the novel by Jeff Lindsay

*Die Hard* (1988) Screenplay by Jeb Stuart & Steven E. Sousa, novel by Roderick Thorp

*Dog Day Afternoon* (1975) Screenplay by Frank Pierson, article by P. F. Kluge and Thomas Moore

*Don Quixote* (1605) Novel written by Miguel de Cervantes

*Doubt* (2008) Written by John Patrick Shanley, play by John Patrick Shanley

*Edge of Darkness* (2010) Screenplay by William Monahan and Andrew Bovell

*Elizabeth* (1998) Written by Michael Hirst

*Enchanted* (2007) Written by Bill Kelly

*Erin Brockovich* (2000) Written by Susannah Grant

*E.T.: The Extra-Terrestrial* (1982) Written by Melissa Mathison

*Fargo* (1996) Written by Joel Coen & Ethan Coen

*Fight Club* (1999) Screenplay by Jim Uhls, novel by Chuck Palahniuk

*Finding Nemo* (2003) Screenplay by Andrew Stanton & Bob Peterson & David Reynolds, story by Andrew Stanton

*Firewall* (2006) Written by Joe Forte

*The Firm* (1993) Screenplay by David Rabe and Robert Towne & David Rayfiel, book by John Grisham

*(500) Days of Summer* (2009) Written by Scott Neustadter and Michael H. Weber

*Fletch* (1985) Screenplay by Andrew Bergman, novel by Gregory McDonald

*Flight of the Phoenix* (2004) Screenplay by Scott Frank and Edward Burns, original screenplay by Lucas Heller

*Forrest Gump* (1994) Screenplay by Eric Roth, novel by Winston Groom

*48 Hours* (1982) Written by Roger Spottiswoode and Walter Hill & Larry Gross and Steven E. de Souza

*The 40 Year Old Virgin* (2005) Written by Judd Apatow & Steve Carell

*The Fugitive* (1993) Written by Harold Ramis & Douglas Kenney & Chris Miller

*Fur: An Imaginary Portrait of Diane Arbus* (2006) Written by Erin Cressida Wilson, book by Patricia Bosworth

*Gandhi* (1982) Written by John Briley

*Ghost* (1990) Written by Bruce Joel Rubin

*Ghost Town* (2008) Written by David Koepp and John Kamp

*Gladiator* (2000) Screenplay by David Franzoni and John Logan and William Nicholson, story by David Franzoni

*The Godfather* (1972) Screenplay by Mario Puzo and Francis Ford Coppola, novel by Mario Puzo

*Greenberg* (2010) Screenplay by Noah Baumbach, story by Jennifer Jason Leigh & Noah Baumbach

*The Green Mile* (1999) Screenplay by Frank Darabont, novel by Stephen King

*Groundhog Day* (1993) Screenplay by Danny Rubin and Harold Ramis, story by Danny Rubin

*Hancock* (2008) Written by Vincent Ngo and Vince Gilligan

*The Hangover* (2009) Written by Jon Lucas & Scott Moore

*Heat* (1995) Written by Michael Mann

*Heathers* (1988) Written by Daniel Waters

*Hitch* (2005) Written by Kevin Bisch

*House of Sand and Fog* (2003) Screenplay by Vadim Perelman and Shawn Lawrence Otto, novel by Andre Dubus III

*The Hudsucker Proxy* (1994) Written by Ethan Coen & Joel Coen & Sam Raimi

*The Hurt Locker* (2008) Written by Mark Boal

*Inception* (2010) Written by Christopher Nolan

*Inglourious Basterds* (2009) Written by Quentin Tarantino

*Insomnia* (2002) Screenplay by Hillary Seitz, original screenplay by Nicolaj Frobenius and Erik Skjoldbjaerg

*Iron Man* (2008) Screenplay by Mark Ferbus & Hawk Ostby and Art Marcum & Matt Holoway, characters by Stan Lee & Don Heck & Larry Lieber & Jack Kirby

*The Jacket* (2005) Screenplay by Massy Tadjedin, story by Tom Bleecker and Marc Tocco

*Jaws* (1975) Screenplay by Peter Benchley and Carl Gottlieb, novel by Peter Benchley

*Juno* (2005) Written by Diablo Cody

*King Lear* (1606) Play written by William Shakespeare

*Knocked Up* (2007) Written by Judd Apatow

*Kung Fu Panda* (2008) Screenplay by Jonathan Aibel & Glenn Berger, story by Ethan Reiff & Cyrus Voris

*L.A. Confidential* (1997) Screenplay by Brian Helgeland & Curtis Hanson, novel by James Elroy

*Lady and the Tramp* (1955) Story By Ward Greene, story by Erdman Penner & Joe Rinaldi & Ralph Wright & Don DaGradi

*Last Action Hero* (1993) Screenplay by Shane Black & David Arnott, story by Zak Penn & Adam Leff

*Leaving Las Vegas* (2001) Screenplay by Mike Figgis, novel by John O'Brien

*Legally Blonde* (2001) Screenplay by Karen McCullah Lutz & Kirsten Smith, novel by Amanda Brown

*Leon: The Professional* (1994) Written by Luc Besson

*Life or Something Like It* (2002) Screenplay by John Scott Shepherd & Dana Stevens, story by John Scott Shepherd

*The Lord of the Rings: The Fellowship of the Ring* (2001) Screenplay by Fran Walsh & Philippa Boyens & Peter Jackson, novel by J.R.R. Tolkien

*Love Actually* (2003) Written by Richard Curtis

*M\*A\*S\*H* (1970) Screenplay by Ring Lardner Jr., novel by Richard Hooker

*Macbeth* (1606) Play written by William Shakespeare

*Magnolia* (1999) Written by Paul Thomas Anderson

*Maid in Manhattan* (2002) Screenplay by Kevin Wade, story by John Hughes

*Mamma Mia!* (2008) Screenplay by Catherine Johnson, musical book by Catherine Johnson

*Man on Fire* (2004) Screenplay by Brian Helgeland, novel by A.J. Quinnell

*Man on the Moon* (1999) Written by Scott Alexander & Larry Karaszewski

*Mary Poppins* (1964) Screenplay by Bill Walsh & Don DaGradi, books by P.L. Travers

*The Matrix* (1999) Screenplay by Ed Solomon, comic by Lowell Cunningham

*Men In Black* (1997) Screenplay by Ed Solomon, comic book by Lowell Cunningham

*Miami Vice* (2006) Written by Michael Mann, TV series by Anthony Yerkovich

*Midnight Run* (1988) Written by George Gallo

*Million Dollar Baby* (2004) Screenplay by Paul Haggis, stories by F.X. Toole

*Moll Flanders* (1996) Screen Story & Screenplay by Pen Densham, novel by Daniel Defoe

*Mr. & Mrs. Smith* (2005) Written by Simon Kinberg

*Must Love Dogs* (2005) Screenplay by Gary David Goldberg, novel by Claire Cook

*My Best Friend's Wedding* (1997) Written by Ronald Bass

*National Treasure* (2004) Screenplay by Jim Kouf and Cormac Wibberley & Marianne Wibberley, story by Jim Kouf and Oren Aviiv & Charles Segars

*No Country for Old Men* (2007) Screenplay by Joel Coen & Ethan Coen, novel by Cormac McCarthy

*Norma Rae* (1979) Written by Harriet Frank Jr. and Irving Ravetch

*The Notebook* (2004) Screenplay by Jeremy Leven, adaptation by Jan Sardi, novel by Nicholas Sparks

*Notting Hill* (1999) Written by Richard Curtis

*The Number 23* (2007) Written by Fernley Phillips

*Ocean's Eleven* (2001) Screenplay by Ted Griffin, original screenplay by Harry Brown and Charles Lederer, story by George Clayton Johnson & Jack Golden Russell

*One Flew Over the Cuckoo's Nest* (1975) Screenplay by Lawrence Hauben and Bo Goldman, novel by Ken Kesey, play by Dale Wasserman

*101 Dalmatians* (1996) Screenplay by John Hughes, novel by Dodie Smith

*On the Waterfront* (1954) Screenplay by Budd Schulberg

*Open Range* (2003) Screenplay by Craig Storper, novel by Lauran Paine

*Ordinary People* (1980) Screenplay by Alvin Sargent, novel by Judith Guest

*Out of Africa* (1985) Screenplay by Kurt Luedtke, books by Errol Trzebinski, Judith Thurman and Karen Blixen

*Outbreak* (1995) Written by Laureence Dworet & Robert Roy Pool

*Panic Room* (2002) Written by David Koepp

*The Pelican Brief* (1993) Screenplay by Alan J. Pakula, book by John Grisham

*Peter Pan* (1904) Stage play by J. M. Barrie

*Pinocchio* (1940) Screen story adaptation Ted Sears & Otto Englander & Webb Smith & William Cottrell & Joseph Sabo & Erdman Penner & Aurelius Battaglia, story by Carlo Collodi

*Postcards From the Edge* (1990) Screenplay by Carrie Fisher, book by Carrie Fisher

*Pretty Woman* (1990) Written by J.F. Lawton

*Primary Colors* (1998) Screenplay by Elaine May, novel by Joe Klein

*The Proposal* (2009) Written by Pete Chiarelli

*Pulp Fiction* (1994) Screenplay by Quentin Tarantino, stories by Quentin Tarantino & Roger Avary

*The Punisher* (2004) Written by Jonathan Hensleigh and Michael France

*Rain Man* (1988) Screenplay by Ronald Bass and Barry Morrow, story by Barry Morrow

*Ray* (2004) Screenplay by James L. White, story by Taylor Hackford and James L. White

*The Rock* (1996) Screenplay by David Weisberg & Douglas Cook and Mark Rosner, story by David Weisberg & Douglas Cook

*The Rocker* (2008) Screenplay by Maya Forbes & Wallace Wolodarsky, story by Ryan Jaffe

*Rocky* (1976) Written by Sylvester Stallone

*Romancing the Stone* (1984) Written by Diane Thomas

*Romeo and Juliet* (1593) Play written by William Shakespeare

*Runaway Bride* (1999) Written by Josann McGibbon & Sara Parriott

*Sayonara* (1957) Screenplay by Paul Osborn, novel by James Michener

*Scarface* (1994) Screenplay by Oliver Stone

*Serendipity* (2001) Written by Marc Klein

*Shadow Boxer* (2005) Written by William Lipz

*Shakespeare in Love* (1998) Written by Marc Norman and Tom Stoppard

*The Shawshank Redemption* (1994) Screenplay by Frank Darabont, story by Stephen King

*Shrek* (2001) Written by Ted Elliott & Terry Rossio and Joe Stillman and Roger S.H. Schulman, book by William Steig

*Sideways* (2004) Screenplay by Alexander Payne & Jim Taylor, novel by Rex Pickett

*Signs* (2002) Written by M. Night Shyamalan

*The Silence of the Lambs* (1992) Screenplay by Ted Tally, novel by Thomas Harris

*Sister Act* (1996) Written by Joseph Howard

*Six Days Seven Nights* (1998) Written by Michael Browning

*Some Like It Hot* (1959) Screenplay by Billy Wilder and I.A.L. Diamond, story by Robert Thoeren and Michael Logan

*The Sopranos* (TV Series, 1999-2007) Creator David Chase

*Spider-Man* (2002) Screenplay by David Koepp, comic book by Stan Lee and Steve Ditko

*The Spitfire Grill* (1996) Written by Harold Ramis & Douglas Kenney & Chris Miller

*Stranger Than Fiction* (2006) Written by Zach Helm

*Star Wars: IV-A New Hope* (1977) Written by George Lucas

*Sweeney Todd* (2007) Screenplay by John Logan, book by Hugh Wheeler, play by Christopher Bond

*Syriana* (2005) Written by Stephen Gaghan, book (suggestion) by Robert Baer

*The Taking of Pelham 123* (2009) Screenplay by Brian Helgeland, novel by John Godey

*Thelma & Louise* (1991) Written by Callie Khouri

*There's Something About Mary* (1998) Screenplay by Ed Decter & John J. Strauss & Peter Farrelly and Bobby Farrelly, story by Ed Decter & John J. Strauss

*3:10 to Yuma* (2007) Screenplay by Halsted Welles and Michael and Michael Brandt & Derek Haas, short story by Elmore Leonard

*Titanic* (1996) Written by James Cameron

*Tootsie* (1982) Screenplay by Murray Schisgal and Larry Gelbart, story by Don McGuire

*Training Day* (2001) Written by David Ayer

*The Truman Show* (1998) Written by Andrew Niccol

*27 Dresses* (2008) Written by Aline Brosh McKenna

*Twister* (1996) Written by Michael Crichton & Anne-Marie Martin

*200 Cigarettes* (1999) Written by Shana Larsen

*Unforgiven* (1992) Written by David Webb Peoples

*Up* (2009) Screenplay by Bob Peterson & Pete Docter, story by Pete Docter and Bob Peterson & Thomas McCarthy

*Urban Cowboy* (1950) Written by James Bridges and Aaron Latham

*The Usual Suspects* (1995) Written by Christopher McQuarrie

*V for Vendetta* (2008) Screenplay by Andy Wachowski & Lana Wachowski, graphic novel by David Lloyd

*Waiting for Godot* (1956) Play written by Samuel Beckett

*Walk the Line* (2005) Written by Gill Dennis & James Mangold, books by Johnny Cash & Patrick Carr

*Wall Street* (1987) Written by Stanley Weiser & Oliver Stone

*WALL-E* (2008) Screenplay by Andrew Stanton & Bob Peterson & Jim Reardon, original story by Andrew Stanton and Pete Docter

*Waterworld* (1995) Written by Peter Rader and David Twohy

*Wedding Crashers* (2005) Written by Steve Faber & Bob Fisher

*When Harry Met Sally* (1989) Written by Nora Ephron

*White Palace* (1990) Screenplay by Ted Tally and Alvin Sargent, novel by Glenn Savan

*Wise Guys* (1986) Screenplay by George Gallo and Norman Steinberg

*Working Girl* (1998) Written by Kevin Wade

*The Wrestler* (2008) Written by Robert D. Siegel

# INDEX

❧

## *b*

# ABOUT THE AUTHOR

ERIC EDSON has written seventeen feature screenplays on assignment for such companies as Sony, Warner Brothers, Disney, 20th Century-Fox, ABC Motion Pictures, Lifetime, Showtime, NBC, and TNT. He has also written for episodic television. He is Professor of Screenwriting and Director of the Graduate Program in Screenwriting at California State University, Northridge, and lectures through the UCLA Extension Writers' Program, the largest screenwriter training center in the world. Eric holds a Master of Fine Arts degree in Screenwriting and Film Directing from the American Film Institute, and a Master of Fine Arts in Playwriting from UCLA. He lives in Calabasas, California.

Eric can be reached at
*thestorysolution@gmail.com*

# THE WRITER'S JOURNEY - 3RD EDITION
## MYTHIC STRUCTURE FOR WRITERS

### CHRISTOPHER VOGLER

## *BEST SELLER*

See why this book has become an international best seller and a true classic. *The Writer's Journey* explores the powerful relationship between mythology and storytelling in a clear, concise style that's made it required reading for movie executives, screenwriters, playwrights, scholars, and fans of pop culture all over the world.

Both fiction and nonfiction writers will discover a set of useful myth-inspired storytelling paradigms (i.e., "The Hero's Journey") and step-by-step guidelines to plot and character development. Based on the work of Joseph Campbell, *The Writer's Journey* is a must for all writers interested in further developing their craft.

The updated and revised third edition provides new insights and observations from Vogler's ongoing work on mythology's influence on stories, movies, and man himself.

*"This book is like having the smartest person in the story meeting come home with you and whisper what to do in your ear as you write a screenplay. Insight for insight, step for step, Chris Vogler takes us through the process of connecting theme to story and making a script come alive."*
> – Lynda Obst, producer, *Sleepless in Seattle, How to Lose a Guy in 10 Days*;
> author, *Hello, He Lied*

*"This is a book about the stories we write, and perhaps more importantly, the stories we live. It is the most influential work I have yet encountered on the art, nature, and the very purpose of storytelling."*
> – Bruce Joel Rubin, screenwriter, *Stuart Little 2, Deep Impact,*
> *Ghost, Jacob's Ladder*

CHRISTOPHER VOGLER is a veteran story consultant for major Hollywood film companies and a respected teacher of filmmakers and writers around the globe. He has influenced the stories of movies from *The Lion King* to *Fight Club* to *The Thin Red Line* and most recently wrote the first installment of *Ravenskull*, a Japanese-style manga or graphic novel. He is the executive producer of the feature film *P.S. Your Cat is Dead* and writer of the animated feature *Jester Till*.

**$26.95 · 448 PAGES · ORDER NUMBER 76RLS · ISBN: 9781932907360**

# SAVE THE CAT!.
## THE LAST BOOK ON SCREENWRITING
## YOU'LL EVER NEED!

**BLAKE SNYDER**

## *BEST SELLER*

He made millions of dollars selling screenplays to Hollywood and here screenwriter Blake Snyder tells all. "Save the Cat!." is just one of Snyder's many ironclad rules for making your ideas more marketable and your script more satisfying – and saleable, including:
- The four elements of every winning logline.
- The seven immutable laws of screenplay physics.
- The 10 genres and why they're important to your movie.
- Why your Hero must serve your idea.
- Mastering the Beats.
- Mastering the Board to create the Perfect Beast.
- How to get back on track with ironclad and proven rules for script repair.

This ultimate insider's guide reveals the secrets that none dare admit, told by a show biz veteran who's proven that you can sell your script if you can save the cat.

*"Imagine what would happen in a town where more writers approached screenwriting the way Blake suggests? My weekend read would dramatically improve, both in sellable/producible content and in discovering new writers who understand the craft of storytelling and can be hired on assignment for ideas we already have in house."*
　　　　　　　– From the Foreword by Sheila Hanahan Taylor, Vice President,Development at Zide/Perry Entertainment, whose films include *American Pie, Cats and Dogs, Final Destination*

*"One of the most comprehensive and insightful how-to's out there. Save the Cat!. is a must-read for both the novice and the professional screenwriter."*
　　　　　　　– Todd Black, Producer, *The Pursuit of Happyness, The Weather Man, S.W.A.T, Alex and Emma, Antwone Fisher*

*"Want to know how to be a successful writer in Hollywood? The answers are here. Blake Snyder has written an insider's book that's informative – and funny, too."*
　　　　　　　– David Hoberman, Producer, *The Shaggy Dog* (2005), *Raising Helen, Walking Tall, Bringing Down the House, Monk* (TV)

BLAKE SNYDER, besides selling million-dollar scripts to both Disney and Spielberg, was one of Hollywood's most successful spec screenwriters. Blake's vision continues on *www.blakesnyder.com*.

**$19.95 · 216 PAGES · ORDER NUMBER 34RLS · ISBN: 9781932907001**

# MEMO FROM THE STORY DEPT.
## SECRETS OF STRUCTURE AND CHARACTER

### CHRISTOPHER VOGLER & DAVID MCKENNA

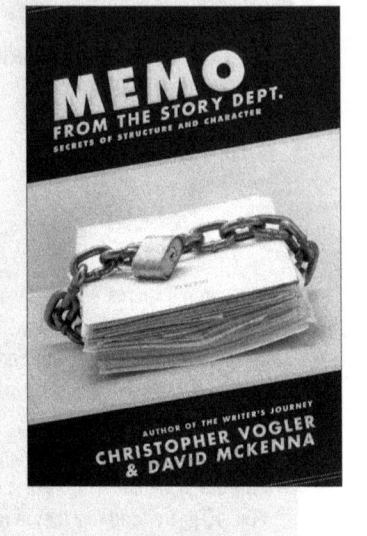

*Memo From the Story Department* is the long-awaited sequel to Christopher Vogler's immensely successful and influential handbook on mythic screenwriting, *The Writer's Journey: Mythic Structure for Storytellers and Screenwriters* (more than 250,000 copies sold). Vogler and his colleague, Columbia University film professor David McKenna, have produced an authoritative guide to advanced tools of structure and character development for screenwriters, novelists, game designers and film students. Users of the book will find a complete set of precision tools for taking their stories, step-by-step, through a quantum leap in writing quality.

*"Story structure is 90% of the game in screenwriting, though it's invisible on the page. Great movies have great structure — period. Nobody understands that better, and communicates it more brilliantly, than Mr. McKenna. His insight is a key reason I'm a working writer today."*
— Mark Fergus, Oscar-nominated co-screenwriter, *Children of Men* and *Iron Man*

*"The way that Vogler and McKenna tag-team this book – it keeps you on your toes. Sometimes when you're yelling in the wilderness – it's good to have two voices. Certainly they'll give you perspectives on screenwriting that you've never seen before – and in this world of multiple screenwriting book choices – that's a good thing."*
— Matthew Terry, filmmaker/screenwriter/teacher – columnist for
www. hollywoodlitsales.com

CHRISTOPHER VOGLER is the top story analyst and consultant for major Hollywood studios and talent, advising on projects as varied as *The Lion King* and *Fight Club*. He wrote the script for the animated feature *Jester Till* and the story for a Japanese-style manga comic, *Ravenskull*. He was executive producer of the feature film *P.S. Your Cat is Dead* and has worked recently on projects for Will Smith, Helen Hunt, Roland Emmerich, and Darren Aronofsky. He travels widely to lecture about mythic structure. With Michael Hauge he produced the instructional DVD *The Hero's Two Journeys*. His book *The Writer's Journey* has been translated into ten languages and is one of the top-selling screenwriting manuals in the world.

DAVID MCKENNA is a stage director, acting coach, voice-over artist and film professor at Columbia University and Barnard College. He is an expert on the films of Clint Eastwood and film genres including horror, westerns and war movies. His influential classes on screenwriting have stimulated a generation of young filmmakers and writers.

**$26.95 · 280 PAGES · ORDER NUMBER 164RLS · ISBN 13: 9781932907971**

# SELLING YOUR STORY IN 60 SECONDS
## THE GUARANTEED WAY TO GET
## YOUR SCREENPLAY OR NOVEL READ

### MICHAEL HAUGE

### BEST SELLER

Best-selling author Michael Hauge reveals:
- How to Design, Practice, and Present the 60-Second Pitch
- The Cardinal Rule of Pitching
- The 10 Key Components of a Commercial Story
- The 8 Steps to a Powerful Pitch
- Targeting Your Buyers
- Securing Opportunities to Pitch
- Pitching Templates
- And much more, including "The Best Pitch I Ever Heard," an exclusive collection from major film executives

*"Michael Hauge's principles and methods are so well argued that the mysteries of effective screenwriting can be understood — even by directors."*

> — Phillip Noyce, director, *Patriot Games, Clear and Present Danger, The Quiet American, Rabbit-Proof Fence*

*"... one of the few authentically good teachers out there. Every time I revisit my notes, I learn something new or reinforce something that I need to remember."*

> — Jeff Arch, screenwriter, *Sleepless in Seattle, Iron Will*

*"Michael Hauge's method is magic — but unlike most magicians, he shows you how the trick is done."*

> — William Link, screenwriter & co-creator, *Columbo; Murder, She Wrote*

*"By following the formula we learned in Michael Hauge's seminar, we got an agent, optioned our script, and now have a three-picture deal at Disney."*

> — Paul Hoppe and David Henry, screenwriters

MICHAEL HAUGE is the author of *Writing Screenplays That Sell*, now in its 30th printing, and has presented his seminars and lectures to more than 30,000 writers and filmmakers. He has coached hundreds of screenwriters and producers on their screenplays and pitches, and has consulted on projects for Warner Brothers, Disney, New Line, CBS, Lifetime, Julia Roberts, Jennifer Lopez, Kirsten Dunst, and Morgan Freeman.

**$12.95 · 150 PAGES · ORDER NUMBER 64RLS · ISBN: 9781932907209**

# THE SCRIPT-SELLNG GAME - 2ND ED.
## A HOLLYWOOD INSIDER'S LOOK AT GETTING YOUR SCRIPT SOLD AND PRODUCED

KATHIE FONG YONEDA

*The Script-Selling Game* is about what they never taught you in film school. This is a look at screenwriting from the other side of the desk — from a buyer who wants to give writers the guidance and advice that will help them to not only elevate their craft but to also provide them with the down-in-the-trenches information of what is expected of them in the script selling marketplace.

It's like having a mentor in the business who answers your questions and provides you with not only valuable information, but real-life examples on how to maneuver your way through the Hollywood labyrinth. While the first edition focused mostly on film and television movies, the second edition includes a new chapter on animation and another on utilizing the Internet to market yourself and find new opportunities, plus an expansive section on submitting for television and cable.

*"I've been writing screenplays for over 20 years. I thought I knew it all — until I read* The Script-Selling Game. *The information in Kathie Fong Yoneda's fluid and fun book really enlightened me. It's an invaluable resource for any serious screenwriter."*

> — Michael Ajakwe Jr., Emmy-winning TV producer, *Talk Soup*; Executive Director of Los Angeles Web Series Festival (LAWEBFEST); and creator/ writer/director of *Who...* and *Africabby* (AjakweTV.com)

*"Kathie Fong Yoneda knows the business of show from every angle and she generously shares her truly comprehensive knowledge — her chapter on the Web and new media is what people need to know! She speaks with the authority of one who's been there, done that, and gone on to put it all down on paper. A true insider's view."*

> — Ellen Sandler, former co-executive producer of *Everybody Loves Raymond* and author of *The TV Writer's Workbook*

KATHIE FONG YONEDA has worked in film and television for more than 30 years. She has held executive positions at Disney, Touchstone, Disney TV Animation, Paramount Pictures Television, and Island Pictures, specializing in development and story analysis of both live-action and animation projects. Kathie is an internationally known seminar leader on screenwriting and development and has conducted workshops in France, Germany, Austria, Spain, Ireland, Great Britain, Australia, Indonesia, Thailand, Singapore, and throughout the U.S. and Canada.

**$19.95 · 248 PAGES · ORDER NUMBER 161RLS · ISBN 13: 9781932907919**

# THE MYTH OF MWP

In a dark time, a light bringer came along, leading the curious and the frustrated to clarity and empowerment. It took the well-guarded secrets out of the hands of the few and made them available to all. It spread a spirit of openness and creative freedom, and built a storehouse of knowledge dedicated to the betterment of the arts.

The essence of the Michael Wiese Productions (MWP) is empowering people who have the burning desire to express themselves creatively. We help them realize their dreams by putting the tools in their hands. We demystify the sometimes secretive worlds of screenwriting, directing, acting, producing, film financing, and other media crafts.

By doing so, we hope to bring forth a realization of 'conscious media' which we define as being positively charged, emphasizing hope and affirming positive values like trust, cooperation, self-empowerment, freedom, and love. Grounded in the deep roots of myth, it aims to be healing both for those who make the art and those who encounter it. It hopes to be transformative for people, opening doors to new possibilities and pulling back veils to reveal hidden worlds.

MWP has built a storehouse of knowledge unequaled in the world, for no other publisher has so many titles on the media arts. Please visit www.mwp.com where you will find many free resources and a 25% discount on our books. Sign up and become part of the wider creative community!

Onward and upward,

Michael Wiese
Publisher/Filmmaker